Final Call

Colin Hilton lives largely in cyberspace. This is his first book. Just three and a half people have read it, here is what they had to say about it:

'Only Richard and Judy will interview him now'

Tony Mason

'It's a winner'

Captain Bob Williams

'Really interesting, even gripping in parts'

Heather Doyle

'Who gave you this number?'

Danny Fyne

THE AUTHOR...

... first became aware of aeroplanes from the *Airfix* models hanging from the bedroom ceiling, like mobiles suspended above the cradle. He consolidated this interest by looking up at the skies and listening to communications from over Strumble Head, where 707s and DC-8s departed these shores for North America. He also bought books of registrations published by *Ian Allan*, visiting Speke and Ringway to underline the aeroplanes dropping in ~ thanks to Brian Robinson. These included piston-engined Dakota DC-3s belonging to *Dan Air*, as well as Viscounts from *British Eagle*, some of whose pilots he joined on the flight deck thirty years later. Among his earliest flights was one around Lands Head in a de Havilland Dragon Rapide, at a cost of fifty pence. He learned to fly (though little else) at university and eventually eschewed the office to punch buttons on autopilots instead. His next book describes his attempts to build and operate a flying car, in time for the Wright Brothers' centenary.

Final Call

This edition first published in 2003
First published in Great Britain by
Global Media Domination
87 Heyes Lane
Alderley Edge SK9 7LN
www.colinhilton.com

10 9 8 7 6 5 4 3 2 1

A catalogue record for this book is available from the
British Library.

ISBN 0-9545598-0-0

Printed in Great Britain by
Printout of Halifax

For Anja

Ladies and Gentlemen, welcome on board from the captain. My name is Colin Hilton and I shall be doing the flying this morning. Our route takes us from the airport to the wider world of aviation, with perhaps a glimpse of a personality or two enroute. Judgment will occasionally be clouded and I anticipate a little turbulence in relationships, besides odd flashes of inspiration. Do not let such rumblings spoil your enjoyment of the service.

The crew today will be on hand to assist your journey. They will happily answer queries on aspects of flight safety. These may not all appear on the card in the seat pocket, neither should you expect the commercial pressures attending us to feature in the in-flight magazine. Once in the cruise we might see the origins of flight, while I shall speak to you later on the consequences of flight at 35,000 ft to our health and environment.

In the meantime, do please sit back, relax and enjoy the read.

CONTENTS

PREFACE

It is customary to acknowledge all those who have made a book possible. It is also insufferably dull and from the perspective of the reader, only marginally more exciting than looking at holiday photographs. Belonging to somebody else. With this in mind I should especially like to thank my Apple computers, who have been constant companions, along with my Peugeot 306, which has been good enough to drive me around the country without complaint.

I would like to thank the captain at my previous employer who extracted as much money as possible on my behalf and in doing so, perhaps contributed more to the understanding of aviation than he might otherwise. Also Linda who helped compile my *roll of honour*, listing those among my fellow pilots who survived the experience. I should like most unfashionably to thank Bill Gates for the software with which this was composed. More fashionably I would like to thank Mum and Dad for providing lodgings and making no mention of the illicit sex that appears as early as the third page. Bob Williams and Tony Mason were so good as to take the material for a test-flight and issue the subsequent Certificate of Airworthiness, while on the technical side Heather Doyle ensured the text was up to the job. Mostly though I wish to thank all those who enjoyed flying with me as much as I did with them. This is for both of you.

The book is a personal snapshot as well as an instantaneous view of the wider business of commercial aviation, one hundred years on from the Wright Flyer. It marks the end of my flying, certainly at Heathrow and ideally for the foreseeable future. It will stand I hope as a cheap monument, the sort that falls over within the year. Accordingly it is flimsily researched and like my university dissertation, largely invented during the course of a pub lunch. I hope you enjoy it as much as I enjoyed the steak and kidney pudding.

Skelmersdale, April 2003.

PRE-FLIGHT

Throughout the acres of press and miles of videotape accompanying the collapse of the Twin Towers, the view from the flight deck was conspicuously absent. It was as though Agatha Christie omitted the cook from an investigation into poisoned soup. Interviews with experts who write about aviation without ever flying, or with captains who had long ceased flying, were the *menu de jour*. Acting airline pilots would be less free to comment.

Aviation is a specifically male preserve with methods dating from a more romantic age, when the jetset boarded Caravelles across sunlit aprons. Perhaps it is the preponderance of older men involved that sets its tone. If there is a section of society who like to wear the badge of flexible thought without changing their ways, it is that of old men like me. The naivety of the post-war years, when commercial flight was born, was truly profound. Archibald Russell of the British Aircraft Corporation recalled asking BOAC how many seats they required in his latest aircraft. The answer was an explicit thirty-five. He was told any more than this and the capacity of the airport coaches would be exceeded. British aircraft were especially handicapped by the whimsy of the state airline, run as a branch of the civil service and staffed by retirees from the Forces. Greater commercial imperatives in the United States produced a successful series of aircraft initiated by the Boeing 707. The 737 is the most successful descendant and the bestselling airliner, yet has a cabin with the original outline. It is as if your next car used the chassis of the Ford Prefect.

Nonetheless the design of these aircraft testifies to a generation of aviation engineers who knew no computer. Asked to comment upon his favourite building, Norman Foster elected the 747, an aeroplane of over six million parts. Wartime bombers might comprise 'only' a hundred thousand parts, but could be assembled inside the hour. The aircraft we travel in today are their legacy and while the advantages of legacies are often apparent, drawbacks take longer to emerge. Recent accident investigations have specifically pinpointed the risk of explosions in fuel tanks and cargo holds, while catastrophic fires have resulted from short-circuited wiring. The exposure of the flight deck to hijack has been re-focused by recent events, though the Airbus which narrowly avoided ditching after running out of fuel went largely unnoticed, except by investigators. They criticised the fact airliners have no system specifically alerting crews to fuel leakage.

The way the entire industry in the UK is structured stems from gentlemen's agreements forged in the corridors of the CAA, or the lobbies of the RAF. The original routes to Africa and South America were actually pioneered for BA by the former leader of the 'Pathfinder' squadron. The prime mission of staffers at the CAA continues to be the security of their index-linked pensions. Their policies have a deadening effect on air traffic control services to customer airlines. On occasions they galvanise industry with bewildering initiatives, like raising the age limit for command to sixty-five, out of step with Europe, leaving UK airlines with captains who cannot cross the English Channel. (More bizarrely again, in Australia employment rules dictate captains can fly at *any* age so long as they are considered to retain their faculties. Where *did* I put those spectacles?)

In common with the governmental department charged with overseeing transport, the CAA can generally be relied upon to fix the previous problem. It is abetted by the airlines, whose prime directive is maintaining the *status quo*, as it is this that most likely guarantees them revenue, without troubling them with the innovations required by competition. The management of airlines is notoriously divorced from the workforce and specifically the pilots, who rightly suspect they would be taken to the cleaners if the opportunity arose. Though the rift is concealed from travellers, the last CEO of BA publicly conceded that while relations were bad, they were not *as bad* as elsewhere. At the lowest ebb of the last dispute, he reportedly required personal protection when moving among his staff.

The situation was not so bad when airlines were nationalised, principally because pilots enjoyed a privileged existence and uninterrupted employment between the confines of the fighter cockpit and those of an airliner. This clubbable aspect of recruitment continues on the continent, where entrepreneurs like Richard Branson have had problems applying freewheeling brands to the congested airways of the European Community. Restrictive practice is still manifest in the wider world, where promotion is tied to joining dates in the form of a *seniority list*. This was inherited directly from among steam locomotive drivers and their firemen. Such seniority of promotion and transfer is exploited by airlines in the way unions and proprietors excluded competition in Fleet Street, which was also unsuited to change. Whether *no-frills* airlines can circumvent the arrangement is unclear. There is though one constant in the business equation of any airline, which is soon uncovered by anyone in the industry: pilots are never happy.

If it had a definable start at all, my own flying career might have begun the summer I squeaked graduation and stayed in Richmond with the family of a Lloyds underwriter. They had taken my girlfriend under their wing and I was there for surreptitious sex in the bunk bed, like a recalcitrant cuckoo. I also had a milk round, involving a training course not dissimilar from that of airlines. Here too, expectant youth was pervasive. I was one of the more privileged cadets in having a place to live. One man lived in a Ford Cortina and we wondered did he leave a gap at the top of the window for letters? There was a visit to the depot, with its array of parked milk floats, hangared expectantly and smelling not of castor oil and leather, but of yoghurt. I felt like David Niven in *Dawn Patrol*. Perhaps realising this, the foreman moved his charges swiftly along to the bottle-washing plant.

The experience was echoed years later, during an inaugural tour by one airline around its ancestral headquarters in Derbyshire. By this time I had been an unwitting participant in various career strands, of which flying was the latest. Aspects of the tour had obviously been little adapted from the days fresh-faced lads with good Physics had been initiated. The ancient building had many stairs and passageways, along one of which was a room piled high with the paperwork from a thousand flights. Sat here was a veteran you might have encountered in The Hobbit, a flyer now surrounded by clouds of tobacco smoke. There was one other chair in the room, proffered by the co-trainee with whom I had spent the previous evening at clubs in Nottingham. Pausing between breaths drawn through a walnut stem, the veteran leaned forward to say the key thing to remember about flying was (and here we leaned too)...*not to burn the candle at both ends.* I was thirty-eight.

To return to this student summer in Richmond, I was hitching home via Richmond Park one day, more in hope than expectation. The deerpark is not the sort of place you expect to see hikers, as you might on Route 66. Perhaps as a result of this incongruity, someone offered me a lift. These days it would be a crazed psychopath and I would be recounting these memoirs from within a velveteen-papered cell. On this occasion it was a well-dressed businessman in a Volvo. When I described my circumstances and my hopes of endorsing my civilian flying licence, he let slip he had spent a number of years in the military ferrying a variety of aircraft from one place to another. In those days he said it had been like hiring a car at Palma Airport, sitting there for a while figuring out the controls. He would be assisted by a brief flight manual and checklist, which he usually studied walking over to the aircraft. Hearing of so *louche* a lifestyle from one so outwardly successful only served to fuel my ambition. As I got out of the car, after a ride of some six minutes, he called out "Good luck in life". The sort of thing Shane might have said before riding out of town, or in this case out of Richmond Park.

Quite how to convert my training in the RAF into a civilian licence was not obvious. The nearest airport was located, inconveniently I felt, twenty-five miles away at Biggin Hill. After studying the network of public transport connections I realised that railways, or what was left of them, were designed only to get people *into* London. The single most important contribution of Henry Ford to mankind was allowing it sideways movement. Personally I had no car and instead resorted to borrowing a bicycle from the youngest daughter of the family, who had long since grown out of it. I therefore peddled to Biggin Hill and back, only once, on a pink bicycle with flowered mudguards. This was not how the films led me to believe it was supposed to be. I should have been living a life of abandon above a local hostelry and arriving at the airfield, along with my Labrador, in an open-topped sports car. The training aircraft here were something else as well. Just thirty-five years previously, young men had shoehorned themselves into state-of-the-art fighters, which Mitchell had been exhausted designing. Beneath you were slender elliptical wings and ahead of you twenty-seven super-charged litres. Civilian training in the remaining years of the century would be carried out in confinement with an obese instructor with bad breath, hauled by the type of engine used on canals.

All of this effort culminated in a flying test rated *above average* by a mature examiner called Cyril, whose brother not long afterward flew into the side of a railway viaduct while avoiding cloud. (This was because he had crossed the channel where the fuel was cheaper, one way I guess in which arbitrary taxes distort the lives of citizens.) Where would *my* fledgling wings take me? To a range of jobs not the least enjoyable of which was washing dishes in a Surrey hospital. It was best to live a little before working as an airline pilot and probably best to live a little afterward. The best career-end I came across was told me as I sat queuing for forty minutes before take-off from Heathrow. In America, domestic flying is huge and the weather contributes famously to delays. During one of these, one captain extended the aircraft stairs and after apologies to the passengers, simply walked out on life. Now that *is* style.

CHECK-IN

Though the airport is the first point of contact for travellers, for aircraft it is literally the final point of contact. The French term for taking off is *decollage* and as I pointed out to one of my co-pilots while awaiting take off in Paris, I thought this also meant cleavage. Of course it does, meaning literally a parting of the ways. There is nothing crews enjoy more than a little smut prior to take-off. Toward the end of the book I offer French aircrews (known as *equipages*) an award for the most creative use of the word *decollage* within the airport perimeter. The prize is a cheeseburger at a Michelin-starred restaurant.

Whilst touching on the topic of Frenchness, I might add that one of the interesting things about flying in the UK is the licensing of crew has been unified across Europe. Or at least as unified as a crème caramel topped with pepperoni. Implications of this change for me included flying with a co-pilot called Gregoire. He could be invaluable during night-stops at airport hotels. I would hand him the wine-list with a flourish, while interrogating the waiter on the quality of the *poulet* used within the chicken-in-the-basket. Gregoire might be discussing the various merits of different corkscrews, while crinkling his nose at the mere sight of New World wines, like he had spotted a maggot in the lettuce. He was a man with whom you could share either flight deck or Chateau Neuf de Pape.

During the day I might respond to his request for say flap setting five, not with the customary "Speed checks, flaps at five" but with "Mange tout, Rodney", borrowing a catchphrase from situation comedy. Were these departures from standard terminology to be picked up by our superiors, we would be castigated for enjoying ourselves on duty. After landing the 737, the electrical supply was transferred from engines to on-board generator, the co-pilot reporting "APU available" and the response being "On the buses". One captain would reply "Reg Varney" at this point, after the star of the programme *On the Buses*; though it was clear from his demeanor he ran the risk of Soviet-style censure.

A less savoury aspect of the harmonization of EU laws is that airlines like Ryanair might undermine your employment prospects by shipping in pilots from the Balkans, avoiding the war that is usually going on there. The reason so many Croatians qualify to operate the Boeing 737 is because the purchase of airliners for most countries is one of the few remaining instruments of *realpolitik*. Should the Chinese ambassador have offended his American hosts at a banquet, say by refusing the chicken-in-the-basket, the next day Peking would have faxed for another 737.

Ryanair is considered to be the mother of all flag-of-convenience operators. If they could employ Philippine rickshaw haulers, they would. For their entire postwar history, states have tried to forestall such developments. The Chicago treaty of 1944 established commercial aviation for what it is, by warranting freedom of movement through the airspaces of otherwise sovereign territories. Whilst the sovereignty of the various national air traffic control bodies remains intact, shorter haul airlines in Europe at least are increasingly allowed to fly not just over wherever they want, but also *from* and *to* whichever countries they want, no matter where they are based in the EC. The only remaining strictures are those related to ownership (like the way American airlines have to be three-quarters owned by domestic stockholders) or the way governments restrict access to routes or airports to their own carriers, usually on a reciprocal basis with whichever country they might fly to. This is what politicians call *bilaterals* and what you and I call a cartel. The practices are designed precisely to avoid recent experiences with either liberalised shipping, with its liberally dispersed loads of oil, or similar outcomes with networks of trains and buses. The politics of aviation though is something that fills the business pages, whereas the history of the airport as a social factor or a machine of the modern age escapes them. Let me make up for this omission.

In common with much of aviation, the airport is a historical besides a physical departure. Its name is derivative and this is often an aspect of new developments, being described in terms of the old. The *car* was named after railway trucks, which in turn were named after a contraption some Indian goddess sat upon. Such terms derive from customary use, even though people like Ford might have preferred *Quadricycle*. Could you have imagined a generation of teenagers saying things like, Check out that guy's quadricycle? In a similar vein terms like *aerodrome* or *airpark* are now disdained as old-fashioned. They are simply not sophisticated enough for ourselves. We laugh at them in the way we laugh at pictures of people on the beach in striped costumes and sandals, appearing to enjoy wholesome entertainment instead of discarding used syringes. For people like Hercule Poirot, jumping into a cab and shouting "To the aerodrome!" was the height of style.

The aerodrome itself was a French concept, like so much of aviation. They developed it in the way only Europeans could: as an extension of the things extraordinarily rich people did in Paris of a Sunday afternoon. It might augment pastimes like cruising the Bois de Boulogne in carriages and hats, or watching small Argentinean men doing much the same thing in airships. To the French everything is an aesthetic exercise. Anybody knowing the reaction of Marcel Proust to his first sighting of an aeroplane (he fainted) will appreciate the affinity the French have for pursuits both technical and artistic. In America meanwhile they were developing aeroplanes for ghastly uses like transport.

Use of the word 'aerodrome' was eventually expunged from French and English, becoming *aeroport* in one and *airport* in the other. This might have been because their role had changed. Aircraft had initially been a curious fashion before the descent into function. Accordingly we cannot utter the word *aerodrome* without our imagination taking flight to a world of dashing aristos, whom women would like to see in bed and servants in a ditch. Eventually though the place became the age-old point of departure or *port*. Though you immediately think of boats, six terms of Latin left me secure in the knowledge that it is actually the Roman word for a door. What they probably meant here were those big doors at intervals around walled towns. (Two things occurred to me during a visit to Pompeii. First, they all seemed to be getting more sex and from every possible angle. Second, for all their sumptuousness, these were dangerous places to be. You would no more go out on Saturday night in Pompeii than you would in Stevenage).

Here is another illustration of how modern terms stem from ancient practice. I once read in one of those newspaper sections, in which readers submit queries and others attempt an explanation, the question "Why do we enter aeroplanes from the left-hand side?" The only response came from a buffoon at British Airways, saying it was because it had always been like this. (I have to divert here briefly, or die laughing. As a result of demographics at BA, cabin crew adopted the names *Wrinkly* and *Nigel* for captain and first officer respectively. These names crept into air traffic communication around Heathrow, viz:

BA   *Could I ask the Midland to pull a little further forward?*

bmi   *No you couldn't, Nigel.*

BA later took to calling us *Barry*.) We are likely to board from this side because this is what happens with boats. These are entered from the left or *port* side, probably because most of us are right handed. Before rudders were fitted to the stern, boats were steered by hanging an oar over the right side, known as the *starboard,* or the steering side. Not only do we get to use ditching stools on you left-handers, we get to tell you which side of aeroplanes to get on. And don't give me this "We gave you Renaissance art" crap.

The great contrast between seaports and airports is we get more say as to where to locate them. It has never been easy to accommodate shipping in places where there is no sea, though they certainly tried this in Manchester, in order to service the cotton mills. They found though it was quicker to sail across the Atlantic than the thirty-five miles between Manchester and the sea. In this positive choice of location, as with many of its other aspects, aviation was emblematic of the twentieth century. Whereas Victorian technology was considered to be a gift from God for husbanding nature, for us it was more a case of "It's our planet and we get to play with it."

A curious echo of this early attempt in Manchester to defy the natural course of events is the modern trend to locate airports in places where there is no dry land. Many of these plans are like a hippopotamus and surface at sporadic intervals. I think during the twenty-first century we can expect to glimpse them more frequently.

For example, a favourite spot for the perpetually new London airport is the Thames estuary. As the British are better at theme parks than earth moving, expect nothing to come of this. As someone who often manoeuvred Airbuses around seagulls on the way into Belfast, I can think of no more stupid place to land aeroplanes than the coast. The hierarchy will be horrified by this confession. "You're supposed to fly through them, idiot. How else are we supposed to jeopardise lives?" Well get this: at Rome one night I slowed the aircraft to let a mouse cross the taxiway.

New York or *JFK* was a prototypical attempt at building a terminal on land otherwise of use to only grebes and love-struck teenagers. Whether this was an attempt to displace the collisions above New York and visit fiery wreckage upon colonies of waders instead, I do not know. What I do know is speed was limited to 250 knots around airports precisely because of these collisions. You can almost hear the guy at the Federal Aviation Authority. Okay guys, that's the last coffee and pastry of mine you get to spoil...

JFK was followed by an ambitious installation off the coast of Hong Kong, ironically a British initiative. This new airport was a tremendous disappointment to pilots, mainly because it was so easy to land at. Prior to this you pointed a 747 at a washing-festooned hillside before executing a wall-of-death turn, to locate the runway. During the procedure the whites of eyes could be observed. The new airport, which I cannot be bothered looking up, is I think called *Chep Lap Kok.* (Looking at it, this may be what I ordered with a beer last night.) The new airport was something of a legacy gifted by the British prior to handing over the colony to the Chinese. My own government is adept at gifting peoples around the world in this way and asking me to pay for it.

Moving on, there is Schiphol airport in Amsterdam, where my favourite people are. The air traffic controllers here are so laid back and yet at the same time so switched on, you feel they would be happy with you smoking weed, so long as it did not interrupt the sequence. Inevitably there are plans afoot here to build an airport out to sea. This is not so peculiar as it seems, as the Dutch spend a fifth of their GDP in expelling seawater. Even Schiphol is twenty feet *below* sea level, so that if you dig into the concrete of the apron, which sadly I never did, the hole fills rapidly with water. You can see the thought processes dawning in the minds of the planners:

Q. Where do we go to escape the omnipresent fear of inundation?

A. The sea. Next on the agenda, please?

The logic behind this seaward trend is a ruthless function of population growth, beside competition between airlines. Both of these inexorable developments add to passenger numbers. They might be termed an explosive mix, but never use such an expression as you pass through security. Also, as aeroplanes get larger to carry all of these passengers, the runways required to raise them into the air get longer. The situation has the rationale of an arms race or the average road-building program. (Anybody doubting the fact larger aircraft require larger runways should take the kids to watch swans failing to get airborne.) Conversely, providing longer runways in advance is an open invitation to manufacturers to build bigger aircraft. It is what my professors used to call a 'positive feedback loop'. Or at least this is what I would have heard had I been there.

Long, straight lines are at a premium in the developed world, however. For the aviation engineer, this is a great shame, being about the only limiting factor to the size of aircraft. Helicopters are limited by the fact their lift-off is an exercise in raw weightlifting. In contrast the performance of aeroplanes is limited only by the speed of take-off. A Boeing 747 might spend more than a minute engaged in this phase. From the view of aesthetics, the concrete used to accelerate four hundred tons to two hundred miles an hour is likely to be ugly viewed from any angle. Though viewed from the flight deck, runways can look strangely enticing. That at Madrid is so long it disappears into the horizon in a heat haze. Others have attractive features in middle distance, like Heathrow 27R, which affords a perspective on Windsor Castle, or else Brussels 25R, from where the dome of the basilica can be seen. Occasionally 'spectaculars' seem to be staged to entertain pilots awaiting take-off, like the firework displays at Legoland, visible from runway 27L at Heathrow.

Earlier during the twentieth century the length of runways, or even the requirement for a runway *per se* was not a problem, as aircraft were smaller and lighter. This was because of shortcomings in two separate spheres of development. The first was the persistent use of the sort of engine fitted to your car. In aviation terms, this was as useful as a sparkler at Legoland. The second shortcoming was the collective failure of humankind to get to grips with really big things. The Romans had a crack at these with piles of bricks, as did the cathedral builders whose edifices frequently collapsed. We can only guess at this, because headlines like CHURCH CRASH CRUSH awaited the invention of the press. Outside places of worship there was no pressing need for any sort of congregation until the expansion of sport and commerce. The need was answered by skyscrapers, which were made possible by a metal framework. Around the same time, the Germans became dab-handed at using giant Meccano sets to build airships like *Graf Zeppelin*. The first all-metal aeroplane, which again was credited to Germany, was the Junkers, which looked like the sort of sheds you see on allotments, but with wings.

Fortunately, a little later the jet engine was developed. This was a close call, with Frank Whittle just outpacing von Ohain, in the brown shirt, by a whisker. Needless to say this invention did not prevent British post-war aviation from focusing upon use of an engine first outlined by James Watt and improved upon by an eccentric called Otto. The grand post-war airliner envisaged by the UK government, the Bristol Brabazon, was equipped with piston engines and as a result, at a different time or in a different place, it might have been called the *Millennium Dome*. I am in no way dismissing those who built it, but whereas governments build things for self-aggrandisement, companies prefer to build for customers. The jet airliner was thus ushered into use by the *Comet*, designed privately by a company not a mile from where I live.

Before these developments, during the 'twenties and 'thirties, aircraft remained small, along with the demand for their services. This contrasted sharply with the vision of architects like the Futurists, who had discovered steel and its use in reinforced concrete. This produced some interesting anomalies in their plans. In artful sketches of the coming metropolis, biplanes jostle for airspace with tubes that appear to suck commuters between breakfast table and office. Eighty years on, my wife is still waiting. The modern architect Le Corbusier often featured amorphous spaces for landing personal aeroplanes, between or on top of office buildings. In his plans people can be seen spilling from airborne carriages in the way I would emerge from East Croydon Station with my fellow somnambulists.

A key to all of these projects was the aircraft envisioned like the car as a means to shift backsides from home to place of work. Architects can never be persuaded that where most people want to be is on the beach, or that the last sort of home they want is one designed by them. Nor would the future metropolis offer convivial arrangements for those preferring to sit on a bench contemplating society over tins of extra-strong lager. What it did offer were arrangements for the aeroplane, if only because leaving such a machine out of modernism was like leaving turkeys out of Christmas.

Notwithstanding all the concrete around at the time, aircraft generally ran about on grass, which was both cheap and plentiful. Aircraft at the time needed no brakes, which is also cheap unless you hit something. They simply took off like the birds, directly into wind. These modest demands meant aerodromes could splash out on circular fields. Nothing quite like it has been seen since, this urban requirement for big round spaces. Most big things these days tend to be rectangular and even baseball stadiums simply set a margin around a diamond. I suppose the nearest modern equivalent was something that caught my eye when I flew over the prairies: those round fields irrigated by an arm on wheels. Artesian irrigation systems like this in the desert are large enough to be seen from space. Plus they are like a DVD, in that you can fast-forward to your favourite vegetable.

The field being circular, you could point the aeroplane in any direction the wind chose to blow from. Even now the Americans still call an airport a *field*. Like Boeing Field, where they make triple-sevens, or Miegs Field, where your Microsoft ™ flight simulator takes off. The brightest among you will be asking, OK, so where do you put the clubhouse? The accommodation would be of modest proportions, like everything else at the time, with the exception of parts of Errol Flynn. Naturally the buildings went around the edge;

ideally that opposite where prevailing winds came from, so aircraft did not overrun the members in the bar. You will have noticed from newsreels that on aircraft carriers, the terminal (or whatever naval types call it) is virtually off the deck for this reason.

Turf lost its attraction for aircraft soon after the dawn of reinforced concrete, which could support their weight. Newer and heavier airliners have to distribute their weight over many wheels (the 747 has eighteen) so as not to damage the surface, while concrete laid down to form the maneuvering areas has to have a required PSN, or pavement strength classification. Nonetheless it offends even modern sensibilities to punctuate the landscape with circular expanses of concrete several miles in diameter. There had been a brief flirtation with runways designed to rotate around an axis, so as to point wherever you liked. This had the obvious disadvantage that the area over which they swept might as well be surfaced anyway, eliminating every possible source of breakdown. As a scheme it appealed especially to modernists, who would have them pirouette on top of skyscrapers. Eventually reality sank in and the planners returned to models promising reliability, like men turning from the excesses of the Moulin Rouge.

The compromise was an angular arrangement of three runways, each of which generally crossed more or less around their middle. The longest would point into the prevailing wind direction, with the two shorter fixed at angles offset by 120 degrees. It was pointed out to me that all of the runways in Frankfurt are precisely the same length, to the metre, though you would have to be German to understand why. Few airfields retain all three runways, because the tolerance of modern aircraft toward crosswinds is much better. Many airfields have been left with just one runway (or two, if they have since expanded) pointing into the prevailing wind. A classic is Paris Charles de Gaulle, which has four such runways. The two on the south side are given a different identification, implying they point in a different direction, though in fact it is merely a case of terminology, to distinguish them from their northern counterparts. Until I knew this I used one of them once, as it appeared to help during a raging gale. Just imagining it did probably helped.

It soon transpired three runways had been wildly excessive and devised with the sort of exuberance we feel in the off-licence when planning a party. Come the next day you still have sixteen litres of Cinzano. I think the problem was draughtsmen were like children in enjoying appealing shapes and star-shaped airports kindled fond memories of the beach. The reality came too late at Heathrow, which has 'hidden' runways long since disused, but loved by many of us with the affection reserved for secret gardens.

This trend toward geometrically pleasing arrangements became complex when paired runways came into use for parallel approaches, or for separate take-offs and landings like at London Airport. These runways might be imposed over others at offset angles, producing Star of David shapes. Runways nowadays often point in different directions simply to accommodate them to the surrounding landscape, or to make it easier for aircraft to move around on the ground. A consideration here is arranging for aircraft to move from gate to point of take-off with the minimum disruption. Heathrow fails quite miserably in this respect, as in many others, though we still love it like we do our grandfather, even after finding him drunk upon the lawn. An example of a layout adapted from the start in this way is again Frankfurt, two of whose runways are westerly while another is aimed uncompromisingly toward the south. The reason I say *uncompromisingly* is that the classical arrangement in the UK, which has a typical maritime climate, is for runways to point toward the southwest, where the nastiest of winds come from. Another would face southeast, for summer breezes and another vaguely northerly, for the snow-laden winds punctuating winter. Modern environmental arrangements for runways now have little to do with where the winds come from, but rather where the angry residents come from.

Before such considerations became uppermost, there were other reasons why runways pointed in odd directions. One is demonstrated amply at Shoreham and Southampton, where the runways point due south, from where sea breezes emanate. Another reason might be the constraints of surrounding terrain. In places where only one strip of land is available, that is the direction in which you are going to have to land. Coastal strips are a nice illustration. The sands at Southport used to constitute an official landing site, though principally for sightseeing tours. Until fairly recently the island of Barra, off the coast of Scotland, used to host a regular air-service from the beach. There were two problems with this, the first being an irate cockle-picker who, depending upon his mood, might not remove himself from the 'runway'. I lived for the day when I could tell the passengers we were diverting to Glasgow, where there were less cockle-pickers. The other problem was the larger aircraft which made the service at all viable, were prone to sinking into the sand. This is where I could say, Gentleman please offer your jackets for use beneath the main-wheels and children make sandcastles until further instructed.

I do though miss the seasonal qualities of grass airfields. They make a lovely sound in the wind before they are mown and smell nice afterward. They encourage wild flowers and birds. This is possibly the best reason for preserving airfields: like the landed estates of the English aristocracy, they are one of the few green-belt areas that retain a wealth of flora and fauna. Stansted near London even has a horticulturist tasked with selecting and encouraging strains of wild flower to grow within its confines. These do better here than they do in the wild, which is comprehensively attacked by spraying, if not grazing. Nobody much cares what grows or moves around the grassy spaces of even the busiest airfields and foxes, birds of prey or larks ascending are a frequent sight. I was once instructed at Warsaw to cancel the take-off due to "Dogs on runway". Wild ones. At more exotic locations, the printed aerodrome information casually advises pilots that Impalas might disrupt the landing run.

On the other hand, grass airfields do get a trifle muddy. Mud is an omnipresent threat to wars and village fetes alike. One sepia-tinted memory of mine is of perusing the original diaries of the first RAF squadron formed in 1916. You are thinking, but that is halfway through the war? Yes, but before this point they were known as the Royal Flying Corps and technically a division of the army. In the diaries are pictures of the assembled crews, posed between rows of tailfins extending into the distance. Beneath all this and as they say at the Oscars, "without which it would not have been possible", is ample wooden decking. Alan Titchmarsh would have had a field day. Decking was as ubiquitous to the Great War as was pierced-steel planking (PSP) in the Second. Even now, artificial means of support have peculiar manifestations. On the rare occasions upon which jets end up in fields, they have usually to be dismantled. I remember one case of a business jet in this predicament being salvaged by a modular runway, of the sort you might see at a flower-show. Though it enabled the aircraft to take-off again, it probably cost nearly as much.

Like flower shows, aviation had once been principally a summer pursuit, associated as it was with leisure. Once it became a method of moving exasperated passengers who would rather they were relaxing at home, concrete came into its own. Especially the aggregates reinforced by steel rods, invented I believe by a Frenchman. Upon one visit to Mallorca, I could not help noticing the concrete apron appeared to be reinforced by random inclusion of fibres. If anybody saw a man in uniform walking around an Airbus like he was missing money, that would be me incidentally. The immediate advantage of concrete for flying was it allowed for swifter acceleration for take-off. This reduced the potential distance required to get airborne, which in itself was important in view of the cost of paving surfaces. The downside was the renewed importance of brakes for stopping after landing, or for changing your mind during the take-off. There are various reasons for returning to the terminal. One captain I know did this to retrieve his hat. Others have left the strict confines of the runway for the sound reason they just died of a coronary.

If you are wondering whether concrete really makes that much difference to the rolling performance of the average airliner, an illustration from the industrial revolution might help. It was a rule of thumb among travellers that a horse could draw a ton on the road, two tons on rails and *forty* tons on water. This explains the affection of Europeans (and European horses) for canals. Besides this element of *rolling resistance*, jet engines are most effective at the top end of the range of speeds at which they turn. They share this at least with spin-dryers. At lower revolutions, lacking direct traction, they make a lot of noise but little progress. I have at times used sixty-percent of available RPM to surmount lumps in the paving. During ground testing of the first jet aeroplane, seen by its inventor, the engine ran at over eighty percent of available RPM, but produced a speed of only twenty miles per hour. Whittle described this worrisome surface as "soggy grass".

Another aspect of the location of airports, unlike ports on water, is it is prone to whimsy. There are airports even in the Swiss Alps, the highest being Samadan at two thousand metres, though seaports have proven consistently to operate best at sea level. You might have thought the position of Heathrow was also a testament to rationale. You would be wrong. It was co-opted from a civilian aircraft manufacturer, Fairey, during the war. The people doing the co-opting were civil servants, who foresaw a need for an airport near London to replace the one several miles away in Croydon. They used the conflict as an excuse to push through planning permission. Spitfire pilots used RAF Heathrow when they got lost, or fancied a sandwich somewhere different. Fairey themselves selected the place by serendipity, helped by an employee whose biplane once conked out nearby. He recalled how flat and loamy the area was, so the busiest international airport in the world was conceived by an oily spark plug and later commandeered by oily civil servants.

This event spurred progress in the way only random failure could. At the time the fashion had been to locate airports downtown, especially if you were an architectural visionary. This of course was precisely the wrong place to put an airport. Wrong on three counts. Never outside of dreams were we ever going to fly ourselves to work. The proper use for central real estate is coffee, banking and sex emporia (in that sequence). Thirdly, cities are the most vertical developments known to humankind and airports the most horizontal.

The aircraft manufacturer De Havilland in north London demonstrated amply how airports are slowly displaced from towns by future demands on real estate. You could have picked any of the other pre-war manufacturers: Sopwith in Kingston, Fairey in Heston, or Vickers in Weybridge. The chances of finding an airport amongst the affluence of Weybridge these days are about as great as finding the Taliban decamped to Golders Green. Beside these historic aircraft names there were engine manufacturers, like Rolls-Royce just beyond Watford. All of these once-great names are now only reflected in housing estates, in the way Wolsingham was once the most powerful man in Elisabethan England, but is now a cul-de-sac in Hatfield. The old Rolls-Royce site at Leavesden, while largely used for housing, retains a hangar used by George Lucas, the erstwhile Star Warrior. As I passed it each day on the way home from work, I would silently enunciate, May the Force be with you George.

In a way it all made sense. The first airports were designed for manufacturers themselves and not passengers. If you build a flying machine you have to be able to (a) get it out and (b) get it airborne. We have then this historical evolution of the airfield, beginning as a location for building aircraft, to a site of recreation and only eventually becoming the place that launched a thousand s***s. Indeed, some airfields were designed only for the launch of aircraft destined never to return. That at Leeds-Bradford was constructed for the factory next door, which manufactured bombers for dispatch to their various bases. Bristol was located on a hill chosen for the density of fog. It was used to perfect 'blind landing' equipment for the Air Force. These experiments produced a legendary cinefilm in which an aeroplane was flown at the runway through successively thicker layers of fog. Watching it once my brother turned to the old guy next to him and asked whether he remembered these days. Not just that, he replied, but he had been flying the aeroplane.

It just so happens the history of De Havilland is better known to me, though the site is being redeveloped as I write. Last summer, seeing a Trident parked here unceremoniously, once the fastest jet airliner in the world, I stopped the car at the old entrance to the factory:

Can I have a look?

> *No, because you are entering a hard-hat area, without a hard hat.*

Do you have a hard hat I could borrow?

> *No, but if you drive out back and climb the fence, no hard hat is required.*

From the health and safety point of view the visit was a disaster, because I climbed a fence in order to get a better photograph and as

I took it, fell from the fence and impaled my hand on a steel spike. This produced the bizarre spectacle of an old man sat in mud, next to an ageing airliner, weeping silently into his sleeve. Later I climbed into the hold, which was easily within reach. I know a girl who engaged in sex with baggage-handlers in such places, but more on that later. In the baggage holds of this Trident I discovered a kind of loft hatch into the passenger cabin. Naturally I let myself in, half expecting to be attacked by an itinerant axe murderer. In much the same way, since watching *Jaws* I can never swim without fear of shark attack, even at leisure centres.

I have to tell you, there is nothing stranger than working your way around musty places where so many dreams were invested over so many miles. You almost feel the passengers and crews are still there. At least you would have until the aircraft was broken up with a jackhammer a week later. Then they were left to drift the world again, disembodied spirits with no final destination. At East Midlands airport there used to be a derelict aircraft in which a number of people, including the crew, met their end. At night it could occasionally be seen lit, even after removal of the power. On one of these evenings an engineer returned to the flight deck and found him there, sat in his seat: the first officer. No longer with us, but wondering how he came to be in that place, so young and at so wrong a time. Peace, child, for I grew old there. It gets no better than that first time.

De Havilland were tied up with the first developments of commercial, military and business jets, culminating in the wing for the Airbus 320, curiously the aircraft I last operated. The firm established a name producing the Moth, the most successful trainer, with a name deriving from its wings, which folded for transport. This in itself tells us it dated from the nineteen-thirties, when they believed we were all destined to have an aeroplane in the garage. All that twenty-first century man actually has in his garage is a broken lawn mower, a vice he never got around to fitting and Aunt Ethel's armoire.

De Havilland was originally established in Edgeware, before this became part of the suburbs of London and too expensive to occupy. Stag Lane. Is the lane still there? Are the stags? I shall include all your replies in a box and then leave it at the bottom of the drive for the bin men. Or as managers now prefer them to be called, refuse collectors. The English have a peculiar resistance to this sort of thing, as the Anglo-Saxons did when invaded by Normans who wanted everyone to speak French. At that time for instance, Van Gogh's sketch the *Potato Eaters* would have to be known as the *French-fry Eaters*. For a more recent example of this famous intransigence, take an exchange I heard of recently during a protest march down Whitehall:

Policeman	*Sir, you cannot go beyond the cordon, it's a sterile area.*
Protestor	*What's that?*
Policeman	*I don't know. B******s, isn't it?*

With the advance of suburban London in the nineteen-thirties, a consequence of the underground railway, De Havilland had to move further out to Hatfield in Hertfordshire. Not so much because the local council required it, but because the firm could make as much money that way as it could making aeroplanes. In Hatfield they were to be taken over by Hawker, already consolidated with Armstrong-Siddley, itself a product of the amalgamation of separate companies. I think at one point a prior incorporation of Armstrong and Whitworth was an amalgamated entity going back to Whitworth himself, the man who dreamt up his own gauge of thread, which I am not sure the Americans do not still prefer. (There was a town in America recently put up signs in kilometres. Nobody liked them, so they took them down again and put the old ones back up, the sort of behaviour that might give a French bureaucrat a coronary).

Hawker pinched all the best designs from De Havilland and appended their own name to them, before being taken over themselves by British Aerospace, who decamped further north again to a place near Manchester whose name you need not know. Not that it has the power of voodoo, but more I could not be bothered telling you. When I say the best designs of De Havilland were appropriated, I should add that everything after the Moth was equally groundbreaking, if only from crashing into it so often.

These then represented successive migrations to the middle of nowhere, in an effort to balance the opposing imperatives of cheap land against the need to get staff into work. These were times after all when everybody relied upon public transport. Tell that one to your children. Another veteran my brother flew with pointed out the old air force base at Honiley and said when he had flown fighter jets there he had commuted by bicycle. I too recall a celebrated photograph in which a farmer turns from ploughing to watch a supersonic jet about to bury itself in the ground. The most remarkable thing is the tractor. Its wheels are tyred with metal, as they might have been a century earlier.

The old aerodrome in Hatfield was vacated in the nineteen-eighties, costing four hundred jobs. I arrived to live there not that long afterward and it still had the air of a town where something catastrophic had happened, but you were not sure what. The fellow who had previously occupied our house had worked there and amazed me by saying he walked to work each day: how many people are able to do that since we stopped mining coal? A lady who had worked along with her husband for many years at the firm ran the bric-a-brac shop on the corner of the old town. Her husband travelled the world selling BA146 commuter aircraft and loved it. Before I removed it there had been a wall-chart in my own house bearing little flags at strategic sales points around the globe, like a battle plan. "Did you know" the lady asked me, "that at eleven each day I would take Sir Geoffrey de Havilland a cup of coffee and a banana?" No, I had not known.

A captain I knew had been apprenticed there as a graduate and assured me the firm had long since been moribund. Before redevelopment the airfield was used by Spielberg to produce war movies. Indeed Tom Hanks said the best thing about Hatfield, was it was near to London. The use of airfields for such productions capitalises on their best assets: they are an accessible and flexible space ideally suited to the needs of either industry or house builders. We can no more resist their development than Canute could defer the tide, but we might still look at disused airfields in a different way, a way that satisfies our need for redoubts of quiet greenery. Such urgent needs are more easily accessed by all of us than any nostalgia for past glories in aviation.

There was no need for such green belt during the Second World War, when most of the country was rural anyway. A prime imperative at this time had been to construct airfields. Seven hundred littered the landscape. Many were unfinished at the close of war, by which time bases like Great Easton had eradicated great hunting forests. This was next door to Stansted anyway (which was itself underused) and never saw an aeroplane. Conveniently, it was given over to farming after the war, being an enterprise that turned somebody a profit. Likewise it will soon be sold to a developer to make another comfortable living. Until he retires to a place in Spain, to enjoy a landscape of 'ancient untouched forest'.

The situation was complicated in Europe by the shortage of unoccupied territory from which US aircraft could be launched. This had consequences both happy and grave, depending upon how you view airfields. If there were seven hundred, considering Britain is also seven hundred miles from north to south, then if they were arranged contiguously, you need never leave the airport shopping mall; in the same way, during the Middle Ages a squirrel could travel the country without recourse to forest floor. Much development was along the flat eastern side of the country and concentrated upon the Great North Road. This is the natural spine of Britain, the axis of its first major road and railway. The reason for this development was that fuel, which aeroplanes have an enormous thirst for, could be shuttled up and down this artery. A pipeline has long since replaced this logistical exercise.

Unfortunately, these low-lying areas are prone to fog and the singular worry of every departing bomber pilot was colliding with another from a nearby airfield. If you survived the reception party thrown by Goering (known affectionately as Hermann the German), then you arrived back a day later in the same conditions, when it was not possible to land. You then had three options:

(1)   Fly on until the fuel ran out and then crash anyway.

(2)   Crash deliberately in the sea.

(3)   Bail out and endure a lingering death.

(4)   Rely upon crazed boffins to get you down.

This was not much of a choice and is partly the reason why fifty-two thousand crews are not here to read this book. We are here to read it and we salute their bravery. I have just finished reading a book of wartime reminiscences and believe me, there were countless occasions upon which departing flight crews knew intuitively they were not returning and yet they went all the same.

As to the option you were immediately drawn to, the fourth, this comprised a range of ideas for dispersing fog. The most spectacular involved lining the runway with barrels of fuel and setting it alight. Doing this today would send you way over quota on the green-house gas front, but at the time the arrangement rendered a passable imitation of the sun, in its customary role of clearing fog. Inevitably the French felt they had to modernise the idea after the war. They used jet engines instead, which have a *fatigue life*, at the end of which you are left with an expensive toy capable of producing tons of thrust. You could try fitting it to a car to break the sound barrier, but ideally not without adult supervision.

What the French did was to fit them at the end of runways, to blow away fog. Californian vineyards are often kept frost-free by burning fuel oil, though not with the mother of all hairdryers. My only comparable experience of this was circling Stansted upon return from night flights, to await the departure of the first schedules, which would usually clear the runway long enough to permit our landing. This may depend on optimistic assessment of the meteorological situation from our friends in the control tower, who after all had no particular vested interest in my untimely death: or at least not until reading this.

Where did we get to on our journey to the airport? We were building them in towns and discovered that was a mistake. We eventually found building them on the mainland when they could be at sea was equally misguided, with the future in view. And I do say *could* be at sea, because there are still flatter parts of the world affording space for airfields, though mainly within continental interiors. The new airport at Denver is an example. This came with a financial package that is going to take forever to repay. Continental interiors are perfect for airports, for the simple reason that nobody wanted to go there in the first place. Culture seems since antiquity always to have been associated with water, because that is what people drank, washed in, watered their cabbages with and sailed boats around on. Think Venice, New York or London and not Denver, Milton Keynes or come to think of it, Moscow. There has at least to be a navigable river connecting the place to the sea, like at Paris. German technical supremacy stemmed from the waterways of the Rhine and not from Goethe's pen. Discuss.

There are two aspects connecting aeroplanes with water. One I touch upon later is actually landing them upon its surface, which at one time was considered a stylish thing to do but is now rightly viewed by most passengers with abject terror. The other is simply the fact that the coastline often coincides with the flattest part of most countries and this has considerable advantages when it comes to taking off or landing. Take Heathrow itself, which sits at just eighty feet, only about the height of two houses above the sea. The highest point for several miles in the take-off direction is Windsor Castle, which is not a great deal higher, which can sometimes be a good thing. The pilot of a jumbo jet, which had suffered engine failure on take-off and was dumping fuel feverishly in order to lighten the load, was instructed by air traffic he should not be dumping fuel overhead the town. The American captain reportedly replied that the Queen could choose to have the fuel, or else "the whole damned aeroplane".

Where airports are concerned, the flatter the surrounds the better and there are few things in life quite as flat as the sea. This is important when it comes to taking off, which is usually a breeze, unless one engine goes BANG and you had only two in the first place. This is especially true should you be fully laden. When I say fully laden, this is usually with every seat occupied and *only then* with as much fuel as you can carry. Aircraft are not like cars (as the manual says, CAUTION: AIRCRAFT ARE NOT LIKE CARS) and you cannot fill them with both fuel and people. This is not so much nowadays because they might not get airborne at all, but more in the event of losing an engine, they might drift slowly downwards.

You never want to be drifting downwards in any aeroplane, unless this is what the pilot intends. Some of the passengers do not like going up, while others fear the coming back down again even more. Like the grand old Duke of York, it is the neither being quite up nor quite down that passengers fear most.

In view of this requirement for flat terrain there are numerous airports located along coastlines, which allow aircraft to take off toward the sea, or to make an approach from the same direction. The only conceivable hazard on the sea is shipping, which these days can be as tall as any high-rise building. The fact it represents a moving target and cannot be displayed upon any map rather complicates the threat to aircraft. At Corfu, where we take off over the bay, I recall the aerodrome booklet warning us of the proximity of masts. I imagined any collision would be more of a surprise to the sailors involved than to those of us on the airliner. Merchant vessels are an entirely different matter. Get too low on the approach into Barcelona and you could be saying "Ola!" to the sides of a container ship. During one arrival I was told by air traffic that the *return* on our radar screen (which is not actually radar, but very similar) was not another aeroplane, but a naval vessel instead. Presumably it put out the same sort of identification code as aircraft so as to be obvious to naval aircraft around it, or to gather its charges after every exercise like a mother hen.

For pilots, take-offs out to sea, as if from an aircraft carrier, are a joy. I would usually ask the co-pilot to perform these, so that I could look out of the window at the lovely palms and parasols and wish I was down there with them for the week. Was I not scouring the instruments? Scouring is not required. Listening plays a part though. Even operating the largest aircraft, as with your car, the cues that tell you trouble is afoot are much the same:

(a)   Something does not *smell* right. Hoovering up a bird produces a pervasive smell of roast chicken. Good on Sundays, but bad in aeroplanes.

(b)   Something does not *sound* right. In the 737 the toilet sited just behind the flight deck might be flushing. You get used to it after about the third time.

(c)   Something does not *feel* right. Those perturbations or vibrations that were not there yesterday. Acknowledged by the term "What the **** is that?"

(d)   The passengers are *screaming*. A good cue, though not infallible. Many businessmen scream in thunderstorms. (I usually let them know they can scream all they like, as we are all going to die anyway.)

(e)   Oh yes, something does not *look* right. Visible cues range from the motion of a needle on a dial, to a Canada Goose through your windscreen.

(f)   Something does not *seem* entirely right. You are having a moment of existential doubt. Get on with the flying.

Turning to the actual approach to the airport, aircraft engaged in this descend along a three-degree slope. If you can remember your protractor from school, that Perspex thing that cracked when you sat on your pencil case, you will recall it ranged from zero to ninety degrees at the top. Three degrees looked as nearly flat as a rejected pancake. Viewed from out front of an airliner however it looks generally precipitous and at times quite alarmingly so. Occasionally approaches are designed into places like London City, with angles almost twice this, because of the high-rise surrounds. This feels, as one of my colleagues once remarked, like negotiating a very steep staircase. Even the three-and-a-half degree slope at Nice, designed to over-fly the residents of Cap Ferrat at higher levels, can result in much heavier landings. The rich can only guess at the suffering they cause.

In a perfect world all airfields would be nearly flat, along with the approaches to them. It so happens that the places most people want to be on their holidays, at least in Europe, are places that are least flat. Islands are a good example and those featured in that Bond film, within the Andaman Sea in Thailand, are often mountainous specifically because they *were* actually mountains, whose tops have since been submerged. This is also true of those around Europe. The alternative scenario involves volumes of drifting sand or coral forming attractive piles in the Indian Ocean or Caribbean Sea. These are fast disappearing anyway with the advance of global warming. Aside from island destinations, there are the ski resorts. That these will also be located near high ground is something of a no-brainer.

You therefore find airports in impossible places. The perils of arriving here are not elicited for the travelling public with as much relish as for the pilots themselves. The crew may be advised by pre-prepared literature that the *approach to runway 05 is constrained by high ground, largely unlit and rising to 2000 ft within three miles of the aerodrome. Severe turbulence can be expected on the final approach when the wind is from the North West, while the weather at night in July and August is usually thundery.* This is our own personal view of your arrival in the Greek Isles. In the brochure yours will invite you to "...admire the richly attired olive groves, gilded by the rays of the sun setting languidly over the Ionian Sea", though the sun will actually have set about five hours previously.

Only during radical manoeuvres do you begin to suspect these are designed precisely to avoid a closer inspection of the richly attired hillsides. For the crew though this is all as straightforward as ABC. Category 'A' destinations, are about as perilous as taking the car out of the driveway and beloved by crews for the absence of forethought required. As I get older I find thinking and enjoyment are mutually exclusive exercises. Then there are category 'B' airports, which you ought to brush up on. Occasionally it happens as a pilot that you land at one of these, wondering why the experience was not as pleasant as you anticipated, before discovering it actually had conditions attached. The most demanding are category 'C' airports, perched upon mountainsides and reserved for pilots from the training department. This suits all of the parties concerned, for the trainers invariably assume they are better than regular crews, while the regulars would rather be at home.

I did promise I would say something about taking off from water. Among the earliest incarnations of the aeroplane was a machine upon floats, which was called variously a seaplane or more normally nowadays a floatplane (as it lands on lakes and rivers too). This was an aeroplane with a pair of buoyant pontoons and actually the first type that William Boeing produced. This was not wholly improbable because Seattle, where Boeings are built, is by the seaside. These aircraft evolved into the 'flying boat', whose fuselage was boat-shaped and waterproof and rather more exciting altogether. The Art Deco establishment latched onto these in a big way, believing everybody was going to be either liberated by art and mass-production, or travelling the world like Noel Coward.

Travellers arriving at Milan Linate airport from the South might notice a strip of water out to the right. This exists there because Mussolini imagined people racing to the airport in streamlined locomotives and drinking from streamlined teacups, before boarding flying boats and exporting this vision of the future around the world. Except that the British got there first. Their flying boats used to be built on the Isle of Wight, or on the banks of the loch at Belfast. These would make their way at a leisurely pace down to the southernmost reaches of Africa, stopping at places like Lake Victoria instead of Luton. Or they would reach across to the Indian sub-continent, eventually to be abandoned years later in places like Goa, where they are used for purveying pizzas of the microwave variety.

There is your potted and partial history of the airfield. What does it mean in practice? Looking at the terminology, take the *terminal building*. In common with most airports, there used to be only one of these and at Heathrow it was called the Queens Building. It is still there, though its curving frontage, which once overlooked the comings and goings on the apron, now overlooks only a roadway passing through canyons of multi-storey buildings, accrued over the years by entirely arbitrary planning. The expression *terminal* was taken from the terminus at the end of every railway or shipping line.

Airports though are like children in that they rapidly outgrow themselves. As more buildings are added, they have to be distinguished. They may become known as the North or South terminal, like at de Gaulle, which is an amalgamation of two different airfields. More romantically, Heathrow had its 'Domestic' and 'European' terminals, which have now been renumbered with the rather less romantic designations of T1 and T2. Then T3 was added alongside these for long-haul destinations, though it also does dispatch some European flights. T4 was provided for the exclusive use of British Airways, while T5 is also intended for British Airways, or for anyone else who might enjoy playing Monopoly.

The aircraft are navigated around the airport via *taxiways*, which to you and I are roads. The problem with roads traditionally is that they have different names depending on the point from where you set off. The Great North Road emerging from the capital becomes the London Road at the Edinburgh end. To avoid the confusion once people had taken to the road in greater numbers and had to navigate themselves around, the roads emanating from around London were given numbers beginning at '1' and increasing clockwise. The Great North Road therefore became the A1, while the A2 went toward the southeast and the A3 toward the southwest etcetera.

Something similar has happened to taxiways, but is in a constant state of flux along with the rest of Europe. Traditionally you might use the *outer* or *inner* taxiway, or run along the *parallel*, which parallels the runway. In Heathrow all of the taxiways are divided into sections or blocks, so that if you see a sign bearing 79:80 alongside, this means you are just leaving block 79 for block 80. This is quite a logical system, so much so that it is about to be changed to conform to the European model. This nominates taxiways with letters, so one might be the 'hotel' taxiway and then appends another letter thereto to be more specific. If the taxiway leads onto the runway at three points, these might be nominated HA, HB and HC. The scheme looks fine on paper, like they always do over a cup of coffee and a nice warm desk, but in the dark and rain when you are being told to route via "Hotel Hotel to intersection Hotel Delta to take Golf Lima to holding point Foxtrot Echo", instead of taking the inner taxiway to block 79, the idea begins to pall. In Paris I have known American wide-bodies just to stop and await a marshalling vehicle. If we all demanded this sort of service, we would soon get things changed back again.

From the air, runways, taxiways and indeed motorways all look the same. This is why at Dublin you are advised there is "a motorway parallel to the runway" because the implied extension to this advice is that you should not land on that instead. At London Gatwick airport the taxiway is designed for emergency use as a runway, which is probably why people occasionally land on it in error. It is also very long and I was once told that Ryanair were upbraided by no less an authority than the Police, for using it at over seventy miles per hour. Whether they received points I do not know.

Taxiing is the term for what you and I would call driving with due care, in an aeroplane. The taxiway occasionally crosses the runway, though you do not want to do this while somebody is taking off. As experiences go, it is like being in a milk float on a level crossing. To avoid this scenario the ground controller up in the tower often has a radar screen, which detects aeroplanes as little outlines creeping around the tarmac. Interpreting these returns and coming to meaningful conclusions used to require all the skills of a necromancer. The radar now works in conjunction with aircraft *transponders*, which are transmitters that send a reply, while they would also be linked to a computer to help generate a meaningful picture. As a result it has more of the look-and-feel of a Gameboy, along I suppose with the potential pitfalls. For instance, you only get one 'life'. One of my favourite cartoons featured a man at a radar screen marked in concentric circles, interrupted at intervals like those games with ball bearings which roll around inside. "Look," he is saying, "I finally got them all in the middle."

What usually complicates the picture is the amount of roadworks going on, especially at night. You would have thought these would be marked better than they generally are on the highway, but in fact they are not. This is because as pilots you are expected to know or at least to guess what is going on and besides, suing you afterwards is always going to be cheaper than providing lighting. Combine this with the quality of windscreen wipers fitted to aircraft, on a par with those of the Model-T Ford, then you see why a Singapore Airlines captain collided with a digger during take-off with the legendary expletive, "Shit, I think we hit something." In the 747 this impact might only take the form of a mere stirring somewhere in the bowels. It is so large and the flight deck so high (because actually it was designed for freight and had a front door), they had to produce a mock-up first on a rig like a double-decker bus. This could be driven around airports in advance of production, just to see how much fun it would be.

Now let us look inside the terminal. The control tower used to be on top of here, but now it normally sits on a stalk in the middle of nowhere. This provides a panoramic overview to help you guide aircraft on the ground, as well as providing a comprehensive view of the skies around. It also means you can see if pilots are misbehaving. At Heathrow we liked to get in the queue for the pushback nice and early by pretending we were ready, when in fact we might still be loading the catering. This would not be possible if it was obvious from the control tower, or indeed anywhere at airports like Rome Fiumicino. Here they have either video cameras or binoculars, or both, so that when you call and say "Pronto", they accuse you of being a Neapolitan lowlife and tell you to call back after the fuel bowser has been disconnected. Another advantage of video systems is you can see if parking places are occupied. I once sat for ten minutes at London waiting for one of these, which the tower insisted was in use. When I saw a BA aircraft with a good view of the area, I asked *them* if we could ask *him*. This was expressly denied, involving as it did the use of initiative by the people on the ground. Eventually the BA pilot informed me the parking space was free anyway, which gave me a voucher to call the tower on the mobile phone. Complaining over the radio is considered to be worse than farting in church.

Looking inside the terminal, there are shops, shops, shops, shops and a few more shops. Occasionally you might even spot a check-in desk, where they take your baggage in order to send it to the wrong destination. At Heathrow you would often see bags lying around on the roadways beneath the terminal. With any luck they would be picked up before they had been run over by a sixty-ton pushback tractor. And they are that heavy; they have to be to push four hundred tons of aeroplane and four engines at idle thrust. At the lovely new airport at Gardermoen in Norway, from the aircraft you could see the bar-coded baggage being whisked around at hairy speeds on rails, like kids at a funfair. In fact I am not sure I did *not* see one or two kids in those bins.

From here they are disgorged onto the apron and if this requires a change of level, this sometimes involves them negotiating a helter-skelter. The business of moving bags around automatically is not cheap and like many of the other systems, usually involves bespoke designs fabricated at great cost. They do have advantages over donkeys, but not many in my experience. Once on the apron the bags are often loaded into *unitary loading devices* or ULDs. These are alloy boxes the size of garden sheds and when they are not being blown around the airport, they are loaded en masse into the aeroplane baggage holds, by a mobile loader armed with a thousand castors. This is done because it is quicker than throwing them on (though if you fly 737s with Ryanair or Southwest, they are still being thrown on), but also because most aircraft are now too high up for loading to be carried out manually, except by the Harlem Globetrotters.

If the flight is held up because a passenger has not boarded, their bag has to be removed. If you are in a hurry then as far as the handlers are concerned, sometimes any old bag will do to be turfed off. This is why the cabin crew will often be exasperated by passengers who ring the call bell to ask why their Louis Vuitton suitcase is sat alongside in a puddle? This then is what happened to your bags. You personally are required to pass through a security cordon, through to more shops. The security section is something of a bridge of sighs. Statistically, every day somebody when interrogated about his wash bag will inevitably reply that it includes a tube of exploding toothpaste, ha ha ha. In response they will be denied boarding and sent for a coffee with the airport police instead, ha ha ha. I bought my wife a life-size copy of a Rembrandt in Amsterdam and as I passed through in my uniform, did my level best to persuade them it was the original, which I had just stolen. Naturally they giggled, which is exactly why Steve McQueen did get away with it in *The Thomas Crown Affair*. I also challenged them to "Name that Picture!" as it passed through the X-ray machine, which these days produce coloured images. Given a hat and sufficient bravado, there is nothing life will deny you.

We usually arrive at the departure lounge along a travelling walkway at the larger airports. Here there is another opportunity to sell you consumables, this time often free of tax. Within Europe you will have noticed that duty now has to be applied, but that the cost of 'duty-free' goods has barely risen. Given that virtually the entire cost of fuel, drink and tobacco in the UK is a handout to the government, this is an indication of the profits the airport owners themselves were extracting from you previously. This is why airports generate revenue only a little more slowly than security printers. One company, the privatised British Airports Authority, owns all of the major London airports and many others besides. It is precisely because of the footfall of passengers and the money they provide the local economy that secondary airports virtually allow airlines like Ryanair to land for free. The reason in turn that these airlines allow many of you to travel for free is because of the kickbacks from hire car and travel insurance companies, beside the fact they themselves avoid taxes on such niceties as fuel. Think of it as a fairground: airports provide the pitch, the airlines the ride, the government the site and you the money.

Down the air-bridge now and onto the aeroplane, whose doorway is conveniently two or three metres high, which is about where the departure lounge is, which provides an undercroft where roadways and baggage halls can be located. In the old days we used to walk across an apron and know exactly what we were getting into. Believe me, you do not know what you are getting into. Not yet, anyway...

PUSHBACK

This is a phase I almost overlooked in writing this book, skipping it along with that part where we taxi to the runway, if only to get on with the take-off. This is a very masculine thing to have done, like jumping into bed when a woman wants the preliminaries like forethought and flowers. There is a more religious element to the preliminaries involved in flying airliners: rising at monastic hours, donning vestments, assembling in the crew room. Then laying out the instruments of our craft, an office performed not by an altar boy, but by the co-pilot. Finally the arrival of the captain, covered not by a mitre, but by a peaked cap. All is silence, especially at five in the morning, all reverent introspection. What I must do for you now is to preserve this feeling and consecrate it in words. This is life as a pilot, a century on from the beginnings of powered flight. A perfect Christmas gift, for the Wright brothers flew on December 17 a century ago, so as to be able to make it back home for the holiday. Little did they know what they were doing for my sales strategy.

I should add I have been flying *short haul*. This constitutes the bulk of flying, principally because the biggest market for flying is in the USA and most of this is internal operation. It is the same in Europe. The airborne population of the world at any one time is several million. The proportion engaged in shorter-haul flights of limited duration is unknown. What I do know is that during the course of eight hours and four flights between Dublin and London, I might dispatch seven hundred passengers. Meanwhile a 747 spending the same time on a flight between London and New York might carry only half that number. I shall consider the differences between short and long haul more carefully when we are safely settled in the cruise, but not much more so. Meanwhile we have a flight to prepare.

One aspect of short-haul flying that I must discuss are the hours involved, how many there are and just when they fall. Long-haul flights from London are very regular. Flights bound for points west, mainly in America where most of the revenue is to be made, leave at lunchtime and arrive in the early evening. I used to dislike operating flights coinciding with lunchtime, because it is the rush hour at Heathrow, when you might be caught in a queue of fifteen for the runway. This activity also meant you could not be eating lunch at the same time, which you might have done had you already been airborne.

The reason long-haul flights leave westbound around this time are historic and developed like the hours of nine-to-five evolved in the office. Bear in mind that debarring the great escapades around the British Empire, the first route of any note was that between New York and London. Even today, about a quarter of all aviation activity in Europe centres in the UK. Further afield, New York and London have always been the epicentres of world trade. New York *is* the World Trade Center. Consider the history of connections between each urban nexus: the attempts by Marconi to transmit radio signals from Cornwall and receive them in New England and later the first oceanic telegraph and telephone cables. Ignore for a moment the wealth of shipping between Liverpool or Southampton and Ellis Island. Instead skip to Lindbergh and his flight from the northeastern seaboard, arriving over Kerry within a half-mile of the intended landfall. The flight went so well he ignored London altogether and continued to Le Bourget in Paris instead. Also of significance was the previous adventure of Alcock and Brown in their converted bomber, which ended up in an Irish bog. These two characters used to be carved in stone out front of the Queens Building, the original London terminal. Now they have been moved to a point outside Heathrow Business Centre, so as to make way for spaces where coaches can be parked. Unlike Alcock and Brown, the men at Heathrow Airport Limited are more concerned with in-trays than iced-up engines.

Leaving London at lunchtime ensures we arrive in America semi-fresh in late afternoon, with the opportunity of a relaxing evening (or technically a very late night) and several hours of sleep before the rigours of business. The timings for the return trip are arranged so you can sleep overnight and arrive 'fresh' at breakfast time in London, where the boss will have arranged a full itinerary for you. The crew will be going home and having sex. One of the things I noticed when returning from night-freighting across the North Sea, bound for Stansted, is that the long-haul traffic would arrive early on occasions and then circle endlessly until six when they were allowed to land. This restriction is applied for environmental reasons. They would rather you spent forty minutes adding to greenhouse gases and then land in time to hit the traffic and add to it some more. See Naples and die. As for traffic going eastbound, this departs at teatime, again with the intention of your sleeping over during the journey. You then arrive at your Thai brothel suitably refreshed for breakfast and ready for the rigours of whatever business you had planned. Flights to points in the Near East seem to go at any time, incidentally.

We really do have to crack on and get this flight away on schedule. The single most important figure reviewed by the board of any airline each day is the proportion of flights dispatched on schedule, as expressed in percentage terms. 'On schedule' means to *leave* and not to *arrive* on time. On one occasion we had a passenger complain we had arrived in London early. Statisticians will tell you that this is entirely reasonable, because in any human population a percentage of 0.001 of the sample will always prove to be a prat. If ever this happened I would go back and say, I am sorry Sir, do remain here with the crew eating bacon paninis and discussing sex...

The reason the departure time is important stems, like everything else in aviation, from maritime practice. The sea was always considered a dodgy thing to use for getting from A to B, interrupted as it was by giant squid, hundred-metre waves, tropical hurricanes and the edge of the known world. The only reason English sea-salts could be persuaded to travel at all is they were slugged with a baton in Portsmouth and offered all the lemons they could eat. When ships came to be used for carrying passengers, as with the voyage of *The Beagle*, you were told when you would be leaving, but not when you would be arriving. Also you could expect all sorts of disclaimers on the obverse of the ticket, like *The shippers bear no responsibility whatsoever toward passengers consumed by giant squid, nor to their dependants.*

The reasonable assumption was that given the perils at sea, not to mention an absence of favourable winds, you were clueless as to when you would arrive anyway. Nowadays you might be saying, "But my Airbus has no sails and there are no giant squid between here and Edinburgh." In reply the airlines will point out that they operate an effective cartel on behalf of the government and besides, you are spoiling the taste of their coffee and pastry. For the same conventional reasons airlines will not guarantee you a date, let alone a time for departure. This is not a whim, but is enshrined in law. Missed a mega-merger in Tokyo because the co-pilot overslept? Go sue the cat.

As for punctuality, this is supposed to relate to the time when the aircraft pushes back, or when at least one engine is started. Airliners are rather like computers and if they find themselves powered only by their batteries, then as little of the equipment on the aircraft is connected as possible, to prevent these going flat. One way to rectify this situation, like in your car, is to start an engine and provide a generator. At this stage the data recording equipment bursts into life, providing an absolute time when the flight is considered to begin. Pilots are simple but devious, so when the management at BA suspected crews were massaging the pushback times, some of them simply started an engine at the required time instead. Hey presto, on time again!

The first thing I noticed when joining British Midland, was that cheating on departure time was going on wholesale. One reason for this is airlines use the statistics published by the Civil Aviation Authority in their war of words. Easyjet like to concentrate on this aspect, but at bottom all it means is they are better at cheating than everybody else, or better at spinning the facts. I like the enthusiasm of their chairman, but am I the only one with the impression he is one bite short of a kebab? To get around this dilemma, the CAA rightly say they are not prepared to trust any of us and look at the time at which the aircraft gets airborne. This is recorded in the control tower at every licenced airfield, as it is important for all sorts of reasons. It might be done so that on TV programmes they can say:

> The aircraft got airborne at 15:17 and at just 15:19 one of its engines ingested a flock of flamingoes, causing it to ditch into a shark-infested lagoon, where tragically, everyone was eaten. Stay with us until after the break.

What the CAA do with their figure is to subtract what they consider a reasonable time for the aircraft to have taxied to the runway, depending upon the conditions prevailing at that time. At Heathrow this might be ninety minutes on a quiet day. That produces a pushback time, which they consolidate by airline and by month. I think this is the case. If it is not then I would ask you to let me know the right answer after you have found it, which is a reasonable request coming from any aircraft captain.

Many airlines traditionally consider delays upto three minutes as not constituting delays at all. I think we can all go with that one. Pilots like to think in terms of the number that the big hand is pointed to. In practical terms this means you round the time *back* to the nearest number. After all at the end of the day we are getting paid, so who cares anyway? One of my favourite calculations while at a bank was how much I had earned while on the toilet. I feel empathy for those in the Third World who are not paid for this; if anything separates the haves from the have-nots, it has to be this.

With flight crew acting in this way, many of you will have worked out that any airliner pushing back four minutes and fifty-nine seconds late will be recorded for the benefit of the management as an 'on-time' departure. Actually the management does not trust the pilots either and use instead the times provided by the *flight dispatcher*. The dispatcher is the harassed one you see on the jetty. In America where they like that cheerleader crap, the dispatcher wears a red cap. They are known quite brilliantly, as 'red-caps'.

Branches of American handling agents continue this tomfoolery in Europe. The practice goes down well in Italy, where Mussolini attributed his prowess in bedding women to the fact he wore a funny hat. Pilots in Italy are treated like senior civil servants, which for all practical purposes is what they actually are. They wear hats at every possible opportunity. Whenever we worked there we would deflate this pompousness if their crews popped into the flight deck, by asking for a tea with two sugars.

In contrast, over in Holland where the people are overtly grateful to America for saving their ass, not only do they exclusively buy their airliners from here, but they also try to wear their hats in the same way. In America, the veteran flyer would leave a peaked cap on in the cockpit, not to look good, but because he was freezing his nuts off. Once radios were introduced, a headset like a pair of tin cans was worn over the cap, which squashed the sides down. The longer the pilot flew, the more squashed the cap appeared, so in the crew-room the highest reverence was reserved for the most squashed hats. What this means in Holland is they try to make their caps look like this before even starting. This way the pilots feel they all look like Leonardo de Caprio and everybody will wish they had a job like theirs.

In Britain the hats required for any profession are all produced by the same obscure milliner established somewhere in the city since the fire in Pudding Lane. Whether you are traffic warden, prison officer, holiday-camp entertainer or airline captain, you are all going to look the same. To get around looking like a holiday camp redcoat, pilots refuse to wear the hat unless the management hove into view. I wear it when it is raining; but I notice if this is sustained for long enough then it shrinks considerably, making me look like one of the Blues Brothers. There are also sad individuals who get their mums to sew down the sides of their cap in the hope people like me will say to them, Hello, aren't you Charles Lindbergh?

To continue, the role of the *flight dispatcher* is to co-ordinate the arrival of everybody at the aircraft: flight and ground crew, caterers, fuel, baggage-handlers, cleaners and oh yes, the passengers. These people are paid for their performance, so the times they record are fed into pushback statistics and are consolidated, so managers can assess their efficiency. You could probably ask a chimpanzee, "Who do *you* think will record the pushback time more accurately, the pilots who do not care, or the dispatcher whose ass is kicked if her flight runs late?" Managers are not so easily trained and prefer to trust the dispatcher, probably only because of their traditional mistrust of pilots. What this means in practice is that as the aircraft pushes back twenty-five minutes late, the dispatcher asks if we can call it five minutes and blame it on the cleaners as usual and the captain replies, Anyone seen my newspaper?

Short-haul flights usually fall into two work patterns, each as anti-social as the other. There are things regulating the hours pilots are available to work, called Flight Time Limitations. These have to be incorporated in the airline operating manual before the authorities can award an operating certificate and a paper hat. Nowadays the operating manual is actually a collection of manuals on how to operate each type of aircraft as well as how to conduct aspects of the business like quality assurance. At its core in Europe at least is Part A, a host of internally generated and externally imposed practices and procedures. It includes throwaway statements like *so-called designer beards should not be worn* besides more homely advice on what to do if the aircraft starts shouting "Pull Up! Pull Up!" at you. Apparently the thing to do here is to pull up, but it has to be spelt out for the benefit of the law courts and subsequent action should you have pushed down. Possibly my favourite entry read simply:

Passengers who should not be carried: *Salman Rushdie*

It was generally assumed that this entry featured in most operational manuals because of the threat such an obvious target posed to the airline, but I liked to think it was simply because he was so smug.

The body of knowledge immortalised by the Part A, or Civil Aviation Publication number 360 as it is formally known, has been handed down through the generations of airlines and lovingly photocopied by each. Often the logos of one bankrupt airline can be seen lightly tippexed out in the corner and replaced. This is simply because the easiest way of setting up an airline and operating Boeing 737s for instance is to pinch the manuals from someone else. This generally involves little guile as the first airline has probably gone bust and had its offices raided before the bailiffs moved in. Apart from which 737 operating manuals are not way up there among the priorities of the average liquidator. On hearing from radio reports that Air Europe had gone under, the first action of many of the employees was to check into the office and help themselves to a favourite item of furniture. This is why my lounge is divided into cubicles. One 707 pilot in Iran not only debunked himself after the fall of the Shah, but helped himself to one of these aircraft at the same time.

The problem with this endless replication and accretion of airline operating manuals is that sections become ennobled, as if they had been found among the Dead Sea scrolls. When people like myself start asking questions about so-called designer beards, we are told it has simply always been that way. Should we not be careful we are not founding alternative religions in this way? After all the photocopying, many of the diagrams already look more like Aztec totems than aeroplanes under a certain light.

The flight time limitations scheme is a case in point, a tedious scripture I rarely bother to look at. It is widely flouted anyway, depending upon where in Europe you happen to live. This does not stop many pilots studying it like novitiates might study the commandments. The reason is pilots enjoy being disputatious, especially if sticking one in the eye of the management appears endorsed by law. What the FTL scheme might say regarding the number of days available to work for example is something like this:

> You may work six consecutive days, unless this involves getting up before the cat, whereupon you may only work four. In all events should you be asked to do seven, you can stick it in the eye of the management.

As regards shift patterns, these comprise either *earlies*, which being lazy I detested, or *lates*, which I liked because you got up for lunch, went to work and before long found yourself in a hotel bar surrounded by people half your age. Early starts may involve rising as early as four o'clock or in places like Milan, where the clocks run one hour ahead, effectively three in the morning. I used to fly mail at night and the more I look at this, the more it looks like the same thing. One way to avoid unseemly behaviour of this kind is to join a national airline like BA, where you are not expected to rise before the sun, even in winter. I think it is contractual. In the USA, where there is no national airline, you have to join a bloated giant like United or American. These lose dollars faster than they cover air miles, for the same reasons as the nationalised airlines. Companies in other industries engage in partnerships for profit. Airlines form alliances only to spread the losses around. As one analyst put it, companies join alliances when the management have no strategic view of their own, besides what you might expect of an average sheep.

The only advantage of getting up so early is the motorway traffic consists of only airline employees, the bewildered and the suicidal. Harder to negotiate is the trip from the car park. Most crew will be consigned to perimeter car parks; in the way Dante consigned his minor offenders to the outer echelons of hell. In the summer this has its compensations. The air is so quiet that the birds are singing spiritedly, perhaps in the knowledge they are soon to pass through the stages of a jet engine. The sun also rises, albeit over Hounslow. The office staff and senior crews miss out on this experience, as the managers allocate central parking spaces in the following order:

    (a)   Ourselves.

    (b)   Managers from East Midlands, in case they drop by.

    (c)   People who rise after eight o'clock.

    (d)   Senior flight crew with the money to sue us.

    (e)   Anyone brown-nosing to required standards.

Upon arrival, the crew room is buzzing with anticipation and repressed hormones. My brother used to say that at Air Europe, the thing that hit him was the scent of a thousand perfumes. This left me undecided as to whether to join an airline or a Turkish bordello. Entering the building the first officers will be earnestly hoping they arrived first. If they have not, they know instinctively they are scheduled to fly with a flight-training captain. This is the time to get on the mobile and explain you are stuck on the motorway, having been maimed by the bewildered or suicidal. Any first officer who ever arrived late will tell you they apologised profusely and fetched several coffees. Any captain who arrives late will tell you they grunted like a primate and helped themselves to a coffee. Later in the bar they will have worn corduroy trousers in a colour that clashed badly with their suede footwear. They would also have forgotten their wallet.

Surveying all of this activity from their eyrie are *crew dispatchers*, who have a hotline to the *crewing* department. These people publish a roster showing when crews can expect to report for work, along with the where and when of flights they are to operate. The crew dispatchers are therefore quasi-papal figures expected to intercede on behalf of all those stranded in the car. All this is later distilled into a PA for the benefit of the passengers:

> *Ladies and Gentlemen, it appears the first officer is on his way from Milan (Uxbridge) and has been delayed by another carrier (bewildered pensioner), for reasons beyond our control. Do please enjoy another orange juice and I shall speak to you again once I have examined the weather (crossword puzzle).*

Good aren't I?

Already prepared in the crew room for perusal by the captain is a variety of paperwork. Much of the weather is now available from the Internet; during times the cabin crew are not using it to examine cross-dressers in Bangkok. The same facility allows the captain to cast a seasoned eye over satellite images of northern England, before declaring the area free of tropical cyclones. Or he might say, Cor, you can see smoke from Mount Etna! While he does this, or checks his allowances on the palm-top, the co-pilot will examine the weather instead. This is the principal determinant when it comes to deciding how much fuel to carry. There will be other considerations: one of our captains had a bad experience over the Atlantic and for this reason alone loaded an extra ton before even pouring a coffee. This is known customarily as fuel for the wife and kids.

Other paperwork to consider at this point includes the Notams, or *Notices to Air Men*. Notams stem from the days when messages arrived by pigeon to say the destination was mired in mud and everyone had gone home. Now they are packed with self-important information on how the third light along the edge of runway 33R at Milan is operating at half-strength. What they ought to say is the ground radar they bought three months ago will not be installed for the foreseeable future, because the godfather who provided it is otherwise engaged. My gripe with Notams is not so much they consume reams of paper, for many pilots take this home for the children, but they should be called *Notices to Air Persons* or Notaps. People like Emmeline Pankhurst threw themselves beneath horses for this kind of thing. Let me tell you now, no horse comes within thirty yards of me.

What this hour of pre-flight preparation mainly affords us is an opportunity to complain about the management, or the scheduling. This chorus, drowning out that of the starlings, might be triggered by a solitary call, not so much of a chirrup but more "The b******s aren't even out of bed yet." Also around this time we have to introduce ourselves to the cabin crew. Some flight crews telephone beforehand to discover with whom they are working, though I would not be bothered. In a small airline you will recognize everybody, in a medium-sized outfit only some, but at airlines where there are thousands, the chances are that nobody on the crew of a 747 will have met previously. This is the reason for all of those manuals and all of those procedures, so that A knows what to expect of B, C and D. This too gives the airline a collegiate feel, everybody having this kind of unspoken affinity.

The time for flight preparation is fixed at one hour. Depending upon circumstances like the logistics of getting to the aircraft, it can be reduced to forty-five minutes. This might come as a surprise to those passengers who allow at least twice as long to check in a weekend bag, but there you are. Do it every day and you get good at it. During this time a second bus has to be taken between the crew-room and the aircraft itself. Airports just get bigger all the time. For a while we could walk through the terminal building, or down the sides of the apron. The *apron*, incidentally, used to be the bit of concrete sticking out in front of the airport terminal. It was mainly there to prevent passengers from getting their shoes muddy when the weather was wet, or to stop the aeroplanes wearing out the turf like a goalkeeper. Nowadays the apron refers to all of the paved sections not already used for parking (*stands*), for driving around (*taxiways*) or for taking off and landing (*runways*).

To walk around upon the apron two things are required. One is identification, because international airports are divided into *airside* and *landside*. Airside does not mean up in the air rather than on the ground, but refers to where the aeroplanes are parked. As you will have guessed, it derives from shipping. Conventionally goods or people arriving in a port are considered to be of dubious provenance. These people have to be checked by *customs officers*, in order to relieve them of money, or to send them away if we do not like the cut of their jib. The companies operating ships soon tired of sitting around whilst this process was enacted and insisted the port authorities did it some place else. This became a formal no-mans-land that might take the form of a bonded store or customs house, or indeed that part of any airport designated as being 'airside'. It is the only place where you are allowed to apprehend passers-by and accuse them of religious fundamentalism, though this used to be Croydon.

The second thing required, more recently, is a reflective vest. This gives the health-and-safety guys something to get off on. One particularly truculent captain I worked with would wear this like underpants, a leg through each hole, in the knowledge the airport authorities had not specified quite how it should be donned. As a matter of course I prefer at least to be seen in white shirtsleeves, as flight crew are frequently run down. There are many vehicles out there and most weigh several tons. None of them incidentally need to be registered as long as they are used within the airport, but their operators are expected to pass a driving test. They do this at fifteen miles per hour and later drive at fifty, killing and maiming to the maximum effect. The drivers of pushback tugs have less chance of noticing they ran you over than you have of knowing you clipped a hedgehog.

Before boarding the airside bus we too have to pass through security where, like the passengers, we have our hand baggage screened and IDs checked. This is where I always hope my bag will not be randomly searched, not because it conceals weapons of mass destruction, but four days worth of dirty underpants. Actually my wife does consider this a WMD. More exotic characters (mainly among the cabin, as flight crew are unexotic by definition) will reveal a vibrator or set of manacles at this point, depending upon personal preference. This might provide a topic of conversation on the bus, engaging many of the crew, while others like myself prefer to feel like a dog that passed away in the night.

When arriving at the aircraft, one of the principal objectives is to let yourself in. It may already have been attached to an airbridge, or *jetty*. Aircraft that do not stand too high are often fitted with *airstairs*. These are like a loft ladder and slide out of a compartment beneath the forward door. Otherwise we would have to sit around for fifteen minutes waiting for the flight dispatcher and then another fifteen waiting for a set of mobile steps. By my reckoning that is half-hour late your flight is running today. And if you think I am busting my ass to make it only twenty-five... An interesting scenario at this point is for someone to have left any of the escape slides armed. This can normally be checked by peering into the porthole to see if a small pennant has been set to say *Do not open this door if you value your job*. This is the reason you should always nominate someone else to open the door. They will be the most junior member of the team and the captain will provide encouragement at a range of twenty yards by shouting, You know how to open the door don't you, you're fresh off the course? If it is a bad day, then a twenty-foot rubberised animal is about to explode from beneath the door, taking out the junior attendant and a passing caterer. In the immediate aftermath the first officer is tasked with smirking and the captain with losing his temper and demanding the whole thing be cleaned up before he even dreams of ordering another coffee.

On board the crew move around the cabin performing the security checks, in accordance with their earlier briefing. Cabin crew briefings are rigorous and standards of appearance exacting. Flight crew briefings are not rigorous, nor are their standards of appearance nearly as exacting. This earns individuals among them epithets like *Captain Caveman*. This particular individual, with whom I especially enjoyed flying, would take his seat before shouting "Oi! Bitch! Tea *now*!" toward the galley. This was most amusing when newer crews took it for real. In which event he definitely ought not to have drunk the tea. Flight attendants who have fallen out with pilots over such demands are reputed to spit in the drink at best, or rub the teabag around the rim of the toilet at worst. What they do for some of the passengers, for whom they probably have even less fellow feeling, is beyond the imagination of any tea bag. The only time I felt my coffee was spiked, erroneously as it turned out, was a function of the catering stores. For deodorising the toilets, powerfully scented aerosols were used and if these were kept too near to the cups, they were absorbed by the polystyrene.

During this interval before the flight the captain will take his seat, complain he has not been offered a cup of coffee and having noticed it was raining, invite the first officer to carry out an external inspection. If ever I fancied stretching my legs, especially since the dangers of DVT had been elicited, I did this myself. It offered a perfect opportunity for self-importantly staring down the front of an engine, while at the same time wondering what you were having for dinner that evening. If you had encountered the passengers and found they were not particularly likeable, you could adopt an appearance of great concern at this point, or even ask the engineer to raise the panels. Another reason for this form of management by wandering about might be to hurry along the fuelling, because in some airports after some contretemps or other, the fuellers might connect the hose but refuse to flick the switches setting the required quantity or opening the valves. On cold or wet days watching the fuel load is like watching a kettle boil and to alleviate this I would stand as close to the jet tailpipe as possible, benefiting from its residual warmth. In the wet I might shelter beneath the wings, which would often be dripping themselves from layers of hoar frost accumulated during descent from 35,000 ft. Another place to enjoy warmth is below the air-conditioning outlets, having selected the units on before leaving the flight deck (which many pilots help to keep warm by turning up the lighting as much as possible).

The thing about modern aircraft like the Airbus is that learning is skewed toward the manuals. In practice this means you can take someone around the aircraft who has years of experience and point to the air-conditioning inlet, knowing what it is because it sounds like your vacuum cleaner and ask them what it is. Not infrequently they will tell you they do not know. They can always get their own back when it comes to flying the thing.

The aircraft might be parked in front of the departure lounge, as they are in many of the cul-de-sacs at Heathrow. Occupants of the flight deck are then afforded comprehensive views of the proceedings. The cabin crew use the term *flight deck* as a generic term for pilots, incidentally, besides describing where they sit. It had not escaped the notice of one captain that there was a public telephone in the corner nearest the window, whose number might be recorded, so as to contact anyone nearby with a mobile. During quiet moments of pre-flight preparation, he would call this telephone and when the nearest passenger answered it, would say things like:

> *Turn around slowly and look at the man with a brown briefcase currently in W H Smiths. He works for MI6 and is there to intercept a Soviet agent about to board your aircraft. That agent is the man to your left in a polka-dot tie. As you board, let the cabin crew know that the man in the polka-dot tie is under constant surveillance.*

A short interlude and a knock on the flight deck door:

> *Some bloke is complaining about a passenger in a polka-dot tie.*

The captain replies:

> *Don't worry, he's a Soviet agent.*

Before boarding takes place, we have to start the Auxiliary Power Unit (APU). The best reason for doing this is it supplies water pressure, so we can all have a nice cup of tea. It also provides independent electrical power in case one of the ground crew walks up and pulls the plug on your aircraft, simultaneously plunging the passengers into darkness and losing everything the co-pilot has entered into the computer over the last twenty minutes. The correct spoken response of the other pilot at this point, according to the manuals, is "Ha-ha-ha, you'll have to put that in all over again!"

What I have not pointed out at this point is that the pilots have to decide who is going to do the flying and who the radio work. To save arguments the captain usually flies the first *sector* of the day. In short-haul operations you might operate as many as six of these, from one point to another. I have known captains to look at the weather and decide because the landing looks challenging that the first officer can kick off instead. I would only give away the first sector if I felt life had grown stale and needed a spontaneous act like this, or like asking the cabin crew for a *Guardian* instead of a *Telegraph*. The Daily Telegraph seemed to be de rigueur for commanders and one I knew would always reply, I should like a stereotypical *Telegraph* please. How we laughed.

The flying or *handling pilot* will either be thinking through the departure procedure or reading the newspaper, depending upon the circumstances of the day. If it is thundery and dark and mountainous out there, then their perusal of the paper will be decidedly edgy and interrupted by periods of brooding over aerodrome plates describing the initial routing. As Samuel Johnson used to say, when a man knows he is to be hanged in a fortnight, it concentrates his mind wonderfully. Personally I imagine knowing this would prevent you from doing anything useful, if only because there would be so little point. If I were to do the flying I might also listen to the radio during this period, so that if a queue was building for pushback or take-off, I could call up and pretend to be ready. This might have to be done through a mouthful of sausage panini. During the flight it is especially funny over the radio to hear pilots who have been caught short for a verbal response with a mouthful of food. It gets others on the frequency trying to guess whether it smacks of a light desert, or has the baritone resonance of a meat pie.

While all of this is going on the *non-handling pilot* fills out the paperwork, copies the weather from the radio or enters the route in the computer. Meanwhile the cabin crew typically pop in from time to time with pertinent passenger information like "The guy in row three is a right dickhead." All of this sounds quietly orchestrated, though at times when you are running late or chasing a departure slot there can be an element of shock and awe. Eventually though the dispatcher arrives with a *loadsheet*. Taken from shipping again, this assures us the payload is both balanced and secure. Freight tends only to move around if it is not secure, though passengers have been known to move en masse during turnarounds and play havoc with the balance. For reasons of this mobility many pilots refer to passengers as self-loading freight. Should either the freight or a sufficient number of passengers relocate prior to take-off, a newly tail-heavy aeroplane will often get itself airborne. Aircraft doing things themselves are always disconcerting for pilots. The passenger weights are normally standardised; I have known of a flight where check-in staff put a rugby team at the rear of the cabin, to avoid distressing the other passengers, though imbalance caused a return to the airfield and the pilots even more distress.

The only thing that can delay us now is an airway or departure slot, generated in Europe by a computer in Brussels when the access to airways has to be rationed. Slots can incur delays of four hours, but are usually limited to a half-hour or less. They produce such a backlog of flights at places like Heathrow that the controllers get quite exasperated. Then rather than let people call them willy-nilly as normal, they produce a list of who will be contacted for start-up instructions, leaving us all feeling like Miss World contestants:

Midland Three Yankee Bravo, Delivery?

Hushed expectancy as the co-pilot and I discuss who should take the call.

Cleared Edinburgh on a Wobun departure, squawk 7436.

Darlings, we're on.

You will notice from this breathless exchange that we have a call sign by which the air-traffic controllers can address us. It bears no relation whatsoever to the flight number on your ticket, but is thought up by a small man in spectacles who hopes to remain with the company until retirement. It is time for my public address:

Ladies and Gentlemen, welcome on board from the flight deck. My name is Colin Hilton, I'm the captain and my co-pilot Anne, who will be operating the radio as only she knows how, is flying with me this evening. We're going to Edinburgh where it's raining heavily and I don't expect it to take more than fifty minutes. The routing takes us via Nottingham and Carlisle, which you won't see because it's dark. I'll talk to you during the flight, but now I'll hand you over to the cabin crew, who will provide you with a safety briefing. Do look as though you are paying attention.

Hopefully the tug has been connected, because the flight deck is so high up it can literally be overlooked. Then a member of the ground crew plugs a headset into the aircraft side. (In London this is a man in a woolly hat, or in Madrid a girl in shades who should model for a living. And we are not talking toys. Here the first officer will spend the pushback discussing what he would like to do with her, ideally making sure his intercom is deselected so she does not get to hear it all, though secretly he would like that too.) The delivery frequency now passes you over to the *ground movement controller*, to whom the co-pilot says:

Ground, Midland Three Yankee Bravo, A321 on B6 for push...

She looks out of the window in the tower and at the screen showing who is parked where, then considers your prospects of making it to the runway inside the next twenty minutes and says:

Midland Three Yankee Bravo, pushback approved.

Captain relays the news to ground crew and they ask him to release brakes. Forget to do this and the tug will tip the aircraft onto its tail.

Brakes released, you say, Turn two?

Clear two.

TAKE-OFF

Before we can even contemplate taking off, we have to get from the stand to the runway. At one time I had something for flying helicopters and the thing about these is you can lift off like a bluebottle from wherever you are. I read an interesting speculation upon how bluebottles land on the ceiling. Do they get close and then barrel roll upside down shortly before touchdown? Or do they loop-de-loop, so the ceiling sort of coincides with the top of the loop, where the fly is inverted? Video footage did prove they consistently execute landings on the ceiling using the second technique. Do not try it in a helicopter.

During the pushback the steering has to be disconnected, in case the tug steers in one direction and the crew inadvertently steer in another. The crew is supposed to be nowhere near the steering wheel at this moment. (In fact it is called the *tiller* and takes the form of a disappointingly small half-wheel down one side of the cockpit or the other.) You might think this would damage the nose-wheel, but they thought of that and use a breakable tow bar. Even these can cost a hundred thousand pounds each and because they are left lying around, although they are painted to show which airline owns which, they are removed unscrupulously from time to time. One investigation revealed a number had been thrown into the back of a 747 flying between London and Africa.

We have all read stories in the press about how consignments of millions of used bank notes go missing from Heathrow, by the simple expedient of people driving up to say, Can I take these containers out of the way for you? Less brazen thefts centre upon the bonded stores or warehouses owned by freight forwarders who occupy the perimeter. My favourite is British Airways losing a jumbo-jet engine. I offer no apologies for spelling that in full. The engine was not fitted to the aircraft at the time, for that would have been a crime of the century, but on the back of a truck. Imagine the queries on the Monday:

Have you seen the jet engine I left here the other day?

There is every chance BA did not notice for weeks, as they inherited enough equipment during a century of government work to supply a small war. Their carelessness is the stuff of legend, mainly because we are financing it. Their half dozen supersonic airliners were 'gifted' for a pound sterling during privatisation, in the way Ryanair are supposed to have paid the same nominal sum for their office at Dublin airport. The airport in London is riddled with tunnels, some of which cave in from time to time. When one was opened recently it was found to contain a considerable inventory of radial piston-engines from another era. These were made over to BA, who are invariably the recipient of any family silver that may be going.

Of more immediate impact for me was the paraphernalia of aviation the national airline regularly leaves lying around. I almost said the flag-carrier, but I was informed that these days the honour of flying the flag officially has been sold off for a knockdown price to Virgin Atlantic, probably during one of those anguished periods of introspection that BA go through from time to time, when in a fit of pique they spend a hundred million on less ethnocentric branding, before changing it again three years later when more management consultants tell them most of their revenue stemmed from Anglophiles after all. Anyway, this equipment left lying around (and I am not just talking about the aeroplanes) means often that other airlines are unable to park. Occasionally the airport operator is roused from its slumber by this malpractice, like a bloodhound awoken at three in the morning. What it does then is to send somebody to collect the equipment and deposit it in an area that might be described as a 'sin-bin'. A small fine is payable for recovery, which BA will cover by a surcharge on your business-class fare.

Once the tug disconnects the fun really begins. More so than with a car, the imperative with driving an aeroplane is not to scrape anything or catch the kerb. Each contingency involves huge expense, considerable delay, much filling in of forms and a wringing of hands generally. Taxiing is complicated by the fact that even modest airliners are a hundred feet wide and you are usually too far forward to see the wing tips. To alleviate the problem the airport paints a yellow line along the taxiways (illuminated by lovely green lights at night), though this does not guarantee immunity. One aircraft waiting at the runway at Heathrow was struck by another following the yellow line; the problem being that aircraft are growing faster than the man with the brush can paint.

Beside the tiller, pressing the brakes on one side or other assists steering. There are no brakes on the nose-wheel and the pilot operates a pair of brakes, one under each foot, corresponding to the main-wheel on either side. When there are sixteen of these as on a jumbo, it is anybody's guess as to what happens. There might be two tillers, one for each pilot. Using them at the same time or in different directions is not recommended, though today a computer examines the inputs. This would soon realise it was flying with a pair of retards and accommodate accordingly.

I described earlier how very large applications of thrust could be required to get the thing moving. On flights like charter holidays, with two hundred passengers and sufficient fuel for the Canary Islands, the weight of the aircraft is immediately obvious from this point of view. At other times it gets stuck in a rut before you move off. Whenever this used to happen to me as a first officer, I used to try to give the captain the impression he was running over a member of the ground crew. It certainly feels that way, which is why it is crucial for the guy on the headset to step aside and give the thumbs-up. In the rush for the runway, ground crew have been run over by aircraft, sucked into the engine or run over with fatal consequence by the air-bridge as it backs away. None of these are dignified ways to die. As aviation is a human activity then if it can happen, it almost certainly will. Aircraft therefore often move off with the headset and possibly its wearer still connected, or even push back at times while still attached to the fuelling truck.

On the return to the parking stand following a flight, the scenarios tend to be less deadly, as most people are expecting them. For this reason they are usually more comical. The main offenders are the guidance systems that have widely replaced the guy with table-tennis bats known as the *marshaller*. You can still get a marshaller if you ask, on the very modern-day understanding that if he steers you into the side of a catering truck, it is your fault anyway. The problem with electronic guidance systems is they vary. Many are of the variety that might be offered children as a project, comprising one box with red and green lights and another with a fluorescent strip. The red and green lights keep you on the centre on the way in, while in the other box a strip light lines up with marks related to the type of aircraft you are operating once you are far enough in. Remembering which type you are operating is the key here. You may laugh, but sometimes even the same type has different lengths, like the Airbus 318 through 321 series. Although identical from within the flight deck, the longest has forty-feet over the shortest. Should you not pull in far enough, the tail overhangs the apron, so a tug has to pull you in further. It is rarely worth re-starting jet engines. It is noisy, expensive and clues up the passengers to your mistake.

I will not go into the comic scenarios I hinted at upon arrival at the gate, but in a nutshell they typically involve crashing into, or sucking up, elements of the ground equipment or superstructure. Maybe I shall tell you about the 777 that pulled too far in and demolished a van with its engine. Again, perhaps just one more springs to mind, because it seems to me that many managers are promoted as a result of the goof-ups they make, or because of some other characteristic like an inability to communicate, or an absence of imagination. You thought it was different in airlines? One of these pilots, actually a lovely chap, was conducting a flight from Dublin and was advised the ground power-unit was smoking. This was shortly after boarding. He mentioned on the public-address system that there was smoke around, but no danger of fire. The cabin crew heard only the last word of his address and initiated an evacuation. For many passengers this meant the over-wing exits. Once on the wing, it is a long way down: like your first dive, but into concrete. The bulk of the passengers could therefore be seen, to the amusement of all those in the terminal, to be waiting on the wings as if for a papal visit.

When on the move and safely away from the terminal there is little to do except join the first officer in complaining about the roster pattern, the management and the progress of your third divorce. It helps to follow the instructions of the ground-movement controller on the radio. At night this is easy at places like Amsterdam or London, as they set up the little green lights on the centre-line to show you the way to the runway. These include sets of points, like on the railways, as well as stop-bars illuminated by rows of red lights across your path. All is coordinated from the tower by a board looking like a train-set. Using it you can send people up sidings if they are naughty, like the carriages in Thomas the Tank Engine. For this reason there are usually fights over who gets to use it.

There is always something to look at during these perambulations. What Richard Branson might have written down the side of his newest aircraft (*Mines bigger than yours*) else what types of aircraft are dropping in like migratory birds. Usually it is incantations of the several injustices the company happens to be visiting upon us at the time. Aeroplane makers do provide guidance on how to use only one jet engine for taxiing around and while I used to do this to save on fuel, eventually I gave up. This is because there are more things to go wrong if only one engine is running, because most of the aircraft systems are designed to operate in parallel. Running one of everything exposes the pilot to the needless risk of providing miserable people with the excuse to moan some more.

On one occasion though I was holding off from the runway in this condition awaiting take-off, when air traffic announced suddenly we could go and we did, fired up and went. I spent the first minutes checking the gauges, fearing the engine that had so recently been coaxed into life might be overcooking. It was not. Some engines have no such limitations while others require a warm-up period, or crack like an overblown meringue. It was about this time I realised the overriding reason for running two engines was the company and its blame culture, known in management-speak as a *no-blame culture*. It involves giving your employees the impression that, as with your local priest, you can open your heart to confess your sins and omissions; not for the good of the church, but in the cause of flight safety. Then they shoot you. They have at least this in common with the Wehrmacht.

Occasionally on your travels around the airport there are interesting diversions. Yellow Land Rovers inspecting the runway for bits that have fallen from aircraft, or dead birds. What are most likely to fall off aircraft are shards of tyre after a blowout, of the sort you see littering motorways. These inspections can be tedious, especially at Charles de Gaulle where a strip of aluminium the size of your ruler brought down Concorde. What they do here is drive up the runway, then turn around and drive back again. This is fine except it is a six-mile trip. You might be thinking this is only six or seven minutes of your time in the car, but try it in the dark while looking for rulers. This is all I am going to say about taxiing, which is only right because it is among the most boring parts of the job, to the extent there are those who have fallen asleep during this phase.

Before we leave it, what is nicest about taxiing when first practised, is just how high up you are before even getting off the ground. It is like sitting upstairs in a double-decker. This has the same effect it has on drivers of sports-utility vehicles. Psychologically these drivers are attuned to drive not around others, but over them. This sort of power corrupts. Listen to the response of an American Airlines 767 wide-body on the other side of the runway, after being told to line up after our business jet:

> *Glad you told us, we'd have squashed the guy.*

Or the Virgin 747 when told to follow a 42-seater operated by Cityflyer:

> *What, the Tonka toy?*

Aviation is irrepressibly size-ist and always will be, as a diversionary outlet for innermost fears over genital proportions. This probably says a lot about how few women fly. During their most politically correct phase of recruitment around seven or eight years ago, BA put it about that by the turn of the century, a third of their pilots would be women. That proportion stands at around 0.05 per cent. They will now write a furious rebuttal to the *London Times* pointing out it is actually 0.15 per cent and that I am the likely cause of war in the Middle East.

Let us look now at the take-off instead. Now you would have thought that unleashing thirty tons of thrust could not possibly be boring, but do you remember the bit in *The Deerhunter* (or was it *Apocalypse Now?*) where the soldier is staring at the rotary fan, which turns to the sound of helicopters and backing by the Doors? It is not quite like that, but on a hot day when you have been up since dawn, flown four sectors and the engines are spooling up again like a chorus of harpies, you do get to thinking, No more, please.

I began this chapter two years ago, when I felt that despite flying full time, I could still dash off a book. The reason this does not always work is not that we are exhausted by the job, but that life can be too comfortable. Thomas Hardy rose at five each morning to write for a few hours before work. Isaac Newton worked eighteen hours each and every day of the week. Had he been 'resting' on a beach in Bermuda, he might never have discovered the force the Wright brothers spent so long overcoming. At the moment I am undergoing my own personal French Revolution and writing is a breeze. The opening sentence from two years ago reads:

> I have foregone a trip into Rome and coffee in that delightful square outside the Pantheon, for the better part of this chapter. You better enjoy it.

Seeing this I remember I was staying at the Hilton outside Fiumicino Airport. The next chapter was to be entitled FOG and began thus:

> Am marooned, not unpleasantly, in a sumptuous hotel between Linate and the town centre. This is because flight 686 to Copenhagen, an MD-83, better known to a generation of American travellers as the DC-9, collided with a business jet during its take-off. Following the collision at eight o'clock this morning in heavy fog, the airliner careened into the baggage hall, killing four of its occupants, along with everybody on each aircraft.

Re-reading this I recall we went out and enjoyed a pasta lunch. This sounds heartless, but pilots do not think of death much, least of all when they are flying. They know it happens occasionally. They feel for the people and the crews especially, but know there is nothing they can do to ameliorate private grief. When the TWA airliner exploded off Long Island, it was witnessed by a number of other crews who reported seeing it. The radar controllers confirmed it had broken up and just one reply punctuated the silence of the airways. *God rest their souls.* Then you continue the flight. If ever I feared life might be interrupted by inconveniences like death, so that this book might not see completion, it is when driving that I most feared not seeing it through.

You're cleared take-off.

At the push of a button in the Boeing, or in the Airbus by slotting the throttles into a gate, the auto-throttle engages in TOGA thrust, used for Take Off and Go-around. It calls for one hundred per cent thrust, as measured by the speed of rotation of that big fan you see inside the engine. You now want the maximum height between you and the ground, for height is time and time is safety. And you rely on those engines. The ones beneath you now might be CFM-56's, described by one research project as the most reliable engine known to humankind. They are like good friends, always there for you.

The engines are kept at TOGA thrust, which sounds like Roman pornography but is not, until the aircraft reaches a safe height, above a thousand feet. Then you hear them throttle back a touch. If either fails, the other is left running full on for up to ten minutes. Beyond this point, manufacturers do not guarantee it is not going to melt. Anybody who has seen newsreels of Whittle will remember jet engines can be persuaded to melt like candles. Actually the manufacturers are very conservative in their estimates and the operating manuals do say that *in extremis* the throttles can be opened to the stops. This produces one hundred and ten per cent, the full nine yards. (When I talk about the throttles, there is one for each engine and they sit in a centre-console, operated by hand and not by foot, though you could try this. The only other things operated with hand throttles are tractors and luxury motor yachts and for most people these are mutually exclusive accessories.)

We have jumped ahead a little, because just after clearance for take-off the pilot doing the handling will call, like they know what they are doing, something like "Take-off". What else they might be considering at this juncture I am not sure. It is no place for a game of bowls. Then they set the thrust to around twenty per cent, whereupon the other guy confirms both engines are winding up nicely and calls "Stable", at which point the full Monty is applied. This is the reason why, when you are sat there wishing you had taken the train, the engines seem to go:

WheeeeeeeeeeeeeeeeeeeeEEEEEEEEEEEEEEEE!

I have to explain *auto-throttle* before I go any further. These days it is more normally called auto-thrust, as throttles were associated with piston engines, of the sort fitted to your car. Let me talk you through a few of the differences between your engine and those on aeroplanes. Even when aviation was powered by the piston engine, it has always been a very different engine from that under the bonnet. Often it was air-cooled and required no radiator. Air-cooling can be very effective at four hundred miles an hour. People assume the water-cooled engine fitted to the Spitfire was the pinnacle of development, which in a way it was, though air-cooled engines fitted to American fighters were equally effective.

Where aviation engines really differ from the one in your car is they operate virtually flat out. I mentioned earlier that at times of need they are left in a suspended state of over-boost. Now there is nothing in your auto manual to suggest you cannot put your foot to the floor and leave it there, but it might be considered unwise in view of avoiding other road users. Aircraft engine manufacturers make more allowances, as the consequence of engine failure far exceed your last invoice from *Kwik-Fit*.

When I talked about engines melting a little earlier, I alarmed you unnecessarily. The problems are heat-related, though rarely so dramatic. The spinning blades of the turbine section slowly creep like wax when they get too hot. This is not in itself a problem, except they rub on the casings, giving rise to a frisson of sparks. The choice between a display of orange fireworks and a collision with the ground is no contest for a pilot. Alternatively the combustion chamber where the fuel and air are burned may puncture at various hot spots, spewing gas at 900 degrees like an active volcano. Okay?

Auto-thrust then is like cruise control in your car. Let us consider thrust further, as Newton said to the actress. We are used to the word 'power' in relation to automobiles, where BHP or *brake horsepower* freely litters advertisements. Get ready for the boring physics lesson. Power is a measure ascribed to the force pulling things along, or turning them round and round. Amateur physicists should note carefully that while (a) I may be technically wrong, the effect is nullified by (b) my not caring less. The excitement of this discovery could barely be contained by engineers, who found a yardstick in the form of the horse. They felt no compunction to consider the same force in the Orient, otherwise adverts would boast of Mitsubishis with a power of *500 water buffalo*.

The engine in road vehicles puts down real traction, while like King Lear, the jet merely emits sound and fury, signifying nothing. Many of those who saw the first Whittle-engine aeroplane assumed the mother of all vacuum cleaners was sucking it along. This was not wholly fanciful, as many bystanders discovered. The development of the jet sprang from an era of men in hats and many were lost in tragic circumstances. Even today I know of flights grounded by the ingestion of peaked caps into air-conditioning inlets.

Of more significance is what happens at the business end. Even as microclimatology, the jet 'efflux' is impressive. Issuing from older aircraft like Concorde, whose exhaust is dirtier, it shows up as a hurricane force sustained over a hundred metres. It lifts block paving and scatters it like confetti. Quantifying the extent of this potent force is the job of *thrust*, which is conventionally expressed in pounds, though there is a trend toward the use of kiloNewtons. You have to hand it to Newton. Anyone who can turn a fortune with five balls on a length of string deserves our respect. Like him I have struggled to help you picture these pounds of thrust in meaningful terms and now I have the answer. Stand fifty metres short of a cliff. I shall tie one end of a fifty-one metre rope to you and a pallet of cement to the other. When I edge the pallet over the top, you are accelerated with the force of a thousand pounds of thrust and I lose more word-of-mouth sales. Now consider the hundred thousand pounds of thrust generated by modern fanjets. This may accelerate you in ways that would bear recounting by future generations.

In the interview for my last permanent flying employment I was asked to describe the process of taking off. It was a good question. Its essence is to elicit an ability to explain a sequence that through habitual use has become automatic. (Take the three-point turn. For many people looking back, fumbling with reverse gear will be as traumatic as the loss of virginity.) First consider whichever pilot has elected to conduct the flight. The reason we take it in turns to be the handling pilot is so neither of us becomes rusty. While the notion of anyone up front becoming 'rusty' is probably alarming, again we can profit from the analogy of driving. We all feel we have this pretty much cracked, but it does not prevent us from clipping the verge, or having the odd collision. We do not punish ourselves for these lapses in judgment, though the insurers rarely pass up the opportunity. Such lapses are considered altogether less forgivable (and less forgiving) in aircraft.

Returning to the point where we let the engines stabilise before advancing them toward take-off thrust, the reason we hesitate is to ensure each is performing as evenly as the other. Were one engine to hesitate while the other spools up, the aircraft could be driven into the rough like a wayward tee-shot. Any mismatch in the performance of each engine is immediately apparent, not least because their instruments are arranged side by side. This is one reason why pilots have an affinity for dials, as the briefest scan will confirm the needles are aligned. Needles that droop stand out like a wino at a church fete. I am sure countless inventors will have proposed two engines for cars, in the same way we see parallel computers that nobody wants. Financial necessity always outweighs logic in the evolution of products, so this is why only aircraft are left with two of everything: because the alternative of having just one engine is likely to be even more costly in the event of it stopping. If ever we develop an engine as reliable as the sun, the airlines will still say "Amazing. Can we have two?"

This is the less obvious luxury of two engines, that one is a yardstick for the other. Large jetliners are known as 'big twins' and the engines do indeed coincide in their behaviour. Atmospheric conditions upsetting one will invariably upset the other. Eliminating any problems with a newly developed engine is crucial, because they will be replicated throughout the fleet like a bad gene. On a visit to China, Whittle was bemused to find many errors in his original faithfully replicated in their own engines. Another reason for two engines is the surround-sound effect this has on the flight deck. It varies by the day. When the atmosphere is warm and dry, they seem to produce a high-pitched and uniform whine. On more humid days they make a deeper and rasping growl. Newer designs of engine with fewer fan blades make a modulated sound like a chainsaw, which offends the trained ear like mine. Much can be gleaned from these sounds and you get to know them unconsciously, like a mother who intuitively detects each intonation in infant cries. Any mechanical failure of the engine is usually accompanied by a report of some kind, mostly audible at lower speeds like at take-off, when the wind-rush has yet to reach a crescendo.

All that can stop us now, before we leave the ground, is a *rejected take-off*, the RTO. (Aviation is a world of acronym and abbreviation, a WOAAA if you like.) Now it may have occurred to anyone who has watched a swan struggling to fly that artificial means of aviation cannot escape the same dilemma. The word *aviation* itself stems from the Latin noun for a bird. On the subject of meanings I think a dilemma is when you are faced with two separate choices, the outcome of neither of which is satisfactory. This aptly describes the take-off condition; so much so that at times I feel an angel is on my shoulder. The reason the swan struggles is its *power-to-weight* ratio. We all have one of these, though many of us have left it in the bottom drawer somewhere. (I am told the ideal power-to-weight ratio for an athlete is ten stone; anybody querying this might want to spend some time looking at those Olympic videos they were too lazy to watch.) For ourselves we have no need of this ratio that the swan requires in order to get airborne. God provided us with a brain and told us it was about all we needed. When we felt like flying, we would build the aeroplane.

This was not an option for birds. There is a two-pronged debate between evolutionary theorists at the moment: at every convention they go at each other with those things you use to carve the chicken. What it also means is that they think birds evolved from the top-down or bottom-up. Top-down theory suggests reptiles climbed trees to avoid being eaten or to find something to eat themselves. They kept falling out of trees, so learning to glide. My own objection to this theory is small boys would have flaps of skin between limbs.
I am a strictly 'bottoms-up' Darwinian, which means it always seems to be me paying for the beer after the proceedings. It also means I concur with those people who feel small reptiles spent so much time racing down hillsides to escape dinosaurs, those with deformities that helped them glide were on a winner. More recently they

discovered that animals whirling upper limbs like dervishes have more chance of scrabbling up slopes. Add feathers to these limbs and you have the gyro-stabilised grouse. They know this because they clipped the wings of grouse so they could not fly. What they could still do though was scramble up cliff-faces and even overhangs. Take your hat off to the grouse.

It has always paid birds to be as light and strong as possible. They are also able to provide tremendous bursts of power (like TOGA thrust) and enough stamina to cross an ocean. Pheasants are notorious for preferring death on the roads to flying and this is their way of avoiding the energy required; although it seems a poor trade-off. You might have thought aircraft escaped these natural laws, but they do not. All flying things need about one hundred per cent to get off the ground and only twenty-five per cent to stay up there. It is that one hundred per cent that is the problem. As soon as birds or aircraft designers suspect it needs only ninety-nine per cent, they load a little more body-mass or a dozen more passengers. If you think body-mass is of no use to a swan, ask it why none of the other birds seem to get in its face. If you wonder how passengers are of use to airlines, ask yourself why you are reading this on the aeroplane.

The absolute difference when it comes to airliners is the regulators say, okay, you can be that swan, but you have to be it on one engine. Should an engine fail in the take-off, you are still that swan and ought to get airborne, but only theoretically. Let me tell you a story or two to illustrate. The first involves an aircraft simulator, in which our hero attempts to get airborne in a Boeing 737-400 from runway 27R at Heathrow, while being laden to the maximum permissible weight with fuel and passengers. At a point when it will be too late to stop (or else we would run off the end of the runway), one of the two engines will go BANG. I shall endeavour to take off using the remaining runway. No safety net will be used. When I did this for demonstration purposes, we eased off the end of the three-mile runway at the height of a house, which is why there are no houses at the end of runway 27R. This met the legal requirement in full, or would have done in the actual event.

A young man who had worked in the control tower at London Gatwick related the other story to me. Taking off from here some years ago was a four-engine Boeing 747. It lost all power on one engine and a measure of power on another. There is a high ground at the end of the runway known as Russ Hill and in the circumstances this calls for a modest turn toward the left. In the chaos that ensued the turn was not made and even from the tower (which is very high up) the aircraft was seen to disappear below the visible horizon for a period. The passengers must have felt they had checked onto some roller coaster.

The reason neither of these stories should alarm you is the great majority of flights do not depart fully laden anyway. On most short-haul flights you would barely notice the effect of losing an engine, except possibly if it went BANG. Long-haul aircraft climb so slowly at the best of times that, well, ditto. Most have four engines, which is a great place to start if you are going to lose them; I spent a little time reading the diaries of the original RAF squadron, whose Sopwith Camels had nine cylinders, fortunate in view of how quickly each oiled up. However, should one of the four engines actually separate from the wing, there is every chance it will take out its neighbour on the way past, like a lucky strike.

I pointedly said the engine went BANG around the point where there was not enough room left to stop on the runway, but enough left to continue and get into the air. This is entirely what is intended. There was a time, rather more recent than you might expect, when flyers would just 'get to know' the length of the runway, the capabilities of their aircraft and what weight they might take off with in the prevailing wind. It did not always work, especially at times of dire need, like during wartime. The last great aviator (before I appeared) who wrote as well as he flew was Ernest Gann, who himself recalled almost taking the top off the Taj Mahal in an overweight aeroplane. But it was the Second World War, especially after the Americans joined, which really tested the technology of taking off. A million tons of ordnance was dropped on Germany by allied flyers and it all had to be lifted into the air somehow. By this stage the know-how to create stupendous lengths of concrete had been put in place and today when we leave places like London

Stansted on our holidays, we are using the concrete laid down during these times.

The two developments that were key to raising this weight of hardware into the air were the runway surfaces for one and disc brakes for the other. Both are still the why and the wherefore, the Liz Taylor and Richard Burton of aviation. However big your engines, there is to be an ongoing need for more concrete and more carbon: concrete in the ground, carbon in your brakes. As I noticed in Palma de Mallorca, it is possible that the carbon has even joined the concrete in the ground, in a royal wedding of these two desiderata. The great difference about the war years was that, chances were, you were not coming back from Germany anyway. As a result, you were most unlikely to be stopped enroute to the aircraft by a man in a yellow Land Rover saying things like, "You appear either not to be wearing your fluorescent vest, or not wearing it in a manner prescribed by section 4.3, paragraph (ii) of the Health and Safety Regulations of the British Airports Authority. You will accompany me to the works canteen and pay for my bacon panini and double latte, or alternatively face fifteen years in detention."

It also meant that if a thousand aircraft raid was to be launched simultaneously and it was foggy, you were required to go anyway. In turn this meant two or more of the aircraft were lost to collisions before everybody got a chance to meet up in the playground. Another consequence of this nasty business was there would be *just* sufficient runway to get the thing off the ground. Then you had a fighting chance of making the sea, because you were travelling over the flatness of the Norfolk fens at two hundred miles an hour, avoiding the steeples. What none of this accounted for was a loss of power as you rolled down the runway. What bright Charlies would do at this point is veer off and at least take out the adjutant's hut on the way to a glorious death, accompanied by the pyrotechnic effect of several thousand pounds of AVGAS and munitions. We are not messing here: the Lancaster could lift as great a bomb-load as any aircraft the air force has operated.

Careening off the runway into the bookshop at T5 is no longer considered a healthy option. The runways may be the same, but the brakes are more effective. Disc brakes were invented not for your car, but for arresting bombers on the runway. Now they come with multiple discs, like your CD player, while in the newer airliners they are made from carbon. Which they were long before anybody heard of Formula One. They have to be, in order to cope with the tremendous weight of modern aircraft and the tremendous power of their jet engines. These have tiny turbine blades, not much larger than those in your Swiss-army knife, but each extracts more power than the Formula One racing car.

Once the war had drawn to a close, things relaxed and from the aviation point of view, as from every other, nobody had much money to spend anyway. The great rush to develop jet aircraft of any sort slowed up and airlines reverted to the 'seat of the pants' approach to take-offs. Jets became the exclusive preserve of the military, spurred on by awkward developments like the Korean War. Much later on the Comet appeared, which I shall not call the world's first jet airliner, but only because it has become a cliché. When it first appeared, pilots launched it like they did piston-engine airliners, which did not work, because jet engines are prima donnas. They demand respectful attention, or else they storm out. In the parlance, actually they *flame out*.

Nowadays engineers bend over backwards to make jet engines more forgiving, though a smooth take-off technique is still required. What happened with depressing regularity in the early days of jet travel was pilots heaved the nose into the air, into what the military call a high *alpha* position. This has nothing to do with ballet, but describes the angle at which the aeroplane is pointing nose-up. If it is steep enough, jet aircraft have an alarming tendency to act like paper floating over a boardroom table. This is just fine if the table continues as far as wherever it is you happen to be going. Precisely this scenario is what led the American aviation authorities to forbid ownership of high-performance fighters to members of the public. (Military aircraft tire easily due to the punishment they suffer, whereupon they are sold at knockdown prices to millionaires, of whom there are many in the United States. Aviation authorities always prefer to see a little destruction before they act, like you and I prefer the Duck Confit before the Lobster in Truffle Sauce. In this case someone put a fifties-era jet fighter inadvertently into this aspect on take-off and rather than climb away from the runway, it simply gathered speed at a very low altitude and departed the airfield, taking an ice-cream stall and several teenagers with it.)

To recap, there was this situation upon introduction of the Comet when the pilots were heaving at the control column with more gusto than was required at the point of lift-off. As a result the great aircraft was responding like Maria Callas and refusing to give the audience a lift. This had to stop. At around the same time the increased speeds of lift-off were becoming a nuisance. To some extent propeller engines are reluctant to deliver the goods until they have gathered some speed, but jet engines are a good deal worse. After all, they are designed for bowling around at five hundred knots instead of fifty. Just to compound the problem, what wartime specialists had discovered (let's hear it for the Nazi scientists) was if you were to go very fast, you needed a swept wing. And you thought it was to make aircraft look cool. Swept wings however do not perform well at low speeds. Put it all together on a low light and what you have is a situation where jet airliners have to be travelling at two hundred miles an hour before they think of doing anything much.

The problem then is stopping if anything adverse happens, or continuing into the air. When I first learned to fly the Boeing 737, joining me in the simulator was a fellow whose father accompanied John 'Cats-eyes' Cunningham, late of Hatfield, in the original take-off regulation experiments in the de Havilland Comet. They had decided by this stage it was not good enough simply running around with a tape-measure to figure out the magical point on the runway by which you had to get airborne. If for no other reason than it made the passengers uncomfortable. It would no longer be acceptable any more to look at the runway and the suitcases while holding a whetted digit aloft. We all did it at some stage after learning to fly, or else we should have done, but it was going to have to stop.

Those in the know had been encouraged in this development by a series of high-profile incidents, of which the one with the highest profile was undoubtedly the loss of virtually the whole of Manchester United football team on return from Munich. I do not think we could mentally calculate the number of zeroes attaching to any lawsuit that might stem from the same incident today. It would probably be quicker to count the stars in the sky. If I recall correctly the aeroplane had actually stopped off during the return trip for fuel and in wintry weather and against his better judgment the commander attempted a take-off. Three times I believe. During the final attempt the aeroplane passed through the boundary.

Although you might have thought this would have assisted the general public in the clamour for safer take-off performance, in my experience the bulk of humanity regards death by aeroplane as an event akin to an asteroid strike. Nowadays what they call Acts of God are being eliminated from policies by our blame culture and replaced with Acts of Whoever We Can Get Our Hands On. The lawyers are turning their magnifying glasses onto everything involved in aviation that had previously been considered sacrosanct: airlines, airliners, crews, even manuals (or perhaps especially manuals, as they are the one type of witness who cannot change their story).

The only reasonable alternative for assessing the take-off run was to look at the speed of the aircraft and use that as an efficient measure of the point of no return on the runway. Were I to design aircraft alerting systems, they would come up with on-screen messages like *Abandon hope all ye who enter here* or the more prosaic *Dang! You just screwed up*. Probably it is a good thing I do not. Now for another tedious Newtonian physics lesson. The thing about Zak was he worked out why planets including our own run in ellipses. People had known they ran around the sun for years and the church roughed up Galileo for suggesting it. They sent him an apology five centuries later, which as I write sits on the mantelpiece of Chuck Galileo Jnr, in a small town in Connecticut. Everyone came to a compromise in the end and agreed these ellipses were a good thing as they provided us with seasons, so we knew when to go on holiday. Newton was unhappy with this, in fact from what I can tell he appears to have been unhappy generally and no wonder nobody went to his lectures. We do have to thank him for all sorts of things, not least for putting the boot into at least one of his colleagues in order that he got the glory instead. The guy should have worked for British Midland Airways.

What Newton eventually figured was the force with which anything hits you, or with which you collide with a book shop in T5, depends upon only weight and speed. If you conversely know all about the force and the speed you can work out the weight. It is very much like a game of Cluedo and indeed you can imagine Newton saying, It was a force of fifteen kiloNewtons, applied to the lead piping, in my humble lodgings. For our own purposes, knowing the weight and the force applied by our engines, we can calculate how fast we will accelerate and therefore how much runway is used to attain a certain speed. We can also consider the force we are able to apply for stopping the aircraft and decide whether there is enough runway left. Looked at in this way, the prospect both of arresting or continuing a take-off at any point hinges upon our speed at the given moment.

This notion was actually toyed with in a roundabout way by American drag racers. These were originally testosterone-charged teenagers in super-charged cars, racing away from traffic lights, but later the idea developed professionally. The man who taught me to fly the Airbus 320 on the line (or with passengers) was a drag racer who introduced the sport to Santa Pod. The first general criterion for measuring acceleration was sixty miles an hour, which advertisers still use. It will have been chosen because it represents one-mile-per-minute. In drag-racing terms this fence soon fell before they had a chance to think and in place of it they settled on the *standing quarter-mile*. They had discovered speed and distance are inter-related. How long to cover that quarter-mile? What exit speed?

The speeds aviation testers decided to use for determining take-off distances were going to require a new terminology. *V-speeds*. This was not a difficult choice, as conventionally 'V' stood for velocity. Who can tell me what velocity is? Correct. Speed combined with direction, though I may have to check that with the headmaster. As a result, ever since, aviators hurtling down the runway have shouted things like "100 knots" and then if all is going well "V1" and if things are going really well "Rotate". At which point ninety-odd tons of Airbus travelling at two-hundred miles per hour pitches gently to twenty degrees and the laws of physics dictate it eases into a rate of climb, which if sustained would take it over Everest in six or seven minutes, all the while accelerating to three-hundred miles an hour.

TAKE-OFF

At the point when it lifts off, or *rotates*, those glorious Rolls-Royce engines are consuming ten thousand litres of kerosene per hour and giving it large.

At the risk of boring you, let us look briefly at each of those speeds. One hundred knots, we are both happy and barring minor disasters, we intend to keep going. At any point beyond this either of us can still call STOP! At V1, which again the non-handling pilot calls out, we are continuing whatever happens. At rotation speed, we do just that, rotate the aircraft like you drew its picture on a paper plate and turned it around the middle. (Ideally for this exercise, the nose should point into the air. All those with tails sticking into the air and who are not Dalmatians, see me after class.)

Let us fast-forward now, with a FAQ section, or Airbus for dummies:

Q1   Who chooses the 'V' speeds that tell us when to take-off?

They depend on weight and come from tables calculated by computer.

Q2   How do they vary?

They increase as you get heavier.

Q3   Who says, in the words of the Clash, Shall I stay or shall I go?

The commander, who shouts "Stop" or "Go" at the point of failure.

Q4   What happens if commanders decide to stop?

They apply reverse; the aircraft does everything else, the co-pilot freezes.

Q5   What is the capital of Peru?

Lima. I ought to be writing manuals, but it does not pay enough. Should you decide to stop, just before V1, which is the go/no go point, it can be exciting. A series of carbon pads clamp hold of a stack of carbon discs the size of bin-lids, with the strength of a frenzied gorilla. These oblige by stopping the aircraft at the expense of setting fire to the wheels. Above the wings, an array of panels is deployed into the airflow to neutralise lift. Like a spoiler on your car, they are known as *lift-dumpers*. On the engines a set of petals are thrown open with great panache, taking tons of thrust and directing it in the opposite direction. And the navigation computer says, We appear not to have taken off ~ is there anything I can do? In fact everyone has a part to play in the drama:

Air Traffic Control	Is something wrong?
Businessman, Row 3	I wet my pants.
Cabin crew	Don't ask us.
Flight crew, in unison	You're not pinning this on me.
Chorus of passengers	Aaaaaaaaaaaaaaaaaaaaaaaaargh.

And finally, should exploding tyres set the aeroplane alight:

Exit Captain via sliding window, pursued by a bear, or a first officer.

In the eventuality there is little to worry about, as the airport fire crew will be so bored of playing pool they will be painting the scene like Christmas before the tyres even think about exploding. If you do not like those rave parties where you all wear a tee shirt and writhe around in bath foam (known by airline crews as a *nightstop*), then this is the time to get off. Bear in mind there are no refunds. The only criterion that determines the quality of fire cover is the length of the aircraft and not the number of passengers. They make up for any shortfall in cover by their enthusiasm. A friend had to land wheels-up one night at Norwich, where cover was divided between the airport brigade and that in town. Each roared up either side of the runway, before realising they were about to collide with the aircraft, which parted them like a ploughshare. My brother learned to fly in a Chipmunk, a wood and fabric trainer. The only time he had problems, a large fireman leapt from the tender on to the wing, which he promptly fell through to waist height.

Assisting the aircraft in stopping, there is the *anti-skid*. The only thing I am telling you about this is it was invented for aeroplanes before it was ever used in your car. In the peculiar way details stand out, I remember the system on the first airliner I flew was called *Maxaret*. You have to be French to see why.

Meanwhile I realise we are anxious to get airborne, perhaps now more than ever. As a result I am going to gloss over a few weather-related aspects of the take-off and call it a day. You recall everything I said about airfields? I hope so, as there are questions later. (When I used to attend business seminars, it was when hearing these words I would break off staring out of the window and trying to improve the design of the *Hindenburg*.) You will recollect we tried to get aircraft taking off into wind, as this way they covered less ground, even if it meant using a circular lawn the size of Sutton. Mentioning lawns I have come over all emotional, because one of the loveliest airfields you could drop into north of Chicago was *Lake Lawn*, where you could wander across the road to enjoy maple syrup waffles on the waterside. All luncheon offerings attending this plug should be directed toward my literary agent.

As airliners got heavier and accelerated faster, the need to take off directly into wind became irrelevant. The potential disruption of a *crosswind* is diminished by both of these factors, weight and speed. It stands to sense that even when stationary, as a rule the heavier an aircraft is, the less likely it will be dislodged by wind from any direction. The whole point about aeroplanes is they generate their own winds effectively, which apparently blow from the direction opposite to that of travel. As jet aeroplanes are designed to cope with effective airflows of several hundred miles an hour, you will appreciate that crosswinds of twenty miles an hour are not going to be as much an issue as they might have been when aeroplanes were first built.

What has changed is something called the *wing loading*, which is how much weight the wing has to carry, compared to its size. Early aircraft were very light and also had especially large wings. They needed these to generate the maximum lift, because they were not going to derive much of this from speed alone, which is what modern airliners do. The problem with lots of wing area and little weight is precisely the same as you have when walking around in a gale with a golfing umbrella: you are subject to the forces of lift (upward) and drag (along) even when you do not wish to be.

We shall look at *vectors* later on (I can hardly wait), but if you think of an aeroplane that gets airborne at two hundred miles an hour, then a wind of twenty, blowing from any direction, only represents a tiny portion of the overall force of the air. The clever dicks among you imagine it to be only a tenth, but the cleverer dicks will realise it is even less than that, as the effectiveness of winds build out of all proportion as their speed increases. All that this means in practice when I am flying any airliner is that if ever I take off in a stiff breeze which is blowing from off one side, I want to accelerate as quickly as possible so that its relative effect is soon diminished. Hit one hundred knots and everybody up front feels a lot happier, which might be the converse of what you had imagined. The disruptive effects of crosswinds were diminished anyway when they got rid of the *tailwheel* at the back of the vehicle and replaced it with a *nosewheel* at the front instead. This also had the happy side effect of making the aeroplane sit level after stopping, whereas they used to slope upward once rested upon their tails.

The reason *tricycle* aeroplanes, or ones with a wheel at the front, are more stable is they are less prone to *ground loops*. All this means is modern airliners are more like your car; they try to put the mass of weight around the middle. That way if either vehicle slides off a bend it does so predictably. Older sports cars with rear engines like the Porsche were tail heavy and tended to spin off roads going backwards, like a dart finding its way. In fact it was Ralph Nader who pursued the first of the landmark consumer rights cases against precisely this type of car. Anyway, older aeroplanes with tail wheels were much the same.

That is the crosswind taken care of. We could even take off with a wind at our tails, but this eats up so much runway that manufacturers insist on no more than a ten-knot breeze. Other complications include rain (when it is hard to see where you are going) and also fog (when it is even harder). I think this was brought home to me at Leeds-Bradford Airport early one morning. This is sited on top of a hill and the runway is short, with a pronounced dip in its middle where another runway crosses, before you take off toward the northeast and rising ground. There is a minimum visibility in which take-offs can be contemplated, but it relates to the need to see where you are going initially. Should an engine fail before the V1 call, it must also be sufficient to see where you are stopping.

And that is about it. As you trundle down to the end of the runway, at this point you have to turn the aircraft on a sixpence in order to point it in the right direction. The mind is concentrated here by steep terrain off this end of the concrete. Then you are pointed at the gloom, with the fewest centre-line lights visible to show you the way. It is not long since you were out of bed, but then they say it, "Clear take-off". The main fear is, while it is not supposed to happen, someone takes a wrong turn and is crossing the runway. Not so much another aircraft, but maybe a vehicle; there is no ground radar here. It is going to take you more than half a minute to accelerate toward a lift-off, while during that time the co-pilot is scanning the instruments almost exclusively, looking for anything untoward that might dictate that take-off should be abandoned. You will be half-looking at these instruments yourself, because neither one of you can, or is supposed, to trust entirely to the judgment or observations of the other.

There is then, inevitably a sense of unease. Especially for the commander, who signed for the flight, for its passengers and their fate. It would be your name in the newspapers. It is not so much this that creates the unease; done daily, it is something to which you are well accustomed. It comes from knowing that everything you learned, the triumphs and terrors of a long time flying, is distilled into the next two minutes. Do this ten thousand times and nothing untoward will happen. What of the one after that? There have been times while recovering situations when I have thought, This is how I die, at eight thousand feet on a Saturday afternoon, while my wife watches football on TV.

Then you say, Set take-off thrust.

And at 35,000 ft you pull out the Daily Telegraph and say, I could use a croissant.

We are just about going to leave it here, pretty much airborne, nosing over to accelerate, the engines having done their bit and now like us, easing off a little. There is one more peril to consider, though we have left it far behind. That is anything on the surface of the runway, principally weather related, which makes braking less effective in the event of an abandoned take-off.

Within the last two years they resurfaced the runways at Heathrow. Before they grooved them, they began describing them over the radio as 'slippery'. So the long-haul people, those guys that spend a whole minute and all three miles rolling down the field to get airborne, looked at the computerised stopping data we talked about, which told them they were now too heavy to contemplate going anywhere. This is not what aviation is about, so they mentioned this to the airport and they stopped using emotionally charged words like 'slippery'. It was not slippery really, except in the parts where everybody tries to vacate the runway after landing, which get all rubberised.

Where I have been that was slippery was Prague, where snow fell after we landed, during the *turnaround* before our return. This left an inch of snow on the surface of the runway. I left to walk around the outside of the aeroplane, where a man was conveniently selling cheap cigarettes. The first officer scrutinised the performance manual, a bacon panini and a cup of coffee, but not necessarily in that order. I come back and say, OK blue, what do we do? Then I look at the manual and realise we *can* take off from this runway, but not with the passengers, because if an engine failed at the worst point, we would be too heavy to stop and even too heavy to take off. This is because when it snows the accumulation makes acceleration especially laborious and conversely, when up to speed it can also be very difficult stopping again.

I might now wander into the terminal building and say, Hello everybody, we are going nowhere because there is an inch of snow on the runway. At that moment, given a random sample of one hundred members of the public, you know some smart-ass will walk up and say, "We can take off because I read about it in a book." He is likely to be the one we read about earlier in the third row, who wet his pants.

And then you will step up, poke the man in the lapel and say, Actually I read a book once as well and I am saying we cannot take off.

And this is the book.

If you are especially observant, or if every different nuance of sound that you detect in an airliner alarms you, then there is something you might have noticed. After having taken off and climbed precipitously over the airfield perimeter, over all the car parks and hotels, then something happens. The engines wind back a little and on occasions, quite a lot. Often as I commanded this action I simultaneously thought, I would not be surprised if there were passengers back there thinking "Whoa, I knew it!"

For it is an extraordinary thing about flying that everybody thinks the flight they have chosen is the one in a half-million that is pre-destined for an accident. Nobody buys a lottery ticket feeling a jackpot win is something they deserve or something pre-ordained. A lottery ticket is a weak talisman, unless it proves a winning combination. Then it is a precious relic, almost mystical and fingered with the same reverence as a leaf taken from the Book of Kells. Airline flights seem to possess these powers before the start. I think it is possibly the judicial feel of the process: the ticket requiring an appearance, the release of your identity and personal effects, the spell in the ante-chamber, the 'longest walk' down the airbridge, the closing-up of the cabin and the preliminaries from the captain, addressing the assembly.

It is also the only event beside war and natural disaster in which a small population can be obliterated by an entirely capricious event. The only comparable loss used to be that of ships like the Titanic, but whereas in this case twelve hundred drowned over the course of a night, it may be half that number destroyed in the blink of an eye. It is a very modern form of death and suits a world where everything happens more quickly. In contrast to much else about our emancipated lifestyles, however, it is one of the few places where we have no measure of control. In America, while still on the ground, passengers have taken to letting themselves out of emergency exits upon seeing *anything* they do not like.

When airborne this is hardly an option, for a pressure of many tons is applied to each door. Besides, nobody relishes falling from an aircraft, defenestration seeming to have died out with medieval autocracy. The most horrible aspect of the collapse of the World Trade Center was the image of people choosing to jump instead. This was a dislocation in the way we viewed the high-rise building: from a technical wonder, to a terrible means of death. Airliners are much the same, except confinement is absolute. When the doors are switched to automatic, your fate is sealed. The gavel drops not with the words "Take him down" but rather, "Take him up". Prepare to meet if not your maker, then at least your innermost fears.

I am sorry this had to be said, but from what I read of the statistics, the majority of people are afraid of flying, even before going near the aircraft. I imagine once it rides out its first turbulence or flash of lightning, then the figure rises to one hundred per cent. I reckon that includes the pilots. Although this sounds like bluster, it does have daily consequences. Operating the first flight out of Glasgow one morning, I was informed one businessman had entered the cabin, taken a seat near the front, then changed his mind and left. There was no security issue as he had only hand baggage and no luggage checked in. Of greater concern was the fact this man had risen like me at dawn, waking wife and kids, scraped ice from the windscreen and parked expensively in the multi-storey, queued at check-in and sat with an inedible croissant, queued again to board and then.... got back off again. If you are reading this out there, this is dedicated to you. I tried to recall him to the flight deck to say that while it may feel like a fairground ride, the attendant is always watching.

It tends to be males. Not that they are more frightened, just less able to cope. When they finally got around to fitting women into fighter jets (I noticed the driving licence my mother received in 1962 refers to 'he' throughout), they found they were better able to sustain multiple sources of stress. Any woman with children who has engaged in combat at the shopping mall will not need telling. In the role of passenger I suspect women are more fatalistic. When it comes to accepting the inevitable, or empathy and understanding, men cannot really compete. It is like Garrison Keillor said of men at funerals: while the women do the grieving, their spouses are discussing the mileage-per-gallon of their cars.

Men not only scream on flights, they also wet the seats. At times on charters occupied by school children, we might have been advised that one or two had problems in this area. In excessive turbulence however, the condition can spread to business-class. I do have male friends who have empathy, or intimations of their death, though personally I am no more psychic than the average house-brick. Like many men when confronting danger, I have to use the Russell Crowe what-we-do-now-echoes-in-eternity method of defiant resignation. Otherwise I am screaming with the best of them. I once drove a ten-foot truck under a nine-foot bridge. What amazed me at the time was hearing primordial screaming and realising it was coming from me. Fortunately I was driving alone and did not have to tell the girl next to me I had merely been clearing my throat.

On another occasion a holiday flight to Sardinia was fully boarded, leaving only a young couple in the lounge. The dispatcher tells me they have checked-in luggage, yet the guy has decided he does not want to go any more. We can all recognise how the discomfort of the journey at either end of a holiday may outweigh the perceived advantages of lying on the beach. I figured it was going to be quicker talking to the passenger and his embarrassed but sympathetic partner, than it would be rummaging for the baggage. I had already asked the co-pilot in the time-honoured style to tell Heathrow Delivery we were looking to start. I had no choice therefore than to get out of my seat and tell the couple how smooth the weather was along the route and how lovely it would be when we got there. Then he gets on and we go on time, though I am aware this is one more way in which the company will never thank me for going that extra air mile.

I said that a detectable change in engine noise could be expected not long after take-off. This will normally be a lowering in their tone, from a *falsetto* whine to a more *soprano*. Occasionally it might be the other way around. If I encountered turbulence behind the preceding aircraft that departed, I might add a little extra to climb above it. We also said during take-off the engines perform to their fullest extent. This is not entirely true, for in aviation there are always exceptions and if you are offered the command of an airliner, they want you to be flexible, a good all-rounder. We know that if either engine should fail on the runway we are still required to be above thirty-five feet by the time we run out of concrete. If there are fewer passengers we can meet this contingency with a lot less thrust. We pre-set the engines to run that little more slowly. This is called *flex*, because we are flexible pilots who treat engines like our lives may depend upon them. The next time you bump into crew as they emerge from the flight deck, ask if they used TOGA or flex for departure. When they say they used flex, which is also known as *reduced take-off thrust*, tell them you thought as much.

Notice in relation to thrust that I talked about the speed at which the engines are spinning. The terms are almost interchangeable. Try playing around with the settings on your desk-fan while the boss is sexually harassing the intern in the copy room. Everything about jet engines is governed by the speed at which they rotate. How much thrust they produce, how hot they get and critically in the case of taking off, how long they last. This is not just in the event of one engine failing, in which case you may push the other to the stops. It is also in terms of the overall life of the engine. One pilot I flew with pointed out that birds and mammals are allotted a finite number of heartbeats in life. The hummingbird uses its allotment more quickly than the elephant and can therefore expect a shorter life. This guy used this theory as an excuse to take no exercise. Unlike Mexico, jet engines have only so many revolutions.

This is the difference between this engine and that in your car. The powerhouse in your motor car was the same device that drove the industrial revolution: a piston that goes up and down in a cylinder and drives a rotary crank, in the same way your little legs went up and down to pedal your bike. This is not the case with a jet engine, which is like a rocket. A rocket contains a form of oxygen, because chemical energy requires it. This is why breathing is important, for combined with food it will take us to the shops and back. Rockets use a mixture of oxygen and hydrogen, which are loaded as liquids direct from the freezer. This is why in shots of the *Saturn V* moon rocket, what is most evident apart from U-S-A passing before the camera, are the shards of ice falling from its sides.

The clever thing about the jet is it uses atmospheric oxygen like us. It does not have the luxury of liquefying it, but what it does instead is to compress it over a number of stages, beginning with the big fan at the front. This is like the one on your desktop, but behind it are many smaller ones, called *compressor stages*. These might be fewer and larger, else a greater number of smaller ones. The difference is like sluicing water over the back yard. You can brush it uphill with a series of little sweeps, or with several longer sweeps. This analogy was actually not mine, but belonged to Sir Stanley Hooker, who supercharged the Merlin engine for the Spitfire. He had just graduated during the war in maths and joined the Navy in Whitehall. They could find nothing much for him and sent him to Rolls-Royce. They could find nothing either and stuck him in a quiet office where he got bored, but found the outline for the proposed supercharger. He took it home to revise it and was castigated the following day for interfering. Within hours though the same boss returned and ordered him to head up the new supercharging section. How wars are won.

The reason compressing the air can be compared to brushing water is because it is always trying to force its way back again. If anything gets in front of the engine (like a flock of flamingoes) the flow becomes blocked and this reversal is what happens. The compressed air turns about face and the engine stalls with a series of discharges, like BANG-BANG-BANG. These *compressor stalls* are like a dog whose bark is worse than its bite. Usually the engine recovers quite happily, especially if you ease it off a touch. Little damage is generally incurred beyond shredded nerves in the cabin. And the flight deck.

With the air compressed, it is very hot and what we do is tap some of it to heat the cabin, or dispose of ice along the wings. Then what happens is a stupendous amount of aviation fuel is squirted into it and immediately produces an enormous amount of hot gas, like the space rocket. From this point on, it really has only one place to go. Initially to set this explosive mixture of compressed air and JET-A1 alight you need ignition like an oven, though afterward the engine normally stays lit. The oven may go out if you open the door quickly and the equivalent scenario in a jet aeroplane might be flying through volcanic dust or monsoonal rain. Normally your cooker should encounter neither of these.

What starts the ignition as the engine winds up is a couple of sparking plugs like those in your car. On the outside you can often hear them during the start, though within the flight deck you get only a muted version unless you open the window. From time to time I did this on a pretext to listen to the music. It goes something like this:

> *Whirr-whirr-whirr-whirr*   (winding up slowly to 25%)
>
> *Click-click-click-click*   (igniters kick in)
>
> *Boom!*   (fuel ignites immediately)
>
> *Whiiiiiiiiiiiiine*   (winds through 45% and starter disengages)

In older aircraft you might have to talk through these stages. On the Airbus the computer would watch what was happening and if it did not like it, shut the engine down, print off an error report and make you a cup of tea. On occasions I liked to talk it through anyway. The official version went:

> *Start One*
> *Timing*
> *N2*
> *N1 rotation*
> *Fuel flow*
> *EGT*
> *Starter cut out*
> *Engine stable*
> *Start Two...*

Though to cheer us up, sometimes it went:

> *Ten seconds*
> *We have main-engine ignition*
> *We're looking good...*

Conditioning...check
Hydraulics...check
Electrics...check
Launch sequence complete
God bless America.

At times it was only by talking like this that we could make it through the day. Just like yours in the office. To continue though, we got to the point at which fuel ignited and the engine was going fast enough to be *self-sustaining*. The only way to stop a jet engine is to cut off the fuel supply, or to block the inlet with a flock of flamingoes. The first option is invariably more convenient.

Do not dismiss all this as obvious, something anybody could have knocked up in their back yard. To begin with, to compress the air Whittle used the simple expedient of the sort of spiral compressor you have in your vacuum cleaner. Bear in mind your vacuum cleaner is quite like a jet engine, except that the exhaust air does not come out of a tail pipe, but from an attractive grille. The other difference is you do not squirt kerosene into the bag and light it. If you wish to try this, do so out of doors. Alternatively modellers have produced jets with compressors about the size of those in vacuum cleaners and they produce a pound or two of thrust. This is sufficient to drive a bag of sugar down the street at a healthy lick, but do this and you risk being branded eccentric.

The compressor used in all jets today is the *axial* type pioneered during the war by the Germans. This is the one I mentioned at the beginning, comprising a series of fans. The reason Whittle stole a march on these developments was because he used a much simpler compressor, so he could concentrate on getting the burners right. This was the only stage unique to this new engine and that is why it was hard to perfect. The Greeks or Chinese had invented the spiral compressor as a form of water wheel, while the *turbine* (explained later) had been used to great effect by the Victorians; notably in the eponymous *Turbinia*, a reckless boat that gate-crashed the naval flotilla at Portsmouth.

It was tricky though to get the combustor section working, because the flame kept blowing out, or the fuel and air mixture got 'wet', like when your car refuses to start. This seemed so insurmountable the Germans turned to hydrogen instead. After the combustion produces a monumental efflux of hot gases, the clever part is at the back of the engine. Before the tail pipe, there is a fan called a *turbine,* which acts like a windmill. It is like one of those plastic vanes on a stick you buy the kids on the beach and stick in the sand, where it always works well in the sea breeze. Would you believe it, this one is connected to the same shaft to which the compressor fans are attached! It goes around in the flow of gas and they go-around too!

In a way the turbine is a sucker for punishment, because the faster it turns, the faster the compressor will turn and the greater the flow of gas. Before we know where we are, for as long as the fuel lasts we have a continuous *jet blast.* What to do? They use it in boats and trains or to generate electricity, though the best possible use is to go flying.

Let us do that.

Firstly let me recapitulate. Much of what is needed to operate airliners is repetitive, so you better get used to it. We got airborne and after a short interval, at a pre-determined height, we level a touch while the engines relax. This is like climbing a steep hill and letting off the gas pedal at the top, in case the situation runs away with you. What we do here, apart from breathing a collective sigh of relief, is to bring in the flaps. These are bits that dangle off the front and back edges of the wings to make them look bigger, so they are more effective. Check out birds as they land and how they spread their wings. They do this when taking off as well, but it is not as obvious because they are flapping nineteen to the dozen. The only other time they use big wings is to impress peahens at the bar, a behavioural practice familiar to any pilot.

If we do not retract these flaps at this time, incidentally, while we are going at a mere three hundred miles per hour, later on they will fall off anyway. Remember the 727 that plunged from 33,000 ft to 3,000 ft at near the speed of sound, taking the passengers to within seconds of obliteration? The crew blamed the manufacturers, who in turn blamed the crew, while the airline blamed anybody including the lady waiting for the airport bus.

The story from the manufacturers is best, if only because most entertaining. They contend that pilots were as bored as everyone else during the cruise. Pilots being curious chimps, it is unwise to leave them in places full of gadgets. While the flight engineer was away (he is the guy on older 'planes who looks after the engines) the pilots get to wonder about those flaps. Were they to be extended a fraction, would that improve fuel consumption? Those along the front edge are more fragile than those at the trailing edge, yet all operate together. The crew is alleged to have de-powered these devices and dropped the rear set. When the flight engineer returned, he spotted the circuit breaker and went to re-connect it, advancing the equipment along the front edge of the wing at the same time. This broke off along one of the wings, rolling the aircraft upside down and into its dive. It ought not to happen and yet you will not find anybody who has operated multi-crew aircraft willing to bet against it.

We got to the point where we levelled off in the *acceleration phase*. This was really designed for the old days, when if you had two piston engines, like the Douglas DC-3, then you would be going slowly back down again if one of them stopped. Since the more powerful jet engine was introduced, sinking is not seen as a viable alternative and if you fly privately with only one engine to begin with, that is really your lookout. One way of stopping these old aeroplanes from drifting down, as desperate as throwing sand bags from a balloon, was to retract those flaps. (Propeller aeroplanes had these only at the rear of the wing, though with poor low-speed performance the swept wings of jets have them at the front too. They include *Kruger flaps*, like crooked fingers, but nothing to do with Eddie Kruger from the horror movie. He might help you remember, though there is no way of remembering *slats*, that slide down the front of the wing like those at the trailing edge.)

Once you had the flaps in and the landing gear retracted after this propeller engine failed, the aircraft could speed up and you had a fighting chance to stay in the air. Like medics, aviation people tend to be conservative, unless they hit the cocktails. If ever a king walks by in the buff, guarantee the aviation authorities will be up front saying, Nice suit, Sir! Accordingly this level phase of acceleration seemed a reasonable strategy and they stuck with it, which is why after each take-off we level off, reduce thrust, speed up and retract equipment, all at the same time. The only difference is if one of the engines has failed, we do not even think of reducing the thrust from any remaining. Not for several minutes.

Nowadays once these devices are 'cleaned up' our next stop is the sound barrier. Well actually not, because controllers imposed a two-fifty knot limit years ago, after collisions near New York. Let us clear up knots, while we are here. A knot is about 1.15 miles an hour and is used in the twenty-first century, because in the fifteenth century sailors tied knots into lengths of string to see how fast they were going. Humans are *so* into the past.

Jets are incredibly (a) fast and (b) thirsty at lower levels and so we use this initial phase after cleaning up to get the climb going into the rarefied layers of the atmosphere. Alternatively you can use it to accelerate into a sweeping three hundred knot curving trajectory around the southern suburbs of London, which is more fun, especially if you are skimming the tops off a creamy layer of cloud. There is little or no danger of hitting anything, as somebody down there is watching on a radar screen.

I realise I cannot throw in assertions like jets being thirsty at low level without qualifying them, so here goes. Boyles Law. Imagine we are trying to fill a balloon to the maximum, so we can let it zoom across the playing field. If you inflate your balloon with air from the oven and I fill mine from the refrigerator, mine goes further as it has more air inside. Mine was dense and compact, yours was literally hot air. If we left both balloons sealed in the comfort of the lounge, yours looks eventually like a failed erection and mine quite perky. Anyone interested in schoolboy physics should take a bag of crisps onboard and leave it unopened. What has happened to it in the cruise, boys and girls?

Correct. The git across the aisle has eaten them.

Experiment two, advanced level:

(a)   Take one Citation jet and two pilots on a rush job
       to Madrid. On return, turn out all lights so one
       pilot can demonstrate the beauty of various
       astronomical phenomena, including the Leonides
       shower.

(b)   Take two sandwiches. Note the prawns, which in
       daylight appeared pink, are glowing green. This is
       known as phospholuminescence.

(c)   Be sick.

If you look at the temperature in the engine, it sits there all day in
the cruise around the 600-700 degree Celsius mark. This is more
than sufficient to bake your baps. Given the engine only ever heats
the air to this degree, it helps if more enters the front in the first
place. There is more of this air if it is colder and therefore denser;
the oven is on and you can put two potatoes in there or twelve, but
which is more efficient? This is why we want to fly nice and high
where the air is cold and there are more bangs to the buck.

While we want to start climbing to more rarified levels, I wish it
were so easy. We are not yet at base camp, for there is air traffic
control to contend with. When the airfield was circular, people took
off and landed in a fairly haphazard way and flew where they
wanted, constrained only by the fuel in their tanks. Once airfields
became elongated around runways, a basic traffic pattern was
established. Most of the traffic at the time was engaged in training
exercises anyway. Flying has always been learning-oriented and as
aircraft have become more advanced, it is so more than ever. At its
outset trainees at places like Farnborough were sent aloft after a
half-hour overview on the ground and many stayed up there,
gripped with fear, until the fuel ran dry.

Much of the training these days is hidden away in flight simulators.
These are as expensive to purchase as some of the airliners
themselves, but considerably cheaper to operate, as they incur
neither the cost of fuel nor landing fees. I consider them in some
detail later, as part of a general review of training, in view of its
importance. Meanwhile the basic traffic pattern stemmed from the

needs of trainees and featured a left-handed rectangle along which the aeroplane could be flown, so as to provide the maximum number of take-offs, approaches and landings. It involved setting off and climbing ahead, before turning left or *crosswind*, left again and *downwind* and finally once more onto a *base leg*, before lining up an approach.

Flying an airliner today, if it is quiet and you have a reasonable view of the airfield from some way out, you can advise air traffic that you will continue for such a *visual* approach. A lot of the holiday islands you visit have limited radar facilities and flying to Mauritius, for example, on a sunny day, you could expect to slot into such a pattern, even in a 747. The great advantage of this *circuit pattern* over more haphazard methods was that if you were arriving from elsewhere, you could slot into the flow of traffic. This was important because the greatest concentration of traffic has always been around airports, which form the *hubs* of networks, so this is where most collisions occur. Before this regularisation of a means of arrival and departure, the most common accident was one aircraft landing on top of another, because the poorest view from any cockpit is beneath the schnozzle.

This circuit pattern was eventually turned into a circular zone around the airport, five miles wide. You now needed permission from the control tower to do anything in this *aerodrome zone*. Before the advent of radio this would involve men in hats firing off different coloured flares, or waving batons furiously. Then radar was invented (Oh, the British again) and controllers wanted a bigger circle in the sand to play with, if only because aeroplanes were travelling quicker. Then it got to the point where in America, they said the entire sky above 18,000 ft was theirs. People would have been apoplectic had Martians landed and said this, but as it was only the radar controllers they said, Okay.

Control below this level was confined to concentric circles, one on top of another, located over each airfield. This looked like an inverted funnel to those able to visualize it, though because it consisted of layers it came to be called a *wedding cake*, of the upside-down variety. Outside of this AND below 18,000 ft was still considered free airspace. Airliners climbing away from the airfield are expected to remain within this funnel of controlled airspace, though occasionally they exceed the confines, like cows tossed from a tornado.

They tried something similar in Europe too, but here the nations are so small that these *terminal manoeuvring areas* or TMAs ended up overlapping. There ensued another form of land-grab exercise by the controllers, an ethnic cleansing of uncontrolled airspace, so that the London TMA for example covered two-thirds of England. The remaining third was co-opted by the RAF for low flying, leaving a fourth and final third for the good of the people.

That said we are just skirting the southern edge of London on course for Dover, though we can climb no higher than 6,000 ft until released to do so by *London Control*. What has happened so far on the radio is *Delivery* said we could start, *Ground* said we could push back and taxi, *Tower* cleared us for take-off and when they were convinced we were not going to crash, they handed us to *Departure*. What I have not explained, except as veiled reference, is the pamphlet for each airport, called *plates*. These show a map of the airfield and its parking places, along with how to get in touch with air traffic. I have a friend who was unable to contact them for start clearance at London City Airport and so called them on his mobile telephone. This is what pilots call initiative and is what the management and authorities intend firmly to crack down upon.

If we are going to Paris for instance, the firm in their munificence will have given us a piece of paper with all the navigation points joining the two cities, which we like to call a *navigation log*. As you will probably have guessed by now, this is named after a lump of wood upon which medieval sailors could carve their progress. The first point on this log will direct us toward Dover, providing us with basic navigational information, which we do not need anyway, as we have the route stored in the computer. (If you had GPS in the car, would you still part with five dollars for a map?)

If we took off and turned directly for Dover, then air traffic control would be very cross indeed. So much so that they would probably pass the following message:

Midland Three Yankee Bravo, London Control, we are very cross indeed. Turn right heading 185, climb six thousand feet and squawk ident.

What we have to do is to examine a plate from the section called *Standard Instrument Departures.* These tell us the initial routing the controllers would like us to use, to join the airways at the nearest intersection, which in this case is Dover. Think of it as the nearest slip road where you join the motorway. Another advantage is that if the radio should fail, everyone knows where we are supposed to be going. This is what departures were designed for, as extensions of the old traffic pattern. If you fly to the Greek Islands in the middle of the night, you notice most airliners flying around with landing lights on. This is because many of these radar-less procedures are still carried out here in entirety and pilots are frightened of colliding, knowing how bad they are at sticking to the plot.

We have turned then for Dover, along this pre-specified route. The controller could have a slurp of coffee and still know where we are headed. As a matter of fact they normally intervene to point us in various directions, if only because neither pilots nor autopilots are especially good at following these departures precisely. Go a little too fast, for example, and it is like what happens in a car on a tightening curve. You skid beyond the confines of the original radius of turn. This is bad news in a car, but not so much at three thousand feet, where hedgerows are rarely to be found.

The main reason the controllers intervene is it makes the entire system more flexible, so if a short cut is available they will offer it. They are effectively playing chess in three dimensions, except the pieces never stop moving. The reason we are kept low on the way out of here for instance, is because aircraft arriving at the airport are all manoeuvered in the layer *above* six thousand feet, at least around London. If you are holding in a stack, you are always going to be above this altitude. Only when they come to line you up for an approach will they drop you lower. And that is okay because departing aircraft are nowhere near the portion of the sky where the approach commences. The reason is simple: as well as taking off into the wind, aircraft land in that direction too.

It is therefore like one of those production lines, or factories with a gate at either end. The aircraft all come in through one gate and go out through another. To make it easier again for the controllers, the departure plate will say you must stop the initial climb at six thousand feet. It may be a little more or less, depending upon the airport. If it is quiet enough the controller may intercede and tell you that you are cleared say to fourteen thousand feet. In this event before the aircraft even thinks of levelling off, you dial the new number into the autopilot and off it goes. You might remember a flight you have been on when you took off and just never seemed to stop, like a miniature space shuttle. This is one of those. We like these flights too, if only because they make life simpler.

Occasionally the controllers make a mistake and clear you higher, only to change their mind. This happened once and I had to push the nose down and level the aeroplane quite briskly. This is what they do to practise spacewalking, because the aeroplane starts on a descending arc, while the passengers (because of their momentum) just carry on going in the same direction. The cabin crew were just beginning to float with those trolleys, which secretly I think they quite enjoyed. On empty flights, what some of them would do is to sit on a service tray at the front end of the cabin, so that after take-off, when the aircraft pitched up steeply, they would toboggan all the way to the back. Others fit condoms on their feet, which I am assured makes them frictionless enough to contemplate skiing in this way instead. If this is true, I can only pay the maximum dues here to the designers of contraceptives. We salute your johnny bags and the fun they give us in every way.

This is an example of controllers amending a vertical clearance. Direction too can be altered in pursuit of a strategy. If controllers have an aircraft they wish to descend and which is shortly passing over the top of you, they will turn them one way and you the other, so descent can begin sooner. Basically controllers are operators with a screen on which dots arrive as fast as they can get rid of them. It is like *Space Invaders*, as whole series of blobs approach from all sides of the screen, which have to be steered into a sort of plughole, which is the airport. There is a whole other series of blobs emerging from this plughole and destined for the periphery and these are labelled as departing aircraft, which someone else gets to play with.

You have to keep an eye on them in case they collide with your own blobs though. Imagine several people playing draughts on the same board, all with their own set. Perhaps you better not. Though because of this mental dexterity, stock markets often target radar controllers for recruitment. At the end of the day whoever has least collisions gets to play again and if they go forty years, they leave with an index-linked pension and a Christmas pudding.

The only intimation you get of all this from the flight deck is the creeping suspicion that they do not want you around. You get this feeling from communications like this:

> *Midland Three Yankee Bravo, I asked you to head 185. You're still cleared flight level 140 and contact London now on 133.45. You are the weakest link, goodbye.*

Further away from the airport there are airway controllers and this is like a larger version of pass-the-parcel. In this game, radar returns appear at one edge of the screen and get guided by you over to the other side and passed through imaginary gates, like sheep herded through a gap. Successive controllers sit next to each other, as in telesales. This is not so they can say things like, It's that jerk with the hots for me, can you take it? Actually it is so one controller can tell another, say, she can expect the next blob to be a Britannia 757 routing via Berry Head for Glasgow.

In the early days a system rapidly evolved in which these flight details were entered on a strip of card, known imaginatively as *strips*, which were passed from one controller to the next. They would contain all the pertinent details for each flight, along with space for personal comments about the guy not being the full ticket. Each controller would rack up the strips like forty-fives in a Dansette record player, adding them at the top and pulling them from the bottom according to how the blobs progressed. If some dork walked past with a coffee and knocked them over the floor, you are playing 3-D jigsaws with several thousand passengers. This strip system, which sounds exciting when you put it like that, is only slowly being phased out, along with circular radar screens. As with so much old technology, its problem was that it always worked rather too well.

It may surprise you to know that television screens were once circular. This was great if you were watching Al Jolson, but not if you were watching baseball. They were rapidly substituted by square ones, though this did not happen to radar for another fifty years, probably because there was no need. If the controllers wanted to watch baseball, they had a portable in there with them. After all, the screen was linked to the *radar head*, which is the thing like a satellite dish that rotates, so the system itself was effectively circular. It was also analogue instead of digital; a vinyl disc is an analogue system, using a needle wobbling in a vinyl groove, like the way your voice box wobbles. Music produced by a comb and toilet paper is analogue for this reason. You could develop digital toilet paper, but there is a limited market. Digital systems take sound, or radio echoes from aircraft, to turn them into numbers. Then you can do what you like with them, like emailing them to your friends.

The radar continually emits radio pulses like a bat produces squeaks. In between each pulse it stops and listens. Any radio wave bouncing like sound off an aircraft is picked up, like your satellite dish picks up the baseball signal. How *long* the echo took to return tells the radar how far away the aircraft is, while the *direction* is also known, from which way the dish was pointed at the time. During the war, before the development of radar each of the opposing sides constructed concrete 'ears' which were arrayed along the coast to amplify approaching aircraft. They were supposed to work like those old-fashioned hearing aids and while they did not work, people had a lovely time listening to the sea. Depending upon atmospheric conditions out at sea occasionally sails act in this way, providing sailors a surround-sound preview of delights ahead in port. Or they think they lost it altogether.

Nowadays there are radar heads everywhere, linked by communication lines. As you fly over northern Europe, at least five always have a lock on you, as they say. When radar heads are in use, controllers describe them as "turning and burning". It does not mean they are on fire, though the bit in the middle which generates the pulses is very like a microwave. Anyway, with a lock on you the computers can work out both your height and *trajectory*. This is where you will be shortly, estimated from where you are now. This data is added to the niceties once appearing on each strip, principally the *call sign*. Ours is *Midland Three Yankee Bravo* and before we go flying, we have to fax a *flight plan* to Brussels, telling them our destination, aircraft type, route and call sign. If we do not do this and just get airborne, then a rogue 'blob' appears on screens all over the place and the controllers start picking up telephones and shouting.

We are powering away now, or I should say thrusting away, toward the south east coast. We can also see the traffic we are being guided around, because it appears as diamond symbols on our *navigation display*. This is a screen like a PC, with a line showing our flight-planned route and names of waypoints along it, like Dover. Many are five letter codes, in the middle of nowhere like the North Sea, which act as aiming points. Somebody has to sit down and think of names for these and they appear to have had a great deal of fun. In the North Sea they include SKATE, HADOC, HERIN and over in Ireland there is a GINIS. In Norway, for reasons best kept confidential, there is a position called DOGGY. There is also one called COLIN, which I hope to buy for my own use one day.

There was a time when aeroplanes did not climb very high at all. The first flight of the *Wright Flyer* was shorter than the length of a Boeing 747, which is no longer the longest airliner, but still the heaviest. By 2008, if we all survive, it will not be the heaviest either, that dubious distinction falling to the Airbus 380. During the inaugural flight, the *Flyer* barely left the ground at all, taking off from a glorified skateboard that they called a *dolly* and landing on skids. Before the Wright brothers, people designed aircraft to turn like a boat, with the rudder. This is fine in water, because water is thick and this method will turn you on a sixpence. In the air it is like holding your handkerchief out of the car window if your brakes fail. There needed to be a way in which you could tilt the whole machine like a motorbike and apply the full force of those big wings in a new direction and not just upwards. If your 747 stays in the air, then at four hundred tons it means, incredibly, the wings are generating a force of this amount. You only have to redirect a portion of that and you are turning fast. Four tons is only one per cent of the available force, but if I knock you sideways with a four-ton truck, then you are going places.

What the Wrights did which it took them ages to get right, just like Whittle, was to put small doors on the end of each wing, which were hinged so that they swung up or down. The French had developed most of the aspects of aircraft that were already familiar and they took to these like a duck to water and named them *ailerons*, or little wings. Little wings at the end of the big wings. They are still given this name, even in America. You can see them on the airliner you are travelling in, if you look out the window. They hardly move at all during the turns, because they are so effective and we are going so fast.

What ailerons do is to push the wing tips up or down in unison. If we want to turn left, then the one on the right pushes the tip upwards while its opposite number pushes the other tip downwards. Like a cyclist, we tilt to the left and turn in the same direction. Once introduced, this method proved stunningly effective and with a flick of the wrist you could roll the aircraft on its back. Demonstrations of the *Wright Flyer* in Paris were awe-inspiring. Previously flyers would pass by and disappear into the far distance executing a HUGE skidding turn that covered miles. I was there, the one with a moustache and a copy of *Le Monde*. Then the Wrights turned up and could pirouette around the control tower in such tight circles that everybody said, Ooh La La! It even led to *pylon racing*, when aircraft were flown around towers marking the turning points of aerial racetracks.

It was Clive Sinclair who said the Wrights were not first to fly, but the first not to crash, though unfortunately this is how one of them eventually met their end. Once their secret was uncovered, the race for altitude could begin and it advanced quickly. It is relatively hard to make an aeroplane go fast, but relatively easy to take it high. Virtually twelve months later people were threatening to top the Eiffel Tower, which had been the highest thing around since the pyramids five thousand years earlier. In no time at all and certainly before the First World War, they were up at sixteen thousand feet. When I learned to fly in a two hundred horsepower trainer, this is as high as the bravest coaxed it and this was seventy years later. In actual fact what begins to fail at these levels is not so much the engine but the pilot, who begins to suffer from a form of asphyxiation, so thin is the air at these levels. All of this came in tremendously useful for the imminent war, when the machines substituted for balloons in an attempt to spot the movements of the enemy. Besides this, if there were people you disliked, you could shower them with sharpened darts, known as *flechettes*. Ideally these would be people on the opposing team, though I could have used them on several occasions I can think of myself.

This new access to the heights of heaven led to great raptures of poetry, which these days we are inclined to overlook. I used to know some of this by heart. We can only begin to imagine the effect this new perspective on the world had on people. Even from a ground perspective, as I mentioned earlier, the sight of his first aeroplane caused Marcel Proust to suffer a faint, but I guess this is an overtly 'French' reaction. Imagine how it looked to those at the sharp end. Something like this:

> *I know that I shall meet my fate, somewhere among the clouds above*
>
> *Those that I fight I do not hate, those that I guard I do not love*
>
> *My country is Kiltartan's Cross, my countrymen Kiltartan's poor*
>
> *No likely end could bring them loss, nor leave them happier than before*
>
> *I balanced all, brought all to mind*
>
> *(Blah-blah-blah, nothing comparing with...)*
>
> *This life, this death.*

That was the worst rendition of W B Yeats, *An Irish Airman Foresees his Death* you could possibly hope for. It is apropos of the first war, in which so many Irishmen fought alongside the Royal Flying Corps.

Alternatively try this for size, of Second World War vintage:

I have slipped the surly bonds of Earth,
on laughter-silvered wings

(Blah-blah-blah-blah-blah and...)

... touched the Face of God.

I realise many of you by now will be asking for your money back and frankly I do not blame you. That was by a Flight Corporal Someone-or-other of Canadian birth. Let us move swiftly on and talk about the mechanics of climbing an aeroplane. To stay in the air an aircraft, like a shark, has to be constantly on the move. A helicopter does not, because it has wings that turn around, developing lift all the time. It stands to sense that wings do nothing without airflow. They are not anti-gravity devices and if your budgerigar were to spread its wings gently over the sandpaper, it will not levitate. Or if it does, the genes are worth a fortune. The way wings generate lift is not important; indeed a professor from Cranfield recently suggested the theory we had been teaching since the inception of flight is simply wrong. He is probably right: if I learned anything from the halls of academe, it was that scientists reverse their view of the world about as often as they move house.

There used to be this big thing about suction off the top of the wing. It is a very gentle effect and that applied to a 747 wing is as soft as a baby sucking on a straw. Over the expanse of those wings though, that is a lot of babies and a lot of straws. The thing was, everybody said the wing had to be like a smooth hillside, or else it would not work. This was true when aircraft were fitted with lawnmower engines, but not especially so any more. It is just that gently rounded wings are like gently rounded people; they are more predictable in their behaviour. Otherwise with sufficient energy behind it, the wing can be something of a blunt instrument. All that you have to remember is that if you take a plank of wood, a pair of water-skis, or any other plain structure and deflect it slightly, angling it to the flow, then it will produce a sideways force. At low speeds this is a small force, at higher speed a big force but at no speed, no force at all. The reason it gets to be a bigger force at higher speeds is that at any given moment of time you are shovelling a lot more air molecules to one side. Think of the wing as a knife cutting cheese. Run this straight and progress is even; twist the knife and you are off on a tangent.

This diversion of the air is lift and it is what keeps the aeroplane in the air. It is a simple force, pushing it upward. When you are in your car, you do not fall because the ground is holding the car up and the ground is a force itself. Think about it. If the weight of your car is supported by the world, what is underneath the world to support it in supporting your car? It has not got any surface upon which to brace itself, but it is following an orbit under the attraction of the Sun and it is not going to let itself be deflected much by the weight of your car. It is simply the force of one body against another and air itself also has weight, because it is made of invisible molecules.

When you consider it, water is effectively invisible too. If you look around the sea bottom wearing a mask, you can only see the point where it interfaces with the air and disrupts the light. The forces of pressure, or the effect of currents are only more obvious because of the weight of water. There are more molecules to encounter with each sweep of your arm. Move the wing a lot faster though air and it encounters as many of these less densely packed molecules, to produce equally powerful effects. We now have lift and are supported in the air by speed and the way this deflects the air beneath our wings. Think of me as the wind beneath your wings. Even better, think of me beneath Bette Midler.

Believe it or not, the aeroplane climbs inclines like you take your car up a hill, except that in an aeroplane you get to choose how steep the hill is. The force of lift remains constant, just like the ground beneath the car continues to exert a constant force in support of it. If we have energy left over from what we need to drive the aeroplane forward *fast enough to keep it level*, we can use the excess to drive us up a slope. Again like in the car, how great a hill you can manage depends on how heavy you are. One of the first things flyers discovered was the *zoom climb*. Nowadays, unromantically, they call it *improved* climb. Either way, it is like what you do when you see an upcoming hill and accelerate hard enough for the momentum to carry you most of the way up.

The best demonstration I saw of this by an aeroplane was a Douglas DC-8 jet freighter belonging to *UPS* and taking part in the fiftieth anniversary of Heathrow. It took off in short order from the long runway at London Stansted, because it was very light. It used the remaining length of concrete to fly at the height of a house, while gathering great speed. At the end of the runway, over the Hilton Hotel, it pulled into a forty-five degree climb. This could not be sustained for long, because there would not be the energy. It could in a jet fighter, which has sufficient thrust to climb vertically like a space-rocket. Other aeroplanes are like your car though. Try to drive too steep a hill and you roll back.

Aircraft do not have the luxury of rolling backwards, because as you now know, as the airspeed reduces to near zero, then the weight of air being deflected also reduces to near zero and the machine no longer has anything to sit on, no force opposing its weight. Then it does what you or I would do if we found ourselves at a great height and begins to fall down. It does not do this as we would, because it still has wings and although it falls a little haphazardly at first, it soon gathers speed like a downhill skier and hey presto, we are flying again! This is called a *stall* and we spend our lives as pilots making sure it never happens. This is because as the bright sparks among you will have noticed, the ground might intervene before we have gathered sufficient speed to regain control.

Many of you, okay three of you, will be asking by now, But how did pilots know how high they were anyway? Or come to think of it, how fast? Let us have another FAQ section upon flight and navigation instruments. Hurrah.

Q1   How did they know how fast they were going?

> *By a length of tubing filled with water and invented by a Frenchman called Pitot. One end pointed into the airflow, so as you went faster, the liquid drove further up the tube. Modern systems are not very different and retain the same name.*

Q2   And how high?

Using a barometer. These have liquid mercury in them and as in the tube above, this goes up or down as the air pressure rises and falls with the weather. Pressure also rises or falls depending on how high you are. It is highest at the surface and near space, where there is no air, it falls to nil. Nowadays an expanding capsule replaces the mercury tube.

Q3   What about direction?

Using a magnetic compass, like in a ship. Unfortunately in the air this wobbled all over the place and had to be stabilized by a gyroscope. This is like a spinning top, which is nice and steady.

Q4   What about in cloud?

They used another gyroscope, painted blue and brown like the sky and the ground. This stayed the right way up even when the aeroplane was upside-down. This gave the pilots a reliable 'earth reference'.

The instruments described above were about all you needed for the next several decades. When they began flying they had none at all and knew how fast they were going only by the draught. We all know which way up we are, until we enter cloud or fly at night. Then it is a bit like waking from your sleep and not knowing where you are. This is not good for aeroplanes, which are inclined to crash if left in the wrong *attitude* for any length of time. At several hundred knots, this is no time at all. Each of the instruments were soon set out in a pattern called a *basic T* in front of the pilot and stayed that way until fairly recently, with the introduction of the *glass cockpit*. This is one with computer screens instead. The reason the instruments are kept in pretty much the same position is that, like the keys on your keyboard, people get used to them that way. Even on the screens they broadly follow the layout for the flight, navigation and engine instruments.

One thing that caused confusion in the early days was that as aircraft became faster, they arrived from parts of the country where the weather might have been radically different. They might converge on New York from the prairies, where a sustained high-pressure system had kept it clear for weeks, while another pilot might arrive from within a deep low-pressure system, like in Carolina. Each would have set their airborne barometers before they left, to reflect their height above the ground. Unfortunately as each flew into weather systems of a different pressure, this *altimeter* as it was called would interpret the change in pressure as a change in height, even if the aircraft continued to fly level. This is dangerous when there are mountains around and is one of the reasons aircraft collide with mountains on a regular basis. What is worse, when we each arrive in New York, all the altimeters read differently and my five thousand feet is not quite the same as yours. To the casual observer from the ground, I am probably at nearly six thousand feet and you are nearer four thousand. It is similar to the situation where you arrive from London and I arrive from LA and we argue about what time it is, when in fact we are both wrong.

This situation had to be stopped and what the controllers decided was that once pilots climbed above a certain level leaving the airfield, they all had to use the same pressure reference. This datum was fixed at 1013 millibars as an international standard, except when you got to America, where the same setting is called 29.92 inches and represents the height of a column of mercury in a conventional barometer, on a conventional day. Even now, pilots turn to each other and say things like, Set standard...

The process is reversed when descending back to the airfield, because we are now less concerned about separation from aircraft flying at various levels, as we are no longer maintaining any level. We are concerned about the level of the ground though, especially if it is obscured by cloud. During the descent we reset the local atmospheric pressure reference, which literally varies by the hour, along with the weather. Among the first things you still do in preparing a flight is set the atmospheric pressure reference on the altimeter. If this is correct, then the altimeter should tell you the height of the aerodrome, say eighty feet at Heathrow. You always know the height of the aerodrome, as it appears on the plates. The datum itself is known as the *QNH* and is provided over the radio for you by staff in the control tower, with a barometer of their own. They must remember to adjust their datum as they are already sixty feet high, worth two millibars in any language.

These control towers are getting higher and higher every time they build one, like some kind of arms race. That at Madrid is set back from the main take-off runway on the far side of the airfield. It is a high-tech construction, with a silver top like a flying saucer, set upon a concrete stalk. It is floodlit at night and if they painted the column matt black, this would disappear and it would look like it was hovering completely. What would finish it off, along with many of the passengers, would be a coloured set of sequential lights around the outside, which they could use to attempt alternative means of contact. I thought about putting this to them over the radio, but they were busy. I did congratulate the controllers in Budapest on their lovely Soviet-inspired tower, which had two sides and a gap through the middle, like the arch at *La Defense* in Paris. I think secretly they were quite pleased. After several hours in a control tower, especially on a quiet day, you are pleased about pretty much anything.

It can be lonely in the tower, especially at night. I spent many hours at Speke Airport in Liverpool as a child and recently flew with a captain who had worked there in the tower. A renowned socialite, who took part in the air race between London and Sydney in the 'thirties, died at the airport in a way I described earlier. As he came to touch down, another pilot touched down on top of him instead of the runway. He was decidedly unhappy with the situation, even after death, spending his evenings going up and down the tower in the lift. Apparently this put the frighteners up the controllers. Many airfields are haunted in this way, which I am not going to describe for fear they will be onto my case. I have been awoken from many a happy slumber by pilots of one sort or another, most but not all of them fortunately from among the ranks of the living.

You are probably thinking, I sincerely hope so anyway, that *QNH* is an odd term for the figure appearing on the barometer. What does it stand for? Queens Notional Height? Actually it does not stand for anything. Before they invented the telephone, all they had was the telegraph. All this could do was send a series of beeps down the line, shorter ones or longer ones. Over a dinner party at sea one evening, it occurred to Samuel Morse that each letter could be assigned an individual pattern of beeps and not be jumbled up with the others. Frequently used letters like 'e' got the shortest beep, known as a single *dit*. The 'm' got one long beep, or a *dah*. The 's' got three *dits*, leading to the legendary SOS message being carried in Morse code as *dit-dit-dit, dah-dah-dah, dit-dit-dit*, which now sounds more like lyrics by Sting. Many mobiles had a ring tone called SOS until someone noticed it actually spelt SMS, standing for *Short Messaging Service*. The text messages that today make the world go around were not supposed to be a feature of mobiles at all, but merely a messaging system for engineers.

Morse code was around in commercial use for about a century and was last used by BT inside the last ten years. Radio hams still use it and like the telegraphers of old, they tap away incredibly quickly. When cryptographers were listening in to communications during the war at Bletchley Park, they could recognise the 'hand' of individual Morse operators, the distinctive way in which they tapped the keys. I have known of security software that works by analysing the way you tap at your keyboard. When radios were first used on aircraft it was in the form of Morse code and this is how vital information like the airfield pressure setting had to be relayed. There are codes for each numeral as well as each letter, so the radio operators could broadcast the term QNH, followed by the pressure, to give arriving aircraft an accurate picture of their altitude. By the way, the term *altitude* is the distance above sea level and *height* the distance above ground.

We are still climbing away steadily toward Dover, cleared now to a *flight level* on the standard pressure setting, which corresponds to whole thousands of feet, which is how the altimeter appears calibrated. The older type comprising a dial has whole thousands at the top, like hours on the clock. A great deal of effort went into presentation on these dials, as often under stress pilots misread the altitude and collided with the ground, like you sometimes glance at the watch and get it wrong. Nowadays the altitude appears as a continuously moving strip, like a tape measure running down the side of the screen.

Above ten thousand feet the speed limit expires, or earlier if controllers are in a good mood. They will need to know if you plan to go supersonic, like Concorde, in which event you would mention this on the flight plan before setting off. They used to say this aircraft was faster than a speeding bullet, but I doubt this is true of every projectile. The Germans set up a super-gun on the far side of the channel called Big Bertha. From my own mental calculations in the Armouries Museum in Leeds, this appeared to have had a muzzle-velocity three times faster than Concorde. But who is complaining?

What we tend to do is to settle back into a climb speed of around 300 knots, which in the lower layers of the atmosphere at least, provides a healthy climb rate of two or three thousand feet-per-minute. We do not need to work this out using the altimeter and a stopwatch, because we have a supplementary instrument called a *vertical speed indicator*. This is only really monitored for two reasons: if you climb too slowly on the way up, you will upset the controllers and if you descend too quickly on the way down, you are about to crash and upset the passengers.

As we continue along the route, we are passed to a succession of different controllers, some of them French, who clear us to successively higher levels, until we reach that for cruising. Choosing where this should be is the subject of the next chapter. Apart from this, nothing much really happens, except to the environment inside the cabin, which is also considered elsewhere. One thing of significance is the aeroplane runs out of steam at the higher levels. This manifests itself on two instruments in particular, the *VSI*, which I casually dismissed earlier and the speedometer, which is connected to the Pitot system we discussed and is known in the parlance as the ASI or *airspeed indicator*.

The way the rate of climb diminishes with increasing altitude as evidenced from the needle of the VSI will be readily understandable in view of what we know about how the wing shovels air. As we climb the air gets thinner. It is easy to say this sort of thing without explaining it. I have said that the air is composed of molecules, like sand on the beach. At the bottom of the atmosphere, the weight of the air above squashes that below. Think of parties where you all fell down the stairs in a drunken heap. This compresses the air at the surface and packs the molecules really close together, so you get lots of them in the average bag of crisps, if this is where you choose to seal it. Higher up, the molecules spread themselves around and there are generally less of them about. This makes for a crisp bag inflated to the same size, but containing many fewer molecules. It is just that they are all now more active and bounce around in there like Mexican jumping beans.

The aircraft and its cabin still contain as many molecules as ever and weigh as much, but it now has fewer air molecules to push around for support and struggles to sustain height. For a short while you can compensate for this by raising the nose. This set the wings, like the jaws of a mechanical shovel, at a steeper angle, in an attempt to divert more air. All this does is to slow the aircraft down, like a skier doing a snow-plough, so it confronts even less air molecules in any given second. This limits the high-altitude performance of any aircraft. The thrust from the engine is tailing off all the while, though jet engines are good at resisting this, which is why airliners fly high. As much as anything it is the wing itself, the shovel, which becomes less effective. Think of it as clearing the driveway: with heavy snow the shovel is effective, while with powder snow it is not. For this reason, one of the most effective US spy planes was the U2, which has a jet engine and long, straight wings. It was the type shot down during the Cuban missile crisis and is also being used in the second Gulf War, which is beginning as I write.

Our flagging performance in the climb is best shown by the VSI, which shortly after take off evidenced our rate of climb as up to six thousand feet each minute. Now at the top of the climb it might only be a thirtieth of this rate. In *Upper Airspace*, which is above 18,000 ft in America and above 24,000 ft elsewhere, you are required to sustain three hundred feet-per-minute (fpm) as an operational minimum. For short periods your climb rate might actually reverse so that you begin to sink back down again. Over the course of several minutes however you must still average a climb rate in excess of this minimum.

What is scarier is the information appearing on the ASI or airspeed indicator, now often a *speed tape* down the left-hand side of the screen. Occasionally aircraft have both the tape and the dial, before anybody really trusted the screens. Either still depicts 'coffin corner' adequately, where aircraft and occupants are at the upper reach. It may be 35,000 ft when you are heavy, or 39,000 ft when light. What limits all jets up here is encountering the sound barrier, as we know from movies. They designed fighters so they could go through it without ill effect, as they did for Concorde. For everyone else it remains a Berlin Wall.

What restrains us here is a feature of air called *compressibility*. Let me explain. Air is made of molecules, like feathers in a pillow, which may be squashed like at the bottom of the atmosphere (or in very cold places) or else rather more expansive, like around the equator or in the upper reaches of the atmosphere. Compressibility is this bounciness. The best demonstration I know comes again from our experience in the car, when you drive around those country lanes in summer. Did you ever see those fluffy dandelion seeds that float around like parachutes? Notice when the bonnet approaches how they are lifted clear and over the roof? You cannot hit them if you try. That is how air molecules behave. If ever they wanted to smoke during the war on a battleship, they would stand beneath the bridge, because the air here is gently shovelled to each side, leaving a *stagnation point* like the eye of the storm, where your cigarette did not go out.

If you envisage these molecules as tiny bodies like ours, with weight and momentum all of their own, what you find is you can go too fast so they cannot be squeezed out the way quickly enough. They then ricochet off the front of the wing in a 'V' shaped shockwave. You can see this at the seaside, where boats leave the same shape in the water in the form of a *bow wave*. Water demonstrates this nicely, as it is always incompressible, while air only gets to be like this when moving at the speed of sound.

Noise travels as a series of compression waves using this characteristic of air. They lap upon the shores of our eardrum and we turn the vibrations into pleasant sounds. You may ask how we come to hear the crack of a whip, or of a speeding bullet. This is because the supersonic shocks emanate as a series of *subsonic* waves. The best analogy, or possibly the worst, is a giant asteroid. It enters the atmosphere at multiples of the speed of sound but when it collides with the ocean, the waves that ensue do not travel any faster than waves themselves can travel in water, which is scary enough if it is you in the kayak. We therefore hear bullets long after they have passed and if you watch jet aeroplanes as well, the noise they make seems to struggle to keep up with their position.

The problem subsonic wings have with this is that shock waves create stagnation points, those places where it is good for smoking, all over the place. When these coincide with flight control surfaces, like the ailerons, they stop working. Fighter pilots began to notice this in deathly dives chasing Mitsubishi Zeroes. Their engines produced thousands of horsepower. Point it vertically and combine it with the weight of the aircraft and you were going for the sound barrier. As it approached, the control surfaces would enter stagnant air and the joystick, which the pilot used to steer the thing, would flop around. If you were unlucky, that meant you could not even get sufficient response to pull out the dive. Alternatively, bits of the aeroplane would fall off. I cannot recall a case in which a recovery was not made, because as you went even faster the shock waves moved around some more and all of a sudden you might find the controls working again. The thing to do then was to pull up gently and decelerate *back* through the sound barrier.

For the design of aeroplanes what this meant was if you wanted to go back and forth through this region you had to have sharp wings that cut like the blade of a knife. At low speed these are not nearly as fuel efficient as nicely curved subsonic wings, which is why nobody flies Concorde any more: it is too expensive. The closest I get to this in airliners I fly is during high-speed descents. During these moments the airflow around non-critical parts of the aircraft, like the nose, does go supersonic. You then hear a sort of rippling from the shockwaves generated around the area of the windscreen and if you go any faster, you feel a similar *high-speed buffet* gently shake the airframe as the wings get closer to the speed of sound and begin to protest. This is in contrast to *low-speed buffet*, which is what happened earlier when we climbed too steep a hill, ran out of airspeed and began to fall like a leaf.

A nice Viennese man called Ernst Mach discovered how to measure the speed of sound and above 25,000 ft we usually express our speed as a proportion of this. You may cruise typically at Mach 0.80, or four-fifths as fast as sound. This guarantees that by the time people have heard you, you are not there any more, which is what makes jets such potent weapons of war. The only other thing of significance to record is the *swept* wing. This emerged from Germany during the war as a means to go as fast as possible without sending any of the air supersonic. All the sweep does is to make the wing appear thinner and more slender than it actually is to the airstream, or to an observer stood to one side. This concerns its cross section really. If you have ever been paddling at the seaside and been confronted by a big wave, you will know what this means. If it comes straight on it hits like a bus, but if from an angle like a sideswipe, it impacts more progressively. This is what swept wings do for the air. The first British jetliner had nearly straight wings and Boeing decided to sweep these considerably in the 707. How far should they be swept? The task was given to just one draughtsman and he just fixed it, off the top of his head, at thirty-five degrees, where it remained for many years afterward.

Let me dispose of that expression 'coffin corner', because it is an emotional term about nothing much. The speed of sound is actually governed only by the temperature of the air, so as it gets hotter, it actually speeds up. I think this is because the molecules are perkier and moving around more, living it large. They transmit waves faster, like gossip travels more quickly across the dance floor. For this reason the speed records used to be conducted in the deserts of North Africa, because if you had a jet that could travel at just about the speed of sound, Mach One, then this meant it was covering a lot more ground some place warm, as measured by the stopwatch.

As we get higher we know air gets cooler, because it is less compressed and less able to retain heat. Space can be a cold place, as there is no air there at all, or if there is it will likely be frozen. This is why astronauts and mountaineers wear woolly sweaters. If you are a jet engine, cold is good. If you are a wing however, cold is bad, because it brings us up against that sound barrier at much lower speeds. At sea level sound travels (or the air compresses, depending on how you look at it) up to seven hundred miles an hour, but at 35,000 ft it tails off by a hundred or two. That means that approaching the six hundred mark, the wings complain they are approaching the speed of sound and about to enter shock. The engines are not entirely happy about this either, because shock waves disrupt the smooth flow into the *inlet* and threaten them with flame-out.

These dangers all appear on the airspeed dial in the form of a red and white needle called the *barber pole*, which registers the local speed of sound. It is fitted to the indicator along with the white pointer telling us our speed in *knots*. Remember those: just over one mile an hour? Our speed has sat near the three hundred knot mark during the climb, but what happens as the air cools is that the barber pole keeps dropping all the while. This says though we are going no faster, we are steadily closing on the speed of sound. In modern airliners the barber pole appears as an upper portion of the airspeed tape, which is striped in black and red. This creeps downward towards our reference climb speed of 300 knots from above, like a lowering storm cloud.

As we climb higher and our wings are less able to cope in thinner air, they have to fly ever faster to sustain our weight. In other words, the speed at which we would fall out of the sky, the *stalling speed*, is creeping up from the bottom of the speed tape, symbolised by a tiny green circle inching up the computer screen, which is actually called a *primary flight display*. In older jets you did not know this stalling speed was there; you knew it was creeping around somewhere, like a bogeyman, but you were not sure where.

Here we are then flying at a constant climb speed, but as we get higher we are encroached by a striped red line from above, whereupon the airframe shakes with high speed buffet, or by a little green dot from below, whereupon the wings shudder in protest at the onset of the stall, the break-up of that nice smooth flow over the wings. Welcome to 'coffin corner'. This buffet can be experienced in the very largest jetliners in bad situations. Normally it will not occur because jets have an autothrust system, like cruise control, so if you begin slowing up they pile on more thrust. This device failed once in a DC10 wide-body and the aircraft slowed and began shaking violently. For a long while the crew considered this must be an engine breaking up, which might have a similar effect. Like spin dryers, if they get unbalanced they shake like Little Richard.

You do get sandwiched between this high and low speed buffet when you are heavy and trying to stretch the limits of climb performance, say to squeak up to a desirable cruise level. Then that mighty frame judders a little here and there, while the climb rate wavers around zero and makes you feel you are walking upon eggs. In the days of blue-eyed fighter pilots they would hit the highest levels where the wings lost their tenuous grip and their aircraft fell like a Frisbee, in a flat spin. This could take several thousand feet to recover, as Norman Tebbitt, once the chairman of the Tory Party, recalls in his memoirs. It could be especially problematic from the point of view the engines might flame out like candles, unhappy at a blast of air up their backsides. Do not worry about all of this as a passenger though ~ we do not intend to go there.

Before I leave off climbing, perhaps I should say the pilots pay the greatest attention during this procedure to the winding of the altimeter, or nowadays the progress of the altitude tape, so that airlines usually insist the crew call out every time whole five thousands are passed. These altimeter checks originated with a Boeing practice and were designed to ensure that the needle on one or other of the altimeter dials had not stuck. It was a purely mechanical exercise. Pilots do not know where most of their rituals originate from and share this characteristic with any human cultural endeavour I suppose. Nowadays they assume it is to keep each other 'in the loop' or to generate an overall awareness, which I guess it does. At times we stumble across right things for wrong reasons.

There has always been this dichotomy of operational procedures recommended by either the aeroplane manufacturers or the airlines themselves, which often leads to fudge. The makers rightly contend it is their aeroplane and they know it best, while the airlines point out they are the only ones with substantial experience of using it as intended. It is a little like the scientific struggle between inductive thought and deductive reason and is with us to stay, I think. The most important call these days, when 'altitude busts' are of such concern, is "One thousand to go", when the aircraft is inside a thousand feet of the required level in either the climb or the descent. One captain with whom I flew found the call unduly genuflective. Accordingly so as to object to its imposition in the only way he knew how, he would use it at every possible opportunity. On a freight flight one night I released the seat belt during the climb and went back to the lavatory. As I relieved myself blessedly, the tinkling on the pan was interrupted by an address over the cabin speakers.

One to go...

CRUISE

We are thinking about our cruising level long before we get there and so is the navigation computer. On the ground, when we entered the weight of fuel and passengers, it came up with the highest flight level it thought could be sustained, at least for the initial portion of the flight. It also made a best guess as to how high you ought to be, given the distance to our intended destination. As jets only get economical at the highest levels, the computer sends you up there, even if you have to come straight back down again. You might be thinking that 37,000 ft is a big hill to climb if like the Duke of York, you are coming straight down again. The energy expended on the way up is released to some extent on the way down. Plus the climb takes place at lower speeds and this in itself saves on fuel. The energy spent on the way up is what in school days was called *kinetic*, which is a Greek word for something overly active. When we get up there we have lots of *potential* energy. Anybody who has been sledging will recall how much energy was required getting the thing to the top of the hill, but also how that energy could be energetically dissipated on the way back down, or into the side of a tree.

You will also want to know why going faster in your car uses more fuel, especially as you are getting there so much quicker. The reason why is crucial to flight itself, not only with respect to fuel, but with respect to getting airborne at all. I drove back from a friend recently who had put me up in the spare room, along an elevated section of the road between Hertford and Ware. (This was not where the spare room was, but where I happened to be driving.) At great personal risk, as this is an awesome viaduct, I watched a swan flying the length of a canal below. It was using the cushion of air between itself and the surface of the water to assist it in gathering the speed to get airborne into free flight. These swans are not stupid, because air becomes apparently more solid the faster it moves. This of course is relative, as it does not matter whether the air moves past you at high speed, like in a hurricane, or you move through it at the same speed.

114

So solid is the air when encountered at high speed, that it can be distressing to meet it when not suitably dressed. Remember that woman you fancied who caught you in the bar wearing the check shirt and trousers you used for changing the oil? It is worse than that. Like so much else in aviation, it was the last war that brought it home to pilots how much nastier it was outside the aeroplane than in. Almost to the extent that death in the cockpit was preferable. The dilemma might not have been helped by the fact these guys might be fairly well shot up, for one thing the brain does in these circumstances is to start pumping you up with endorphins, so that death will only be of mild concern. At the point of death, stood there on the threshold, some people choose life because they have a family to raise, others because they think they left the water heater on. A peculiarity of trauma is that the brain plays tricks at times of stress, in order to relax you by using the familiar. You could call this the 'security blanket' syndrome. A related condition is the *Stockholm Syndrome*, a tendency of hostages to identify with the aims of their captors, when under duress.

Minds can be susceptible to all sorts of ideas when put under pressure. Hostages get to thinking, Maybe the earth does rightfully belong to a bunch of crazed guerillas. This is why brainwashing is the bread-and-butter of cult organizations like McDonalds. They do believe Ronald exists and one day soon he is going to take them away from all this, with the assistance of a passing asteroid. While on cults incidentally, can I say my wife thinks it is a hoot the way I confuse Charles Bronson with Charles Manson. One is an Oscar-winning star and the other a crazed psycho. I apologise here and now to any distress I might have caused the crazed psycho.

What this means in terms of aircraft crashes is people do the oddest things. One of the few survivors of the *Hindenburg* was a society lady who plunged back into the blazing airship, because she had "forgotten her handbag". It can only have been Louis Vuitton. The explanation of psychologists for this behaviour is the mind goes into shutdown, because it has never known a vehicle ten times the size of a 747 to burn like a firework. It compares this with other experiences, like the New Jersey turnpike on Mondays, before deciding it is of a whole different order of magnitude. This is how airline pilots deal with situations that we imagine would grip them with terror. They are doing it routinely and for the same reason the cabin crew are drilled repeatedly with handling emergency situations, so they have a fighting chance of responding more appropriately than everyone else. They will be better accustomed to shock and awe. Remember this when you give them a hard time for having forgotten the sugar.

What pilots who tried to bail out found was, in view of how slipstreamed aircraft had become, it was virtually impossible to leave. There were suction pressures that either jammed the canopy, or else pinned you in your seat when climbing out. As a consolation prize, those managing to exit the diving aircraft normally struck the tail-assembly on the way past, or their parachute cords got entangled in the same way. Others found they had a parachute which was on fire. The lucky among them would merely be strafed by cannon fire on the way down.

To get around this a number of firms, principally Martin-Baker in Northern Ireland, pioneered the use of ejector seats. To simulate the business of leaving the cockpit of a fast jet, these seats would be fitted to a sled and powered by rockets at tremendous speed. They would decelerate aborted runs in an instant by running it through a trough of water, like those flumes at the funfair, except these are not doing three hundred miles an hour. In the nineteen fifties, if you walked into the crew room and said, Who wants to set some records by surviving impacts with thirty times the force of gravity? then lots of people jumped up. Much the same happened if you said you needed volunteers to sit and watch a nuclear detonation. Sunglasses would of course be provided, along with popcorn.

What they discovered at this time was if you bailed out at these speeds, strange things happened. Loose things like eyelids would be torn off. You and I may not consider these parts of the body to have so tenuous a connection, though it is true. Do not ever take a high-pressure air hose to body parts, even in the interests of sexual gratification. The best people to talk to about this sort of thing (and the air hose) are paratroopers, with one of whom I learned to fly. I think it was this conversation that dissuaded me from an offer by the parachute regiment to join them for a day out. They had a name for any contingency. The one where you never made it out the door, but instead got sucked along the sides of the aircraft, was called the *rivet inspection*. The one where your canopy did not open up, but trailed above you like a pennant, was called a *Roman candle*. I do not remember the name for the one where the guy was found with thigh bones protruding from his shoulders, because I was outside performing the *retch in the grass*.

To get around this loss of body parts at high speed, at first a hood was provided and later a crash helmet with a visor that dropped into place. I wore one of these helmets when I learned to fly and for years I thought great heights gave me a headache. Actually it was the helmet. Flying without it however, or without a parachute, made me feel positively naked. Even with this sort of protection, the aviator who holds the records for ejecting at the highest speed, although he survived, was left in poor physical shape. Let us just say that surgeons of every sort of speciality, but mainly plastic, had themselves a field day.

One of the most recent aviation articles I recall reading was by a pilot who survived the loss of a windshield. He had taken off from Birmingham in a *BAC 1-11* airliner that had been in the workshop overnight for a screen change. For any number of reasons avid DIYers would understand, the wrong screws were used to re-seal the glass. When the cabin is pressurised, these panes support a pressure of air weighing a ton. Or rather, this one did not, and let go with the effect of a screwdriver plunged into an anti-deodorant. The ensuing rush of air took the captain most way out of the window, held only by his lap-strap, which was entangled around his feet, assisted in its role by a steward. Although considered a casualty of war by the co-pilot, who landed the aeroplane, the man was not quite DOA. He was though severely frostbitten and looked like he had said the wrong thing at an annual convention of the Ku Klux Klan.

None of this need worry you as a passenger. Admittedly I was shocked at discovering as a civilian trainee that no parachutes were provided. I was equally shocked to find people flew around in cloud without radar cover, in the hope that whoever was doing the same thing was unlikely to be in quite the same whereabouts. The thinking was the collision would kill you before you had time to think about the parachute. Call me Mr. Picky, but something is not right there. As passengers you at least have the luxury of being most unlikely to collide with other aircraft. Meanwhile bailing out six miles up is hardly an option, when it is sixty degrees below and you meet the air at a speed exceeding any hurricane. Besides, it is dark as well and there is barely oxygen to sustain life for thirty seconds. Plus parachutes do not work at these altitudes. Ask the Japanese guy who tried skiing down Mount Everest. There really is one.

What about an escape capsule? Well the only aircraft I know in which this was included with any success and even then, not much, was the swing-winged F111 fighter jet. This had a nose section that came off virtually intact, along with the crew. They figured this was almost as cheap as using ejector seats, which were becoming frightfully expensive. I had a briefing on one of these seats and it appeared to do everything except fax a message back home. The big mortar shell that used to fire it off, crushing a selection of vertebrae, had been replaced by a sequence of rockets, probably with lovely coloured effects, along with strips of explosive that blew the Plexiglas of the canopy apart in a coordinated display. Eventually they decided all this expense and complexity was probably a better alternative than the prospect of losing the escape capsule from aircraft like the F111, which might leave a ten-ton fighter wandering the skies like a headless chicken. One story doing the rounds when I learned to fly, which I particularly liked, was that the Russians had incorporated an escape capsule into their version of Concorde, the Tu-144 usually known as *Concordski*. The thing was, this was for the use of the crew and not the passengers:

> *Ladies and Gentleman, we appeared to have suffered a slight technical problem and that is why I am speaking to you from a small capsule, which some of you may be able to see out of the left-hand side. There is no cause whatever for alarm. Please follow the instructions of the cabin-crew very carefully. We have left them there for your own safety. Thank you and goodnight.*

Let us consider the environment both inside and outside of your cabin, the aluminium tube you call home. One of the first tasks facing the aviation authorities was 'standardising' the atmosphere. You can imagine how difficult this was going to be. Take standardising the thickness of glass in your car windshield. Probably not that difficult, involving as it does little more than a ruler (actually they use a *micrometer*, which measures gauge like a pair of pincers) and a board-table, around which are sat the principal manufacturers. There will probably also be someone from the *International Standards Organization* there to break up those headlocks.

Now think of the sky. Take its simplest aspect, like the appearance of different clouds, some of which are low and ragged, some middling and fluffy and others high and rather feathery. These things were not put into categories until some curate in the nineteenth century took a yen to the subject. Most of western science seems to have been advanced by country parsons, probably because they were only busy on Sundays. He came up with a scheme for quantifying *cloud cover* and this scheme is still used today by airline crews, along with the names for various types of cloud. The extent of cloud cover is described by dividing the sky into eighths, or *octas*. This sounds a particularly odd thing to in our digital age; the term *digital* is associated with our fingers and thumbs and therefore our propensity to number everything in tens. Nevertheless think of the cardinal points of the compass, four of them. Then it is so much easier of thinking of subdividing these again whilst scanning the horizon to report upon the extent of cloud.

The military still use this categorisation and talk of things like *three octas of cumulus*. This seemed too perfunctory for civilian requirements and around twenty years ago they came up with more user-friendly terms, which I shall now try to recall:

Scattered	0-2 octas
Broken	3-4 octas
Few	5-7 octas
Overcast	Too many octas

Give it ten more years and they will decide these terms also are perfunctory, whereupon we will be talking about a *smattering* instead. People will be saying that the constant use of emotionally charged words like *overcast* led to long-term feelings of angst among employees. I say this only because I see my nest egg coming from this source. Along with the extent of cloud cover, this worthy parson gave names to the types of cloud. To those of you on the ground the types of cloud are not really of life and death significance. They will merely determine whether valet parking will be required at the mall, or whether that dream holiday in Bermuda ends in divorce. To the aviator, knowing which clouds are which and avoiding the wrong ones are a key to survival. There are few clouds that bring down an airliner these days, especially outside of continental landmasses like North America. Nonetheless lightning strikes otherwise causing no damage still require the aeroplane to be inspected upon arrival. This takes time and what time means to the flight crew is they miss the start of that football match.

The principal threats to airliners from clouds are easily categorised. To you as passengers some of these will be more obvious than others and do not forget, I am writing this from your perspective, to calm your fears and satisfy your inner longings. Call my agent on the last one. Firstly, *turbulence* is associated with fluffy clouds and *thunderstorms* associated with even bigger clouds; it is no good pretending not to notice the effect of these when we are flying. Thirdly there is *icing*, which brings down slower airliners with propellers with monotonous regularity. Fourthly *fog*, or cloud at ground level. There is of course the not inconsiderable danger arising from cloud, when you cannot see where you are going. Then there is a clear and present danger of impacting what they call *Cumulus Granitus.*

Let us examine each of these in their gory details. The first was the effect of turbulence. We will consider elsewhere during descent, the turbulence arising from strong winds or *jetstreams*. For now let us consider that associated with cloud and I do mean associated, because strictly speaking the cloud merely marks or intensifies a process that had begun already. In fact by visibly flagging areas of turbulence, this can often be avoided merely with the use of what the military call the *Mark One Eyeball*. Where does such turbulence come from? It comes from heating, of the convective variety that you see bubbling up from the bottom of your saucepan of water. This does not have to be associated with cloud at all if the air is particularly dry. Flying over the prairies of the Midwest in a light aircraft you can be suddenly elevated by invisible plumes, the sort eagles soar upon, which raise you several thousand feet higher than you wanted to be. The only way to correct this condition is to point the nose at the ground and drive down a slope. This becomes like walking down the up escalator and in the end I would usually give up fighting and enjoy the ride.

If you heat a surface like the bottom of your pan, the contents rise in *plumes*. The whole lot cannot be rising, otherwise the contents would levitate out the pan. Only Uri Geller can achieve this. For every point where water is rising like a small typhoon, there are parts where it is descending. These are not evenly spread and in the atmosphere these *thermals,* as they are known, only occupy ten per cent of the ground area. They are rising like the fast elevator in the Empire State. To compensate for this, ninety per cent of the air is gently descending to replace that which took off. The trick if you are an eagle, or if you are gliding across country, is to circle to the top of one of these elevators and then dash across to the next one.

You will be wondering how these birdmen (and birdwomen) know where the thermals are? Principally they look for clouds that form above them, like steam from a chimney. The Polynesian peoples who first navigated the Pacific used to know where islands lay over the horizon, because they could see these plumes at a distance. The alternative is to follow soaring birds, which know what they are about. So much so, they often regard light aircraft as a territorial threat and I have known them turn for me when flying in the Rockies. I had no desire to get close up and personal with a bald eagle. I just made jokes about toupees from a safe distance.

For scientific reasons these bubbles of rising air are considered discrete, entities within themselves for the purpose of analysis. All air contains water vapour in the form of an invisible gas. The solid version of water is called the *ice cube*, while the liquid version is found in great quantities everywhere except Vegas. If it contains quite a lot of vapour, just itching to get out, then a little cooling will persuade it to condense into liquid form, into tiny droplets. These are so small they are like grains of sand and clouds can appear white and wavy like beaches. Given a bit of mixing the droplets tend to collide and get together into larger droplets and then fall as rain. Sometimes it never even makes it to the ground before drying out, whereupon it is known as *virga* or virgin rain that never knew cruelty.

The big problem with water vapour being squeezed out like this into tiny droplets is this process releases heat. Remember how the heat of the sun was required to evaporate those puddles? Well during the reverse process, a sort of devaporation, this heat is released again. My spellchecker did *not* like that one. Because of the peculiar nature of this release, meteorologists who study the weather, call it *latent* or hidden energy, for people stand around saying, Where did the warmth come from? This is also why it gets slightly warmer during heavy snowfall, when after a while the stuff turns to sleet instead.

The problem we have as flyers is these thermals rise and cool, release their water content as cloud and in doing so, release even more heat to reinvigorate the thermal. It is like taking a hot air balloon so far up and then leaving the burner going full blast. The balloon keeps on rising until the gas runs out. Clouds are the same, except they keep on rising until the water vapour is wrung out. Unfortunately if the air was already hot and moist at ground level (which is good in bed, but bad in clouds), if it sailed in from the Caribbean and hit the prairies, then it is really going to motor.

So chaotic is this rising and mixing it can throw up eddies like you see in streams, though when they happen in air they are called *tornadoes*. This is why they are associated with masses of moist and rising air called *thunderheads*. They now think tornadoes can be triggered by traffic sliding in different directions down the interstate. This gives the air that initial twist, which is picked up and invigorated by the effect of earth rotation. Spinning effects are very powerful and self-sustaining. Ask any ice-skater.

Now it will come as no surprise to you that if these vortices can pick up a cow and take it on the journey of a lifetime, they are not going to be especially comfortable in an airliner. To my knowledge, just one of these has been brought down by a tornado in Europe, a Fokker F28 in the vicinity of Amsterdam. I used to fly with a captain who left the weather radar off altogether, on the basis no aeroplane ever broke up in Europe. I found this amusing until contact with the first thunderhead. The correct name for these is *cumulonimbus*, which in Latin means heaped thing bearing rain and not dances with wolves. Updraughts in these masses of air are what cause hail the size of melons, for as raindrops fall they are countered by rising air and taken back to the top to freeze all over again. This happens several times, which is why hail is layered, until eventually they get so heavy they drop from the cloud anyway and kill a dog. Unfortunately much the same thing has happened inside these clouds to flyers bailing out: can I introduce *Henry, the Human Hailstone*? Updraughts can travel vertically at seventy miles an hour, sufficient to take anything the wrong direction, especially with a parachute, which becomes a kite in the circumstances. The thing to do is to enjoy the ride and look upon it as the opportunity of a lifetime.

That deals pretty much with convective turbulence, as evidenced by those ugly black clouds outside the window looking like decaying cauliflower. The thunder they are associated with is so loud, at times I have heard it above the noise on the flight deck. I have had two lightning strikes, both sounding like someone kicking the side of the aeroplane. Occasionally lightning travels the length of the cabin as a sort of shimmering flash passing right by, which of course is exactly what it is. Typically it enters the nose and discharges along the length of the aeroplane, or out via the wings. To assist its passage there are little rods at intervals along the back of the wings, called *discharge wicks*. On the Airbus these often fall off, especially those in line with the jet exhaust, which is exactly what manufacturers intend so as to capitalise on those spare parts.

These static effects are fabulous though. Sailors used to call them *St Elmo's fire*, an eerie glow around the head of the mast. Pilots I know have seen it form trails around propeller tips, like a Catherine wheel, though the first signs are usually fingers of sparks spreading from around the edges of the windscreen. Flying at night along the tops of thunderstorms I have seen a plasma form around the edges of the windscreen outside, sort of showing up the airflow nicely, like smoke in a wind tunnel. Looking at these things you do not know whether to be awestruck or frightened by foreknowledge of the lightning they normally presage. Others pilots I have flown with have known a huge plasma field envelope the entire aircraft, a greenish glow, to the delight and consternation of passengers. They must have imagined they were about to be abducted by aliens. Do not expect this sort of service from the no-frills carriers. The best I ever heard was a colleague who witnessed a strike in the form of a lightning ball, which hung like a phosphorescent fart for a second in the flight deck before exiting *through* the door into the cabin. I imagine the call bell going and some passenger saying, I never ordered this.

The most obvious effect from inside the cabin (as many passengers have no window and are unable to enjoy the lightning) is undoubtedly turbulence. This is not overly difficult to explain. Many passengers say they hit an *air pocket*. As descriptions go, this sucks. What they are trying to say is they kind of dropped down a hole, though the reverse is true. We already know the air is punctuated with sorts of chimneys of fiercely rising air. When the aeroplane flies into one of these, because of its momentum it continues on the level, while the wings flex like Fat Jock hit the springboard. You can simulate the potency of this action with plastic ruler and desktop. All this energy has to be released somehow because it was provided for free (remember *potential* energy?) and it releases itself by springing the cabin onto a higher plane shortly afterward.

While the cabin continues on this upward trajectory, the wings are the first to feel the effects of descending air beyond and do much the same thing again with reverse effect. This feels altogether in the cabin like you hit a humpback bridge, or even a whole series of humpback bridges. Should you leave your seat belt off, the game the wings play with the cabin is played out between the cabin and your humble person. This is to say that by the time the cabin is being dragged back down unwillingly by the wings, you are still on an upward trajectory that is only interrupted by the ceiling. This is not too bad in itself, as it gives a different perspective on life. Then you fall like a drunken fruit bat and that is when breakages occur. A DC10 rolled over after landing recently and this left the entire cabin upside down and occupants suspended from the new ceiling, very much like fruit bats. They stayed there some considerable time and investigators attributed this to the conformal nature of society in the Orient, where it happened. I imagine the first passenger to unbuckle became known as *Jonathan Livingston Fruit Bat*.

As we saw earlier at times this vigorous turbulence is not associated with clouds at all, but with clear air, whereupon it is known as *clear air turbulence*. We look at it later in relation to winds though pilots avoid it altogether if possible. I have known some to lose four thousand feet to it while crossing the Pyrenees, because it can appear from nowhere. Defences we have against visible evidence of turbulence, besides the obvious appearance of different types of cloud, include the weather radar. This is a smaller version of the one air traffic use and takes the form of a dish the size of that connected to your TV. It hides inside the nose, right out front of the pilots and oscillates from side to side, sending out radio pulses that reflect back from large raindrops. Heavy rain is a sure sign of rising air, as the thermals have to be powerful enough to levitate the drops. Rainstorms appear as coloured jellyfish on a display that used to be self-contained, but which is now superimposed over our intended route on the ND, or *navigation display*.

You then ask the controllers if you can go off-route and skirt these thunderheads and they normally assent, as their own radar tends not to pick up rainstorms. Like naughty boys, pilots have been known to pretend they are skirting the weather, to connive a short cut. Then the allegations start to fly over the radio between one airline and another. Those with the oldest aeroplanes get angriest because they do not have the TV screens showing potential weather miles down the route, even from the ground, so they do not believe you. You have to tell them politely your equipment is superior to theirs and they can pay due diligence to your posterior.

What I have omitted thus far is a feature of the weather unknown to the passengers, but a terrible reality to the pilots. Hailstones hit the windshield at several hundred knots. Fortunately the glass is multi-layered like that in the presidential limousine, besides being heated. It still makes the noise of death by a thousand snowballs, so much so that heavy rain and hail is deafening and you have to sometimes shout to each other over the din. Beside all the while trying to listen to the flight controllers. Why ever did I get into this job? Though even this effect has its compensations like everything in flying and if you turn on the *landing lights* at night during heavy snowfall, this has a hypnotic effect when viewed through the windshield, like a psychedelic screensaver. The funny thing is, the controllers can hear this noise in the background along with the fear in your voice, or the palpitations caused by continuous turbulence. It must be like listening to exciting drama on the radio, from the comfort of your armchair. I say that, but radar controllers hate bad weather too, because they get requests from aircraft to fly everywhere to avoid it, while they have to repeat instructions endlessly above the confusion. This is why *any* weather in the terminal manoeuvring area around major hubs gives rise to delays, even when the sun is shining when you get off and you toy with suing the airline.

That is convective turbulence just about dealt with. What was next, he inquires while scrolling furiously? I see we disposed of thunderstorms too, but not entirely. These cumulonimbus clouds or *CBs* can extend to the top of the atmosphere around the tropics, where the atmosphere is deepest. You are never going to believe this, but there is a greater depth of atmosphere around the equator because the world spins like a drier and it piles up there. It is almost twice as thick than at each pole. Admittedly this is also because it is warmer and more expansive. Turbulent clouds here rise to forty thousand feet.

As with all these tall clouds, they get so high their water freezes into crystals and spreads downwind into anvil-heads, which is how they are known. As we do not use horses any more, we only know what an anvil is if it falls on us from some height. We need a new name and I am prepared to open it to competition. How about *mother of all rag-tops*? Historians are going to look back and decide the greatest strategic mistake Saddam Hussein made was not to service mark the expression *mother of all*, which is used as a superlative to describe almost any aspect of life in the USA these days. Perhaps this is the ultimate triumph of consumer society, to render even the auspices of war banal.

What is exciting, before we leave this juncture, is that airliners riding over thunderheads have been struck by lightning from *below*. This is stuff J K Rowling could never have dreamt. Scientists have discovered lightning in the form of *sprites* can travel seventy-five miles into space. Airline crews are asked to report them for the purposes of research, as they can most easily spot these traces at night. Lightning discharges are among the most awesome sights described by crews of the Space Shuttle. I cannot say I have ever seen these sprites, though it is not for want of hours spent focused on the middle-distance at night like a zombie.

In the night sky the most apparent thing to occupants of the flight deck, if they turn the lights down really low (if only to get some sleep) are the stars themselves, which nobody on the ground gets to see any more. During recent blackouts in California, LA residents were calling the emergency services to report a change in the sky: the appearance of stars. Among these is the delicate *Milky Way*, now known to children only as confectionery. Seeing the stars is kind of nice, because they assure you the ship is headed the right way, like they did for navigators of old. During the course of long night flights you see them trace a creeping arc across the night skies. There is the odd shooting star, which to the best of my knowledge has yet to strike an airliner, let alone a human, though meteors have accounted for at least one South American dog beside a whole range of dinosaurs.

Then there is the fantastic *Aurora Borealis*, though whenever I flew it appeared only as a smudge of green like an old net curtain above the pole, a franchise outlet for the Milky Way. Other pilots get to see the whole sound-and-light show. Actually, shooting stars do make a whooshing sound as they enter the atmosphere if you listen very quietly. I was told this by a naval flier who engaged in exercises in Scandinavia, where it is very quiet on Saturday nights. Another pilot told me the phosphorescent colours of the Aurora appeared so magical one night he invited the attendant to look. She peered out front at this sight, which is only vouchsafed normally to the most blessed, before announcing, Anyone want a coffee?

We shall examine more effects of thunderstorms later, during the chapter on approaches. I know you are looking forward to it, especially if you are in the air at this moment. For now let us turn to their comrade in arms, *icing*. This is divided into two types for flyers, engine and airframe icing. The former has been pretty well cracked by the manufacturers, literally, assuming you remember to switch it on. Newer and smaller jets have systems that detect ice formation and do this for you. Bizarrely, larger airliners are entrusted to the discretion of crews. If I have learned anything in life, it is never to trust people to use discretion. When the system is on it usually works however, though when that most reliable of jet engines appeared, the CFM-56, it had distinct shortfalls in this area. Both engines and aeroplanes, while they may be resounding successes later in life, can be prone to teething troubles. The Lockheed Electra was an especially fast propeller airliner whose wingtips fluttered like a stalk of grass, to the extent they fell off. Until this was fixed the headline writers freely used phrases like *Mourning Becomes the Electra*. This was a twist on the play of Eugene O'Neill with the title *Mourning Becomes Electra*. It is too abstruse for the newspapers of today, which would lead with *HUNDREDS MEET WITH GORY DEATH* while the subtext would say, And wish they'd gone to Disneyworld instead. But only just.

Anyhow, the CFM-56s as first fitted to the workhorse of internal flights, the Boeing 737, were not nearly so reliable. Inside the sort of clouds we have been examining, the engines would accumulate ice and this would break off and douse the fires, at times simultaneously. Anything happening simultaneously in an airliner with two engines is rarely good news. The first time this happened the crew looked around, spotted a levee (which is a raised canal on the plains), figured it must be flat and landed the aeroplane in the field alongside. Then they dropped the air stairs and invited the passengers out as if they were on a tour of Holland. This particular problem was alleviated by the simple expedient of changing the sharp *nose cone*, at the centre of the big fan, for a bullet-shaped assembly instead.

Most engine anti-ice systems work by taking hotly compressed air from within the engine and dumping it around the front. The same thing is done to dispel ice along the wings, by pumping hot air along the front edge. If you leave this switched on by mistake on a warm day, before you go flying, it has a similar effect on these parts as forgetting the chicken was in the oven. In propeller driven aircraft without an abundance of this hot air, they use a system of rubber inflatable trousers along the front of the wing, where air is directed to crack off ice. Remaindered systems of this type are doing the circuit of gay clubs in LA.

This ice in cloud can build up with astonishing rapidity. When droplets of water cool quickly, they do not have time to think about forming ice until something like an aeroplane collides with them, when they form *contact ice* with enthusiasm. This same process of *sublimation* is what happens when the hot vapour discharged from the engine is instantly surrounded by air at sixty below, so before it thinks about switching from gaseous form to liquid, it freezes into crystals. These form the *condensation trails* behind jets, which cross our skies and themselves lead to layers of cloud. Scientists estimated the sunshine was one percent warmer in its effect after 9/11, because no aeroplanes flew. And imagine the lengths painters like Turner would have to go to in airbrushing them out. On quieter flights in a business jet, we have snaked around to see if we could see these trails in the rear-view mirror. The best most pilots get to see is the shadow of their aircraft on clouds below, accompanied by a trail. There is probably something elemental about this urgent male need to produce a visible efflux, but I am not discussing it here.

Just to record how quickly ice can build, I was descending from high level one evening toward Rome and just a minute or two into the tops of thin and innocuous-looking cloud I had an ugly intuition and shined my torch on the windshield. It was obliterated with an inch of ice, which was surprising because it was heated. As the wings were unheated at the time this rather put the frighteners up me. You can just about see the ends of the wings in narrow-body airliners and to assist with this at night, you put the *wing lights* on periodically and have a look. Watch this carefully as a passenger and you will notice shards of ice being shed by the hot air system. If these are large enough, or if they appear around toilet drains (when they are known as *blue ice* because of the chemicals involved), they may fall to the ground. Then you get neighbourly disputes over who broke whose glasshouse with shards of ice, which fortunately for the airlines soon melted thereafter. Then in the papers the carriers can say things like, Our lawyers assure us shards of blue ice the size of canoes are proven weather phenomena.

Sufficient ice clinging to the airframe will bring an aeroplane down with its weight, along with the drag it produces. A pilot of my acquaintance who shall remain nameless, if only for his attempts to dodge the revenue, suffered this problem in a five-ton aeroplane being ferried to England via the northerly route including Greenland. They sank slowly through a blizzard, the view ahead a complete whiteout, until they realised they had impacted rising ground only because the airspeed was falling even faster. They had very gradually collided with the snow-covered surface and were sledging to a halt, which they survived. I know of two more instances of this in larger aircraft during WWII. This would not have been so bad, except they were dressed for springtime shopping in New York. Eventually they broke the ice from the antennas and contacted a passing jumbo jet. On longer routes you keep a *listening watch* on the distress frequencies for this sort of contingency.

The final weather hazard for consideration is fog, which again I intend to look at more closely in the approach phase. The exception is hill fog, which technically is cloud that caps the mountainsides at any altitude. It is an unfortunate coincidence of flying that the highest places are often wreathed in clouds, otherwise they could be avoided more easily. Dropping into a place like Geneva down a narrow valley, it can be a good thing for pilots *not* to be able to see the mountainsides, as they look so close. Anyone who has used Bryce software, which generates pictures of terrain, will have noticed landscapes have a continuous scale. This software creates mountainous backgrounds on your PC by simple repeating patterns. This is to say that looked at close, even ripples in the sand can look like sand dunes and this recapitulation of forms has become the science of fractals.

It is a dangerous illusion in an airliner, especially in clear air, which provides no spatial reference like haze does simply by getting thicker over some distance. This contributed to the crash of a sightseeing airliner from New Zealand. It collided with Mount Erebus in the Antarctic and one reason for this is airliners take many miles to turn at speed and it is difficult to judge the turn radius by visual estimation alone. I discovered this on at least one occasion flying up a valley; this is especially unnerving if you find the valley floor is climbing faster. What mountain flyers do is to hug one side, so they have a full radius available for a U-turn. What they also do during whiteouts is to drop black bin liners to guide them to a landing. I have been skiing in whiteouts and it is a peculiar sensation when deprived of sight, not knowing whether you are sliding forward or backward.

Otherwise this vantage point, up there in the sky, can be most illuminating. One South American airline pilot figured that a series of impact craters looked just like a glancing blow from an asteroid and upon closer inspection, this is what it turned out to have been. I am not going to say too much about what can be seen from the window yet, as in the cruise this is often very little while there is haze or cloud around. This is why pilots enjoy the clear view over the poles or desert lands: there is little visible moisture, because the air is so much drier and not much vapour to be wrung into clouds by thermals.

Let us look again at that *International Standard Atmosphere*. The first thing that had to be standardised we discussed already, being the barometric pressure of 1013 millibars we fly around with. Another was to decide how thick the atmosphere was considered to be. Further from the ground, which is comparatively warm, air gets cooler. Being thinner up here, like an old duvet, it is less able to retain the heat. Conversely as you descend into the earth it becomes progressively hotter and more uniform in temperature because of its density. I used to fly with a collier-come-captain and it entertained me to think he spent ten years 5,000 ft below ground and ten years above. You may have noticed yourself the underground railway is an even temperature year round, which is why it attracts buskers.

The extent to which temperature rises underground is not very different from the way it falls on the way up, at around two degrees Celsius per thousand feet. If you live in Japan and own the freehold to your house, it is considered to extend all the way to the centre of the earth. I have not investigated the circumstances, but I believe this is in the form of a tapering section, like a slice of cake. Elsewhere I am not sure to what depth your freehold extends, though How Deep is Your Freehold? is a romantic title for a song. Should the Japanese be determined to pursue their fealty to the centre of the earth, they would find it becoming continually hotter. This is not true of the atmosphere, which would otherwise go on cooling into space where we are told there is an absolute temperature to which anything falls, minus 273 degrees Celsius. I have not heard of any absolute limit applied to the top end of the scale and according to Dante we are not supposed to expect one. He assures us the fires of hell exceed the temperature of your sauna by a significant margin.

In the first part of the atmosphere or *troposphere*, the temperature keeps dropping and around 40,000 ft it may be minus 60 degrees or less. A pilot I worked with recently was previously big in frozen foods and specifically Yorkshire puddings. He said the thing with this kind of production is the large-scale equipment required to flash-freeze produce. If ever you want to be that Yorkshire pudding, step outside an aeroplane at this altitude. One of the most unnerving things about flying nowadays is a preponderance of elderly people, seeing as they are the only ones left with any money. Not unnaturally a portion of these, along with a portion of people of every other age, are fruitcakes intent upon opening doors. Rest easy, these fit like the plug in your bath, assisted by the weight of several tons of cabin pressure.

Meanwhile in the upper reaches of the troposphere, the temperature actually stabilises (at the beginning of the *tropopause*) at what the standard atmosphere says is minus 56 degrees. It stays that way for several thousand feet more and later begins to increase for a while again. Unsurprisingly there are no winds in the layer with a uniform temperature, because winds are all about trying to equalise areas of different temperature, like poles and tropics. Concorde flies at this level and its journey times are hardly affected by winds at all. Airliners at lower levels experience *jetstreams*, powerful winds that make huge differences in journey times. Descending once north of Birmingham, I was pleased to calculate we were travelling at seven hundred miles an hour with the benefit of such a wind. Eventually, nearer to space the temperature falls off again and does so fairly quickly; once in space, out of the sun you freeze your nuts off. All of the weather is also confined to the lower part of the atmosphere, that troposphere, though sometimes it climbs so fast like a nuclear mushroom cloud, it punches a little higher.

Earlier in the climb we were undecided about which level to cruise at. Different aircraft types are certificated with a *ceiling* of different altitudes, mainly limited by how much pressure they can contain inside the cabin, which is pumped up like a cheap breast of chicken. For the Airbus 320 it is 39,000 ft and for the older Boeing 737 it is 37,000 ft. Apart from wanting to fly bigger and faster aeroplanes, pilots like to go higher so they can literally look down upon their fellows. When one airline I worked for took delivery of newer aircraft which flew higher, they used to get on the radio to colleagues and say, Hello mate, what are you doing down there? This is the equivalent of going to a cocktail party and complimenting the hostess on her outfit from last season.

We are then limited by the ceiling provided for the aeroplane. Non-pressurised aircraft are limited by the authorities to around 14,000 ft, but they insist you wear an oxygen mask above 10,000 ft, like aviators of old. Otherwise you black out. I once operated one such flight with a cold, having to take my mask off continually to sneeze. What was worse, when I opened my flask in order to make a *Lemsip*, the entire contents spewed out and dropped scalding water into my crotch, as Vesuvius did to the residents of Pompeii. This is because if you reduce the pressure of air, water boils away at a lower temperature. One effect of this is that it is impossible to enjoy a boiled egg up Everest, even by way of celebration, because the water disappears before getting hot enough. By way of consolation for my *Lemsip* incident, the mask incorporated its own microphone, making me sound like Douglas Bader. In view of this I called up the company on the radio and said, Captain bought it over the briny, see you all at teatime, tally ho...

Interestingly there have been occasions when the skin of ageing airliners peeled back like a ripe banana, exposing all and sundry to the delights of the outside world. It happened to a 737 on route to Hawaii, unfortunately disposing of one or two on their feet, who were sucked out. The aircraft had seen extensive service in the corrosive ocean atmosphere, but all this might have been avoided had they listened to one of the passengers, who asked why the fuselage looked wrinkled around the doorway. Aeroplanes do get wrinkled like people and Boeings are prone to this around the rear baggage holds. This is entirely normal and much like the way plasterboard in your new home settles during the first year. Those who flew the prototype Comet jetliner were particularly unnerved when they heard the skin around the nose denting at speed. This was a problem more normally associated with airships, which are much squishier.

Of equal concern is the damage we are possibly doing the environment. All airliners are effectively injecting the upper levels of the atmosphere with a huge quantity of hot air, included with which is an equal quantity of water vapour. Quite what effect this is likely to have in the long term nobody knows. Suffice it to say it does much that automobiles do at ground level, but much more effectively. Bear in mind during a trip across the Atlantic you will each require a barrel of oil, or what you would normally only need for a year of motoring. In addition, aircraft like Concorde travel at the levels associated with the ozone layer. Uncertainty surrounding the consequences is one of the principal factors dissuading firms from the development of future supersonic airliners. If anything, the current trend in leading edge technology is to skip using the atmosphere altogether and spend more of the journey in space. I think most of us probably like this idea.

You might have noticed that even in the earliest days of scaling Everest, oxygen tanks appear to have been required. Aircraft are certificated to fly no higher than 25,000 ft, should they not have drop-down oxygen masks. Technically they can fly much higher and even aircraft during the last world war would regularly scale these heights. To join the *six mile high* club however, jet airliners need to be highly pressurised with compressed air from inside the engines. Because the air comes from here, our noses get a snapshot of problems beneath the wing. The tips of the fan blades are designed to run very close to the walls of the surrounding duct, to prevent air leaking backwards. To make this a really tight fit the fan is surrounded by an *abrasion seal*, which is like icing sugar, so it does not matter if the blade tips rub its surface. If the engine takes a *birdstrike* it can shed a blade or two from the fan and this unbalances it and causes a great deal of abrasion, along with showers of sparks. These are subsequently ingested into the air conditioning and tinged with more than a hint of roasting bird.

In a twisted way this is good news because it means while there is a smell of burning in the cabin, it is nicely contained in its effects.

Once engines were hung beneath the wing they could sustain fires that could not even be put out by the built-in extinguishers. One Airbus 300 in the USA continued its flight for a further twenty minutes carrying a blazing engine. In the days engines sat out front, the way piston engines had to because propellers needed the clearance, this was dangerous because fires lined up with the wing. These are made of aluminium, which has a low melting point, so between engine and airframe they used to fit a *firewall*. Concorde is limited to fifteen hundred miles an hour, because at these speeds, even when outside it is sixty below, friction sends the skin temperature to beyond boiling. A little more than this and aluminium turns plastic, so you must use steel (cheap and favoured by Soviets) or else titanium (costly and favoured by art galleries).

To test the contingency of birds striking engines they fire frozen chickens at the fan while it is rotated at suitable speeds. Rolls-Royce went bankrupt developing the RB 211 engine, principally because they chose carbon fibre for the fan. Metal replaced wood in aviation because it was more durable and yielding, so in this respect carbon was a step backward, for while it is very strong it is also brittle. Also internal fatigue is not so obvious, whereas metals tend steadily to deform. Finally it is harder to repair. I know composite materials are used extensively in Formula One racing, but these people have the money to throw it away when it fails. Aviation engineers prefer metal, because it can simply be patched up like a burst inner tube. If ever the fuselage is punctured by a ground vehicle this is exactly how it is fixed, like an old rag doll. Composites are most useful for parts of the aircraft that generally do not go wrong, like the floor. Airbus first used it for *primary structures* like the tail fin and Boeing have followed suit. Not for fan blades though, upon which frozen chickens had the effect of cruise missiles on Baghdad.

Returning to the oxygen requirement up Everest, the same is true of flying. Out there in the cruise there is insufficient air for you to retain consciousness beyond half a minute. When they invented the gas balloon intrepid adventurers would launch off, protected only by a tall hat. At some point on the way up they would succumb to mountain sickness and pass out. Returning to lower levels as the balloon ran out of lift, they might come round after the hallucinatory 'trip of a lifetime'. On other occasions they returned dead, which is why the opportunity to make the newspapers in this way was more normally offered to passing spaniels. The same practice continued throughout the space program.

We as passengers are prevented from passing out because the cabin is pumped up to a pressure of eight pounds per square inch. The porthole next to you is supporting a quarter of a ton in terms of a weight of air. This is why if it fails the nearest occupant normally goes with it. If this book does nothing else, it will persuade you to leave your lap strap fastened. To regulate the pressure air is continuously dumped out of vents around the floor of the toilets and released by a big valve out back and under the tail. Pilots close this if the fuselage develops a leak, like losing a porthole. It is a condition of the certification of airliners they should sustain most of the cabin pressure following such an eventuality.

Once pressurised the effective altitude of the cabin for occupants, with all the extra air, is reduced from 35,000 ft to nearer 8,000 ft. You have still effectively climbed a mountain in a short space of time and it is twice the height of anywhere in Britain. For this reason you occasionally feel short of breath. I talk a lot in the flight deck and sometimes this makes me see stars, like I stood up too quickly. Thin air contains little moisture too, so you may experience sinus trouble. The best protection against all this, including DVT, is to be fit before you fly. Prepare for the flight like you were preparing for combat. Would you really get drunk senseless the night before the battle? I certainly would.

Should the cabin lose its pressure for any reason, say the valve from the engine fails or the air conditioning overheats, then the pilots commence an *emergency descent* to levels where you can all breath more easily. The most exciting aspect of this is the fact oxygen masks might drop. Some drop anyway upon heavy landings, or if you inadvertently press the wrong switch in the flight deck. This makes you unpopular with both engineers and managers, though does not quite trump the inadvertent release of an inflatable cabin slide.

If the leak causing loss of pressure is dramatic, like a hole in the fuselage, then the air in the cabin vents so quickly it condenses instantly into fog. You may have noticed using a bicycle pump that squashing air adds energy to it and warms it up. Releasing pressure has the reverse effect, cooling the vapour in the cabin rapidly enough sometimes to cloud it for a moment. At the same time the rushing air picks up dust of decades and anything loose around the place and for a while it seems Dickensian London is combined with Hurricane Hilda. The maelstrom may soon subside (though not the noise so much), but if a moment ago you were watching QVC on the seatback, it can perturb even the most stoical. This is the reason bombs are so unwelcome in the cabin, for they add to an explosive situation. If the crew can get to the device it goes against one of the doors to do the least damage and is smothered in seat cushions. During training we are shown videos of the havoc wrought by even small amounts of plastic explosive and the pressure wave it creates. Rather than inspire confidence this always leaves me feeling the careful packing of cushions was as futile as a hedgehog with a reflective vest.

There is little else to say about the cruise phase from a physical point of view, apart from my recalling an alternative comedian saying, Okay I am inside a tube moving six hundred miles an hour... Why? Pilots like this phase though as they get to sit around chatting and reading the paper, looking out of the window, laughing at the management, discussing their investments or ridiculing colleagues. The radio can be switched to speakers so the headset comes off. Below 15,000 ft they insist upon these, so as to attenuate the noise of the flight deck. Most pilots subvert this by wearing only one earpiece, leaving the other free to listen to their colleagues. If you are listening to a weather frequency at the same time as air traffic, while two of the cabin crew drop in for a social, you end up monitoring five conversations, which with practice is easier than it seems. Many see it as a challenge.

From time to time the crew generate crises themselves, like those who experimented with the flaps that fell off. On another occasion, the co-pilot of a DC10 went to adjust his seat, which slid back too far. He reached out to grab the nearest support, which turned out to be the *control column*, the steering wheel. This forced the autopilot to disconnect and pulled the aircraft into a dramatic high-level climb, pinning the passengers to the floor with its acceleration and injuring not a few of them.

At night the cruise can be excessively tedious. Flying up the Adriatic at dawn between Italy and the Balkans, over a steely grey sea, if the co-pilot remained awake I could sleep lightly enough to be aroused whenever hearing our call sign. I do have friends who have been following pre-programmed routes on holiday charters, during which both pilots fell asleep and missed out on most of France. A flight to the west coast of the USA overshot it by the width of a state on one occasion because of this. Since 9/11 the controllers are understandably much twitchier if crews do not respond. Radio calls can be far between, often just to hand you to the next sector controller.

This leaves pilots with a form of sensory deprivation once conversation is exhausted and papers finished. At this point some have even been known to look at manuals. At night this is guaranteed to send you to sleep, especially if you are cleared in a direct line across the sea. I have known captains complete a pipe of tobacco on these routes and then hunker down for the night. Others on freight flights have taken inflatable beds and left the co-pilot to it, which generally suits all parties. The Airbus is especially welcome to many, as it has sheepskin headrests and sufficient carpet behind the seats to lie out flat. In the days when lighter aeroplanes could be flown by single crew members, one pilot who now sits on the board of an airline used to creep alongside other aircraft at night over the sea, navigation lights only a wingtip away. His fellow somnambulists could remain unaware of this for an hour before visibly but silently hitting the ceiling when the reality dawned.

Nowadays if you miss more than a few radio calls you find a fighter alongside. When this has happened recently crews have often not known how to respond in meaningful ways. There are 'speechless' procedures used by the military to intercept civilian aircraft and guide them to an airfield. These are well known in the Forces but generally leave airline crews scrambling for the manuals, especially at night. Military pilots wear white gloves to make hand signals more apparent. Sometimes passing my friends on the ground at Heathrow I would give them a wave wearing an asbestos fire glove like Co-Co the clown. This seemed to go down well. I may have mentioned the gnomes here: around one of the *windsocks* which show the wind direction and strength, ground staff started to assemble a shrine, with gnomes and Buddhas from around the world. I wanted to add a few of those prayer flags Tibetans use, but one day I passed by and sadly all of it was gone.

On longer trips over sea you lose radar coverage altogether and rely upon the aircraft equipment to keep you apart. Over land the aeroplane uses its radio receivers to check where it is by tuning into beacons on the ground, but over the oceans it has to find its way by the satellite *Global Positioning System* or its *Inertial Reference System*. The advantage of the former is it provides global coverage because the satellites are high up and can 'see' so much of the surface. It was invented primarily for dropping bombs down chimneys.

Of as much use as this GPS is the second system, the IRS on the aircraft itself. The way it works is clever, for it plays an electronic version of Blind Man's Bluff. Imagine I tell you exactly in the house where you are and then blindfold you and move you up the stairs and around the first floor. Beside telephoning 999, you would be able to figure out where you were by sensing the rotations and accelerations I expose you to. This is all the IRS does and it has three boxes working independently, so if one gets ideas above its station, like deciding we are on Mars, it gets out-voted by the others. This is democracy in action. The one thing you have to get right is the position of the aircraft in the first place. As the IRS stores your last location after flying it can help you in the process. Enter a wrong position and it queries you, though you may override the message, which is what happened to the Korean airliner the Soviets shot down while the crew scrabbled for manuals.

Voice communication radios also get beyond range and you then have to use the kind of 'HF' sets that radio hams use to contact Buenos Aires. These work by bouncing high-frequency signals off the *Heaviside* layer, a part of the upper atmosphere which reflects radio waves. (It goes up and down as the sun rises and sets around the world, so that you have to select a suitable frequency from a set of graphs depending upon your position and the hour of day. All in all, a truly bizarre way of communicating.) TV signals work like this nowadays, except they bounce off satellites instead. The advantage is that TV signals are clear (which is why aeroplanes are beginning to use the same techniques) while the radio-ham system makes you sound like you are talking down a cardboard tube. I once told a controller this, Be advised you sound like you are talking down a toilet roll. He replied that I had finally discovered his secret... Controllers like a bit of a laugh and innuendo, which is why they like working with pilots. The funniest aspect of their relationship is if they goof up, they think pilots will report them; if the pilots goof up they are convinced controllers will do the same. Actually, complaints between the two are almost unheard of, which is how it ought to be. If you bust a cleared altitude by three hundred feet or more, the computers step in and trigger a report. Computers are like that, always protesting they are only acting under instructions.

There is also a distinct terminology required when tuning HF radio stations, whose signals used to be received by a washing-line stretched over the top of the aeroplane toward the tail. (As with mobile phones, this has since been built in.) It is very like calling Sweden for their score in the *Eurovision Song Contest*:

> *Stockholm Radio, Stockholm Radio, this is Midland Three*
> *Yankee Bravo, DOGGA 35, Flight Level 370, HADOC 47...*
> *Stockholm, come in Stockholm?*

I used to like it because it was often done at night, in the grip of a thunderstorm and miles out to sea, which made you feel like John Wayne in one of his wartime roles. You could also use it to call a station run by British Telecom near Portsmouth, who could 'patch' it through to the telephone system. The first time I was required to demonstrate my competence at this over the Bay of Biscay, I called my wife and asked her to video *Columbo*.

I mentioned the dire necessity of breathable air some time earlier. The loss of it can prove fairly terminal. Business jets are smaller and can be pumped up to fly higher, so Learjets will cruise up to 54,000 ft, where the Concorde operates. All such aircraft have narrower cabins for this reason. I am told these are curvature-of-the-earth levels, the edge of space where the sky turns a deeper blue. (The one thing I have noticed about views in the cruise is that on a clear day they are extensive; way off the North Sea coast I have been able to see the land around Dublin, maybe three hundred miles away. Something else which stands out are snow-covered peaks like Mont Blanc, which is easily spotted at the same distance. What helps at these levels is you are looking through thinner and cleaner air. One of the most obvious things when you fly over towns like London is yellowish pollution trapped by an *inversion*, which is what happens when rising air meets even warmer air and stops rising like a balloon and spreads across the sky, like it does daily in LA or Mexico City. It feels like the aeroplane is wearing shades.)

Anyway, at the sort of levels executive jets fly, any leakage of pressure sends occupants unconscious in a very short time. The pilots are supposed to wear a mask around their neck that they can slip on quickly, but the onset of *hypoxia* can be insidious. As a result, from time to time whole complements of crew and passengers pass out, leaving jets to continue along a route like a guided missile. They may climb higher as fuel burns off but after it runs out altogether the aeroplane gently noses over and consigns its charges to their watery grave. Passengers rarely recover during the descent as they have been deprived of oxygen for so long. When I went through air force selection, I never saw the guy in the next bunk again until years later on the news, after he had scrambled an F4 Phantom to intercept one of these unpiloted aircraft. What they did was to pull alongside while the navigator down the back peered in to see what became of the *Marie Celeste*.

What ultimately determines the longevity of airliners is the number of cruise *cycles*. What this means is the number of times they are inflated for flight and then afterwards deflated. During the climb air is pumped in and during the descent, slowly released. In old jets this did not always work efficiently and after landing the aeroplane would sometimes be under some pressure. As a result the doors might not open by the time you got to the gate. What the captain would do then was slide back the window and let the air out with a rush. The pioneering years of the first jet airliner were brought to an untimely end when a couple of them popped like balloons during the cruise. One called *Yoke Papa* was recovered from the Mediterranean and returned to Farnborough and reconstructed, while another fuselage was submersed in Hatfield and repeatedly pumped up with water to equivalent pressures. Between the two investigations they found the skin had ripped at a corner of a window and then torn like a shopping bag. Boeing had already decided to use a gauge of aluminium four times thicker, but what every manufacturer subsequently decided as well was that rounder windows were less likely to give.

Aeroplane designers do not like windows at all and would like to lose them altogether, but these proposals are inevitably outweighed by passenger concerns. There is an elemental fear about places without windows, whether they are velveteen-papered cells or coffins. We do not need aeroplanes to remind us of these places. After catastrophic failures of this kind, they decided airframes ought to be allowed a certain number of cycles. The engines used to require scrapping long before the limit was exceeded, but the way they are headed these days, they look like outlasting the frames. Together the combination looks pretty good anyway; the B52 bomber has a projected service life of eighty years, which will outdo the service history of all but the best steam locomotives.

I called the ill-fated Comet *Yoke Papa*, as its registration was G-ALYP. Usually aircraft were referred to by the last two letters of the registration, which are often painted on the nose as well, where everyone can see them. Not all aircraft are prefixed 'G', as this stands for Great Britain; in America they use 'N', though I do not know why. I cannot be expected to know everything. In Ireland they use an 'EI' followed by a hyphen and three more letters. I was told of someone who imported an aircraft into Ireland and then hassled the authorities mercilessly to get it registered, so they allocated him EI-SOD.

The letters 'YP' were expressed as *Yoke Papa* according to the original version of the phonetic alphabet, which developed because people could not understand each other over the radio. It also came about to avoid confusion. The best instance of this is pilots who have turned to colleagues and said "Cheer up!", only to find they have leaned forward and brought the gear up, or retracted the wheels. Doing this used to be entirely feasible even when on the ground and in the first aeroplane I operated, they recommended it as a way of stopping quickly in the event of an emergency. On the Boeing you could pull a trigger to override the system and *still* retract the wheels on the ground, though it was not considered clever. The Airbus refuses to bring the wheels up in any place but the air, which has to be the way to go. Nor will it let you land without dropping them.

Thousands of aircraft have landed with wheels left up by pilots, normally under the stress of external events like the loss of a child. The air force used to put a man in a caravan at the end of the runway to fire off a red flare if he saw this about to happen. You may be incredulous, like this should never happen in an aeroplane, like neither should they tip up on the ground if you all rush to the back. They will though and for this reason even the 747 has a big pole to fit beneath the tail during servicing, to avoid it tilting. At times a congregation of cleaners at the back of an aircraft may be enough for minor catastrophe. To prevent tipping, some aircraft with an engine removed for maintenance must have it replaced with concrete ballast to counteract the loss of its weight.

Back to the phonetic alphabet: during the war this was developed using quaint terms you could imagine Margaret Rutherford using, like *Victory, Peter, Queen* and *Roger*. I cannot recall the others, though many remained unchanged in the newer version:

> *Alpha, bravo, charlie, delta, foxtrot, golf, hotel, india, juliet, kilo, lima, mike, november, oscar, papa, quebec, romeo, sierra, tango, uniform, victor, whiskey, x-ray, yankee and zulu.*

Trying to use these in anger is like being an actor with lines: you can easily dry on stage. I panicked from time to time if they eluded me, or if I had forgotten the Morse code for the same letters. The only other reasons for being unable to communicate effectively with air traffic may be (a) a mouthful of sausage panini or (b) laughing helplessly at something your fellow pilot just said, which was often why they said it. One used to do *South Park* impressions at the top of his voice; to the extent I was sure it filtered back to the business class passengers. I like to encourage this sort of thing in a young man.

I leave the cruise with an anecdote, which got David Beatty interested in *Human Factors*, the foibles of the human mind known to cause accidents. He took part in ferrying Halifax bombers during the war to North Africa. All each had to do was fly in a straight line for hours off the coast of Portugal and then turn left at Gibraltar. Instead the guy in front of him turned right, toward the Atlantic, where he was never seen again.

Check in...to the 20th Century

Push back...from Gatwick

Take off...from Wittering

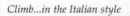
Climb...in the Italian style

Cruise...past thunderheads

Descent...past Etna

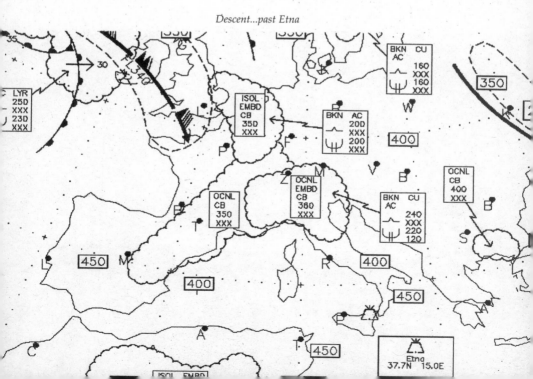

Approach...into Nice

Landing...in the 21st Century

DESCENT

One thing we need to do before we leave the cruise, is look at how high we got and why, before contemplating descent. There is nothing at all wrong with carrying this over into another chapter, as conversely the descent begins during the cruise anyway, when ideally an element of preparedness is involved, a mental contemplation undertaken of what is to come. Many or indeed most pilots will have undertaken one or other descent at some time in their lives with a marked degree of trepidation. For a number were stranded above a dense fog with no means of return to the airfield and indeed no safe way down. Countless numbers have succumbed to this sentence of death. It was the author of *The Little Prince* who spoke of the seductive beauty of this veil of mist that harboured death within its folds. The descent then can be a descent into an abyss.

We have covered the certified ceiling for each type of aircraft; let us now consider the *semicircular rule*. (My proof-reader tells me this is not fully explained until many pages later, so I want you to hang on in there and not forget we mentioned it.) This is the simplest form of collision avoidance in cloud or darkness you could imagine. For denizens of aircraft the most elementary danger is being unable to see. It is akin to a blind man, who compensates from birth by expanding other faculties and later taking advantage of capabilities that have been developed which may be of use. When I am not writing boring books, I like designing things, or just thinking about it, which is much easier. One thing that occurred to me was a white stick able to recreate a picture of the vicinity, as a bat does. This has already been developed. Compensating for its blindness the airliner uses *flight instruments* and *navigation instruments*, along with *radio receivers* and an *autopilot*.

Broadly speaking, flight instruments determine the immediate trajectory of the vehicle, navigation instruments deal with where the aircraft is going generally, while the radio receivers *confirm* the aircraft is going in the right direction. To begin with there were no instruments of any kind and among the first to develop were *engine instruments.* One thing that guarantees aeroplanes stay in the air is money. The next most important is the engine and it is best knowing the quantities of fuel, oil and water available.

Early flyers used the 'seat of the pants' and much can be gained this way. Even in airliners all the senses are used extensively, as often as not with the sixth sense to confirm everything is as it should be. Following the engine instruments, next were flight instruments that detected airspeed and altitude. As flyers were soon in and out of cloud and frequently emerged upside down, they needed gyroscopic references, which like a spinning top are independent of aircraft motion. These included the *artificial horizon*, still the principal instrument today. It sits right in front of each pilot, a representation of heaven and earth itself, an orb of blue and grey. In *glass cockpits*, with screens like those of your PC, the picture of this horizon has an almost devotional quality, like a small renaissance triptych.

Once the *attitude* of the aeroplane was sorted out, early pilots could engage in *blind flying*. The next important thing was to know the way. I have seen a piece of memorabilia from Holland, a strip map provided for the pilots of KLM in the thirties, to help them find their way between Croydon and Amsterdam. Along with Paris and Berlin, these were the only destinations in Europe. The map is printed from a hand-drawn sketch, which showed how to fly south and pick up the railway line to Dover, via Sevenoaks, then across the channel and up the coast. At Sevenoaks, all seven trees were depicted around the village green. Most are still there, though one or two succumbed to the gale of 1987.

This led to the *right hand rule*, which said that as commanders sat on the left, aircraft should travel down the right-hand side of linear features along the ground like railway lines. Remember at this time there would be many more railways than roads. This way you could hope not to collide with fellow-flyers travelling in the opposite direction. Even now airliners about to collide are each supposed to break to the right. Upon the return leg from Amsterdam the North Downs had to be surmounted south of Croydon and to achieve this when they were capped in cloud, pilots would climb up and proceed northward in blind faith for several minutes, as determined by a stopwatch. They would then drop out of the cloud in the expectation they were somewhere near the airfield. This does work well with practice and these pilots were supremely attuned to both their craft and aircraft.

This timing procedure was still used to navigate passage of the Andes after the last war, though they did not know then of the existence of *jetstreams*, powerful winds that threw out the calculations. One aircraft bound for Chile collided with the mountains and was subsumed in a glacier. Around fifty years later, aircraft and contents emerged at its foot, like the Piltdown man. Often aircraft parts are not worth retrieving from mountains and a Scottish flatmate of mine used to regale me with tales of how he and his father would discover huge pieces of undercarriage appearing out of the mist.

The first instrument to assist the use of maps was the magnetic compass, borrowed from the sea. This made sense, for the hard thing about navigating ships is they drift off course in currents the way aircraft get blown by winds. Once you have map, compass and clock, you are supposed to follow routes by referring to features on the ground, along with *dead reckoning* and considerable luck. Dead reckoning is guessing the strength of the wind and compensating by steering further left or right. Charles Lindbergh set off from America and crossed the Irish coast almost where he intended. He was the first to admit this was like winning the national lottery. When they used a spinning wheel or *gyroscope* inside the compass to stop it wobbling about in flight, it came quite unsurprisingly to be called the *gyro-stabilised compass*. The wobbly one was still retained as a backup and in fact is still a feature of the most modern airliners, though I can never figure out why. I think it is like the way we still prefer a fireplace in the lounge after we installed central-heating.

This was great unless you were flying at night. I remember my first night flight, with a Sandy Duthie. This was a flight lieutenant and not a flight instrument. I remember being shown how the lights of aircraft far away seemed menacingly near. The first commercial use of aircraft was for ferrying night mail across the USA and both Charles Lindbergh and Ernest Gann began careers in this way, after *barnstorming*, which was giving cheap rides to townsfolk. To assist passage along coasts they could use lighthouses like ships do. I used them myself when flying down the east coast from Aberdeen. They flash at special intervals, so you can work out which is which from the map.

Then a bright spark had the idea of using flashing lights to guide pilots across country too. The first use of these *beacons* had been on airfields. They may still be used even at major airports like Cologne, where they are an excellent reference for impatient souls like me who wish to take a short cut and fly a visual approach. Water towers are a feature of the landscape in North America and most include the name of the town for the benefit of travellers. Aviators soon took to swooping low to check where they were. For this reason nearly all are painted white with black lettering.

One evening this would have been most useful, I was returning to a fogged-out Chicago Bay with few navigation instruments and little fuel. I dropped down to check one of these and because it was painted with a red background, the light at dusk was insufficient for me to read the name. I can imagine the dork at the council meeting saying something like, Let's make this town stand out so people remember it, let's paint the water tower red! The story had a happy ending, because one of those wonderful radar controllers steered me toward a deserted aerodrome whose runway was lit all night. I landed and checked into a motel to treat myself to a pizza and a six-pack. Know how to celebrate life.

Meanwhile an émigré Italian in London had figured you could use radio aerials for *direction finding* by turning them toward the transmitter. These *loop aerials* were soon fitted to shipping and later to aircraft. Like a mobile phone, they are useless if nobody else has one, so a network of navigation transmitters were strung along the *airways* of America, to go with the beacons. As a result they got to be called *navigation beacons* and after a while they turned the lights off. The aerial was connected to an instrument in the cockpit called an *automatic direction finder*, which was like a clock divided into 360 degrees, with a pointer that swung around to indicate where the transmitter was.

Unfortunately thunderheads generate a lot of electricity and near these the pointer would do its own thing. It is a truism of flying that equipment lets you down when most needed. Around the time of WWII they invented radar, so once it was near to the airfield the controller could see the aeroplane as a blob and pass instructions over the radio on how to get down. At about the same time they developed the *VHF Omnirange*, whose catchy name most aviators abbreviate to VOR. This remains the principal navigation receiver on airliners and it is still the principal way airways are marked out on the ground. Airways are simply imaginary lanes in the sky joining various *waypoints*. The advantage of these beacons was they ran on VHF making them more accurate and less prone to interference. They considered phasing them out in the USA after the advent of GPS, but left them because they are less susceptible to disruption by the forces of evil.

The 'range' part in the full name of the VOR derived from the fact airways were first marked by lighted beacons and then by *ranging* equipment, which was a transmitter pointing down each airway. If you strayed right, you got a series of *dits* through the headset and if left, a set of *dahs*, like a marshaller guiding you into the garage. Its main disadvantage was it only did this between two defined waypoints along the airway. The VHF Omnirange got its name from using very high frequencies while providing ranging from whichever direction you were coming from. It now did this in the form of a dial with a *beam bar* which drifted left or right if you went off course.

The transmitter aerial for these VORs is a thing to behold and I would often point them out on the ground to my co-pilots. They are like a ring of roses. In contrast the transmitter associated with older direction finding systems looks like a washing line. I know this, for during my *instrument rating* training at Bournemouth I drove out into the countryside to look at it, this thing to which I had only ever been connected by a needle. They say you should face up to your demons. I hoped to organise a picnic there for my fellow students, a day at the 'BOH' non-directional beacon, bring own sandwiches, but nothing came of it.

I say the 'BOH' because there were always several beacons around and you had to make sure you were pointed at the right one, like you check the names of towns when driving. The beacon therefore also transmitted a Morse identifier in the form of a three-letter code by which each could be designated. The 'BOH' has long gone, the place it occupied in the world, besides in the hearts and minds of men, now substituted with a Kentucky Fried Chicken. Which I guess we ought to call the 'KFC' and identify by code. One of the first things pilots ask on the flight deck, as often they will not have met, is where the other lives. I was always able to say five miles north of Brookmans Park as it coincided with a beacon ~ BPK ~ known to pilots from anywhere who regularly overfly London. We are strange like that.

Later in the 'sixties they developed the inertial guidance system, the one that plays Blind Man's Bluff. As usual this came about through military necessity. It was used for guiding ICBMs, *Intercontinental Ballistic Missiles*, during the Cold War. They are now assisted by the satellite navigation systems developed in the 'seventies, providing an independent reference as to where they are. These can still be disrupted by radio jamming, which is why inertial systems are retained in aircraft if not missiles. To prove this is so the CAA often tries jamming the signals itself at selected locations, in order they can tell you portentously how right they were to examine your use of a slide rule.

The simplest of inertial systems was based upon a gyroscope and fitted to Hitler's V1 flying bomb. This should never have been called a flying bomb, because it was the first cruise missile. Technically cruise missiles are launched as a missile with a rocket motor, but they soon sprout wings and fire up a jet engine, which is why they are so flexible. Although the V1 was launched off a ramp using its jet engine, it still qualifies to my mind as the first of such weapons. There is one in the RAF museum at Hendon. It has a span of only seventeen feet, the width of your lounge. It was pointed at London and the spinning gyro was linked to an autopilot which merely kept the wings level, so it continued in a straight line. Then overhead London it ran out of fuel like our pilot-less business jets.

The earliest autopilots came about before the war as a means of combating the tedium of flights lasting as long as eighteen hours. They were known colloquially as 'George', so that pilots could switch them on and say George had control. It was important for pilots to know who actually had control of the aeroplane, as both had the same set of controls. When I learned to fly I used to have to say, You have control, Sir. When I flew for a while out of Cushing Field near Chicago, we all sat in a wooden house like the *Waltons* lived in, watching TV. Within a space of ten minutes, two returning aircraft crashed in the maize. No one was hurt, though I thought the episode was funnier than the TV. When we opened the door of the second aircraft, upended in a ditch, the pilots were fighting like *Laurel and Hardy*. You said you would... actually you said you were going to...

Nowadays the autopilot, along with *autothrust*, is comprehensively linked to the engines, as well as the flight and navigation systems. As we see during the approach, there are two separate autopilots so as to create a *failsafe* system, one that cannot possibly go wrong. As a result, it is technically possible to program the navigation computer with a route to a destination and have the aeroplane do ninety-five per cent of the flying. Passengers tell me it is done by autopilots these days, so I tell them they are offspring from a stupid donkey. Let us analyse that a little closer. Only I get the aeroplane pushed back, started, taxied and taken off. Only I retract the flaps and gear, while only air traffic says where we go during climb and descent and often on airways too. They tell us our levels at each stage and both runway and approach for landing. We each intervene to avoid collisions and weather, or to choose alternative levels or airports. I set up the approach and ninety-nine percent of the time, do the landing. I hit the brakes if we are running out of concrete and I drive the aeroplane back to the gate. Apart from this, the autopilot does everything these days.

I am going to round up our look at the semicircular rule before going further. Once the pilots had instruments to pursue blind flying according to *instrument rules*, a common set of procedures for this new level of complexity had to be laid down. The semicircular rule was among the first. Anyone flying to points east, up to 180 degrees on the compass, will cruise at odd thousands of feet and those travelling west through to 360 degrees expects to use even thousands. I hope I have that the right way around or I am out of a job again. This meant anyone headed in broadly the same direction as you would be flying at the same height and anyone flying toward you with a high closing speed ought not to be. These basics were most important until radar came to be widely used. Let me correct a misconception here, for airliners do not have their own radar for detecting other aircraft, though fighters do. They rely only on information air traffic provides, though recently they have incorporated *anti-collision systems*. These work by decoding the information included in the transmissions of other aircraft which relates to their position.

Along with this first rule of avoidance, there were still the old *visual rules*. One of these we saw earlier suggested you turn right if about to collide. While I trained at Redhill in Surrey, two aircraft collided and investigators knew they had tried to break to the right, because each sliced off the left wing of the other. You are also supposed to give way to any aircraft you see closing from the right. A feature of aircraft with which you are about to collide is they remain in the same position in the windshield until point of impact. Any aeroplane that appears to be moving relative to the windshield, even if slowly, will miss you. The only confirmation I have seen of this (because you are not supposed to just sit there watching events unfold) is seeing aeroplanes crossing on other airways separated by a thousand feet. You get closer and closer and then the jet along with its condensation trail flies overhead so close you can see streaks of oil along its underside. This is why for night flights aeroplanes were soon fitted with *navigation lights* like those of a ship, red on the port side and green on the starboard, along with white at the tail. To remember these, think short words and long words i.e. red, port and left, or else green, starboard and right.

As a result, when Elton John sang:

> *Daniel is leaving tonight on a 'plane*

> *I can see his red tail-light, heading for Spaaaaaaain...*

the aircraft was in breach of the *Air Navigation Order* and should have been reported as compromising flight safety. Aircraft do not have a red tail-light, they have a white one or even sometimes three of them: one on the tail cone and another on each wingtip. I think what Mr John had done was to mistake the red stroboscopic *anti-collision light* on the belly for the navigation light and I have written to him requiring an amendment along these lines:

Daniel is leaving tonight on a 'plane

I can see his anti-collision light, heading for Spain on a Bognor departure.

© Elton John and Colin Hilton.

To the semicircular rule an entire legislation was accumulated governing IFR, or instrument flight rules as distinct from VFR, the visual variety. Common law retains vestiges from another age, like I believe Englishmen are free to urinate on one or other wheel of their vehicle upon the public highway without let or hindrance, whereas should they do the same thing on the pavement outside the curry house then they are fair game. So flying rules have their oddities, like ordinarily without filing an airborne flight plan or its equivalent on the ground, pilots may not gatecrash airways; nonetheless glider pilots operating under visual flight rules may cross airways unmolested. This is probably the equivalent of those sort of local byelaws that in theory at least guarantee your freedom to shepherd a flock across the motorway wherever they intersect ancient rights of way. By and large flight by visual rules concerns flying day-trippers around the seaside, spraying crops or operating helicopters just about anywhere.

Helicopters are effectively unregulated in reduced visibility, which is why so many crash despite their limited number. This goes back to the days the RAF were reluctant to accept them at all. Mainly the army and navy use them, neither force having runways to spare. Anyone in the air force considered a go-ahead type was streamed toward fast jets and away from transports or (heaven forbid) aircraft with rotary wings. Accordingly they are under-represented within the CAA, which is amply staffed by air force retirees. They usually crash (occasionally killing executives whose corporations wonder why this happens to helicopters and not airliners) because many of the pilots are inexperienced, operate as single crew and stretch the limits of visibility that the CAA cannot be bothered enforcing. Public ignorance is the chief reason these accidents are not pursued in court.

Instrument ratings for pilots of these machines are as expensive to obtain and maintain as they are for any other type of aircraft, as they require recurrent checks in simulators or the real thing. For this reason there are a proportion of private or business pilots that use the airways anyway, though not qualified, in the same way that some airlines gain access to regulated flight levels by claiming to have equipment and experience that actually they do not. The only helicopter pilots with ratings tend therefore to be those operating in places like the North Sea, if for no other reason because the larger companies for which they work could not afford the loss of their operator certificate. It is a grubby business, really, like any other. Expect any other helicopter pilot to drop into your garden anytime on misty days. In this weather I have seen them creeping along motorways or dropping down to peruse road signs. Airline pilots in contrast have to follow instrument rules, which are like the thread or the means to pursue instrument departure, airway, *Standard Instrument Arrival* and the approach itself. Every phase is highly automated, notwithstanding what I have said about who does what, so that technically you could do it with the windows blacked out.

The chapter commenced, however, with discussing the choice of flight level. We saw we are limited in this by aircraft certification, by weight and by the instrument flight rules. Flying down the length of France you might choose 33,000 ft, referred to as *flight level 330*, by dropping two noughts. On the way back you might select 31 000 ft or 35 000 ft. The choice might be tactical from the view of air traffic control, who may spot a faster aeroplane behind you catching up. Or you might decide the tailwind is stronger at one level than another and ask air traffic for this before anyone has the same idea. A consideration is how bumpy different levels might be and this is weighed against other benefits. The turbulence is usually caused by cloud, which often you can climb above. That caused by winds or *jet streams* occurs almost anywhere, unless you are planning on flying within the stratosphere, which is some way above it all.

The weight of the aircraft can only alter during the course of the flight by burning fuel, unless you feel you want to jettison a passenger or two. In the old days they used simply to cruise at the first level they could make and accelerate as they got lighter, or else creep slowly higher. Concorde operates at levels where there is no other traffic around and it might spend most of the flight creeping slowly ever upwards and then soon it is time to start creeping down again. *Separation* between aircraft at higher levels where altimeters are less accurate (because the air is thinner and less easily measured) was two thousand feet, but reduced to one thousand as instruments improved. As a result, over the Atlantic controllers neither want aircraft to speed up nor drift up, because both would compromise separation. Aircraft are ten miles apart if following each other, or five otherwise, or else a thousand feet apart vertically. During approach to the airport they can be reduced to half this minimum, two and a half miles, in order to expedite the flow of arrivals.

As a result the navigation computer advises the pilots of the most efficient cruise level and then picks a speed to match it. This will be around Mach 0.8 for newer narrow-bodies, or Mach 0.9 for older liners like the 747. As the aircraft burns fuel and gets lighter the computer eases off the gas to maintain speed. It will do the same in the event of a tailwind helping it along. If it encounters a headwind it will drive the engines like ducks paddling upstream. This continual *fuel burn* made it hard to calculate actual consumption at each stage, because for any speed it is governed by weight, which was always changing as fuel was used. To calculate the fuel flow at any point against what you had left in the tanks was a task for a *flight engineer* and a complicated set of tables. Eventually to accommodate the deleterious effect of continual fuel burn on flight engineers, they invented the computer and disposed of the third crew member. I poked around in one of those giant Antonov freighters once and on the upper deck are six armchairs to accommodate two pilots, TWO flight engineers and TWO navigators. That is what I call an aeroplane and the Soviets call full employment.

In aircraft fuel is considered by weight alone, so you fill the tanks to so many tons and it is only the fueller and the accountants who deal in litreage. The equation is complicated by the fact fuel expands on sunny days, so technically you get less in each litre. This is one reason we deal in weight of fuel; if I bought gold I would want that by weight lest it were full of bubbles. One aspect of fuel expansion is that you can fill the tanks right up and later they will overflow through vents with the warmth of day. Then you come back to an airliner surrounded by a puddle of gas and angry firefighters.

Although I said the fuel expands on the ground in the heat, it also has all sort of additives to prevent it freezing in flight, where outside it is sixty below. To assist in this, the fuel is circulated around the engine oil tanks. By a happy coincidence this keeps the fuel nice and warm and the engines nice and cool. At room temperature kerosene, the fuel used, is also delightfully non-volatile. What I mean by that is that if it spills on the floor you can throw a lighted match into it (do NOT try this at home) and it will extinguish. When they built a spy plane called the Blackbird, it went so high and so fast that it expanded and contracted like a rubber band. This made its fuel tanks drip like a sieve. They left them doing that because Jet-A1, the grade of fuel required, is both cheap and comparatively safe.

It is not nearly so when it warms up though, which is true of many materials that appear benign at cooler temperatures. The recent investigation into the loss of the Swissair MD-11 whose flight deck caught fire has determined that the insulation above the flight deck ceiling burned quite readily. What is going on here? This is no loft we are insulating. The inquiry into the TWA 747 that ended up in the sea off Long Island after a mid-air explosion turns out to have stemmed from a related cause, a faulty wiring that sparked off ignition in the fuel vapour of a centre tank. This fire risk has since spread to the fuel pumps themselves and their electrical connections, so that Boeing still impose restrictions on how dry each separate tank can afford to be run. The investigation upheld the non-volatility of kerosene but did discover that if it was warmed in a receptacle above some forty-seven degrees Celsius then the vapour became so much more ready to ignite. It is not nearly at *flashpoint*, when it spontaneously ignites, it is just happy to do so given a little provocation. Which would be true of any of us at this temperature.

It got to be that temperature in the first place because the centre tanks had been close on empty like a greenhouse and sat in the sunshine in New York while a delay was incurred. Combining with this, the air-conditioning packs sit around here (as I say later, the only useful space left for ancillary equipment is the middle) and while these kept everyone cool they had the opposite effect on the tanks. The fuel I think was heated to well over fifty degrees and one of the analysts said it actually had a visible effect upon the expected rate of climb, in the way it would assist a hot air balloon. What spurred on the analysis was the fact that two 737s had already exploded *on the ground* in such circumstances.

Considering fuel in terms of both weight and litreage also has its problems. Firstly it is dispensed in litres, gallons or US gallons and then indicated in the aircraft in metric tons in Europe, or pounds in America. To complicate things, America sells planes to Europe and vice versa. One airline I was associated with was refused the use of a batch of 737s because the switches worked the wrong way, going up to turn them on, instead of down. You might think this odd, but in airliners you do not want to be turning engines off when you thought you were turning them on. This is no basement light we are talking about.

Confusion over the metrication of fuel brought down a Vickers Viscount returning from Spain one night, running out of fuel and putting down in a Cornish field, killing only a sheep or two. The same thing happened to a Boeing 757 over the wastelands of Canada, when fortunately one pilot was an air force veteran and the other a keen glider pilot. This was useful, especially as they were flying a keen glider. The other guy figured there was a disused airfield around some place and eventually they found it, though the aeroplane modellers were most surprised to find the weekly meet gate-crashed by a Boeing.

To avoid this contingency all airliners include, would you believe: dipsticks. There is also a pendulum scale in the landing gear bay to make sure the aeroplane is level first. You used to have to climb out on the wings both to fuel the aircraft and 'dip' the tanks, but these days they have developed upside-down or *underwing* fuelling and this is where the dipsticks are located as well. (They are now called *dripsticks* because they work the other way up.) Of course you have gauges inside the flight deck, but if what they say does not match what the fueller says about the *uplift*, then this is the last resort. It is rarely used, because for one thing it spoils the day for the crew and besides, it is not a confidence boost for the passengers. I used to fly

Alan Sugar occasionally in an executive jet and when things were smoothed out I would go back and sort him out a coffee. On one occasion I mislaid the milk and I can tell you that Alan likes his coffee white, especially after paying five thousand sterling for it. He inquired whether we were sure we had fuel on board and I replied, Yes we did, but it did not taste nearly so nice.

An unhappier story was related to me by one of my older students. Ernie had survived the last shipping convoy supplying the Russians, before Churchill called the whole thing off. He had also worked extensively for the fighter ace, Douglas Bader, after the war. On one occasion he was taken along for a ride in a Victor, a British V-bomber that patrolled the globe before the Trident submarine was deployed in a similar role. This was not so bad, except that the fuel they lifted from RAF West Malling was contaminated with water, so all four engines flamed out after take-off. Jet engines are miraculous pieces of machinery, but they draw the line at running on water. This is the worst possible moment for engines to stop, as the aircraft has neither height nor speed to glide to a safe landing. All perished except Ernie. Later he was invited for a test flight in a Meteor at RAF Boscombe Down. You would have thought he had learned by this stage. During a perilous descent toward the runway the pilot insisted they fire off the ejector seats, but Ernie replied that wherever the pilot was going, he personally was staying right there. They pulled off a successful crash landing, if any crash landing could be described as such. Later he was to survive my flying instruction and was awarded the Distinguished Flying Cross as a result.

To continue with descending, let us look at inadvertent descents. The best reason I know for this is to fly through a cloud of volcanic dust, so the engines stop. There is so much to say about this, in fact, a British Airways captain wrote the book. It was called something like, Forget the Cheese Platter Nigel, Our Engines Have Stopped. It is a thumping good read unless you were one of the passengers, in which case the flashbacks start all over. On the maps meteorologists produce, showing where jet streams or thunderstorms are, active volcanoes are also depicted. The only one in Europe is normally Etna in Sicily, which obligingly is shown with a *Spewing Ash* icon over it and text alongside that reads, Here be dragons...

Basically at night you can see nothing out front, especially if you are asleep. The first you know about these things is that tiny particles of dust interact with the statically charged airframe and get to glow. Did you know airframes get charged like a polyester sweater? This is why the first thing the fueller does is attach a cable to run off any sparks. For the same reason the marines soon found that connecting with a hovering helicopter could be more of an electrifying experience than anticipated. Hit this volcanic cloud and you find you are admiring the glowing discharge, which has the unfortunate effect at the same time of sanding the windshield.

The engines are also unhappy: remember how hot I said it got at that turbine stage, the windmill in the exhaust flow connected to the compressor? Well the tiny blades of these turbine wheels are often ventilated with holes, through which you pump cooler air to give them a break. Block these with volcanic dust and the blades go off limits in terms of temperature. They then *creep* like plasticine and scrape around the inside of the duct. Bear in mind these are running at tens of thousands of revolutions per minute. This adds to the firework show already provided by the super-heated volcanic particles that passed through the engine. If you want your money's worth, choose a seat aft of the wing.

With the engine showing signs of overheating you might have to throttle it back and give it a rest. Though what happens is you get no choice because the fuel nozzles get clogged first. This has happened both to a British Airways 747 in the Far East and to a KLM 747 in Alaska, after Mount St Helens or whichever one it was blew up. The full extent of the danger of volcanoes had not been realised until this time, though it is now. The Dutch aircraft, whose lady commander was later interviewed, got so low among the mountains before the engines fired up again, the aircraft had disappeared from the radar screens.

That is the two involuntary forms of descent considered: volcanic ash and fuel starvation. In the introduction I touched upon the Airbus 330 that ran out of fuel out in the Atlantic. This was a twin-engine aeroplane and a fuel line serving one of the engines had ruptured, so eventually the crew recognised they had insufficient fuel to complete the crossing. There is nothing to tell you fuel is leaking away, unless you continually monitor the contents of the tanks. There is a *fuel flow* gauge, but this is sited on the fuel pump next to the engine and ignores fuel that may be flowing away elsewhere. Pilots do not monitor fuel excessively, because it smacks of paranoia, which is never good in an aeroplane, while modern systems hardly go wrong anyway. This situation did not surprise other pilots, but both the airlines and manufacturers were predictably indignant.

Let us speak of happier things, like planned descents. Perhaps the most surprising thing for me when I transitioned to jet aeroplanes, was that you left them at cruise thrust as long as possible (or rather the computer left them there), then effectively glided all the way to an approach. It is like maintaining ninety miles an hour in your car until a mile from the house, then coasting in. Try it sometimes, it can be fun.

In *turboprops*, aircraft with a small jet engine driving a traditional propeller, you left the engines at cruise power and charged downhill. The disadvantage of leaving jets to figure out where to descend is they usually screw up and leave it too late. Once you have left the descent until the last minute, if air traffic want you down any quicker, it is no good easing off the gas because you did that before you started down. You must point the thing down a steeper incline and as any cyclist knows, this makes you go faster. The aeroplane already decided it was going down at high speed, so a steeper trajectory only has the effect of nibbling at the sound barrier, that Mach buffet we looked at.

As the aeroplane now has the look and feel of a runaway train, there is the not insignificant issue of how you are going to slow up approaching the station. The radar controllers have height readout and they recognise you are going too fast, or else you cannot lose height quick enough and they get as concerned as Mother Hen at this point. They do their best by steering the other chickens out of the way, offering more *track mileage*, a longer route to the airfield, along which you can slow down. Remember those flaps that make the wing bigger for landing, the ones that fall off if you are too fast? Well we need those down, but we are going too fast. Pilots are a testosterone-charged community by and large, except for the women (who therefore tend to be better at flying). They see extra mileage as a form of personal defeat, confirmation of misjudging it.

The man who taught me most about this situation was a man who said little and chuckled if he saw you reach for the speed brake. The speed brake is like a set of panels that spring up from the top of the wing. These always operate after the landing, to dump the lift like a spoiler and keep us firmly on the ground. In flight they have the same effect on speed as your roof rack. Their main function is to declare to the world you screwed up and then retract like a poker player laying down his hand. This captain lived for flying between Edinburgh and London at the highest possible speed and suggested if ever I was high in the descent, I should fly as fast as possible for as long as I dare. I discovered throwing caution to the wind this way was the surest path to success, as in many spheres of life. At the top of the descent the aeroplane has a lot of *potential energy* to lose, which it earned at the cost of much fuel on the way up, so the best way to dispose of this is to engage in the sort of headlong plunge Lord Byron would have been proud of.

This way the airframe is subjected to the maximum drag, clawing at it like a parachute and increasing the *rate of descent*. Also, heavier aeroplanes are supposed to be able to descend quicker, though I could never figure out quite why. I will have a go now. We have all seen the experiment at school where the teacher cannot get the vacuum pump working and we waited an hour for the lab assistant to fix it. Then afterward the teacher assured us that feathers drop as fast as ball bearings and nobody believed him? Well it is very like that. I simply don't believe them.

You knew I was not going to give up that easily, didn't you? Imagine our airliner nothing but polystyrene, painted in the same finish and exactly the same size and shape (BA have a strategy called Future Size and Shape; it sounds like a slimming plan). If we pointed this vertically at the ground, like our own airliner, with engines at idle thrust, can we really see it keeping up? No, I cannot either. In a vacuum I am assured it would. Scientists are said to have developed a *plasma field* around experimental aircraft, which is so intensely hot it thins the air out to nothing in the immediate vicinity, with much the same effect.

During the latter stages of the war in the Pacific, American aircraft had a weight advantage in the dive, though the Mitsubishi Zero they pursued was considered the most advanced airframe in the world. They could therefore chase these things faster in the vertical, while at the same time discovering the existence of the sound barrier. The first aircraft to break this incidentally was the appropriately named X-1, flown by the even more appropriately named Chuck Yeager. It looked like the British had been headed in this direction first with some airframe that I think Handley Page had developed. The government withdrew the funding at an advanced stage, probably because they had a theme park in mind to feature the Glories of British Invention. The key to each aircraft was an American discovery, the *slab tail*. Airliners have one of these and near the speed of sound it adjusts to compensate for its adverse effects. I found that rather cool when first I flew the 737. It was like the spoiler you fitted to your first Ford Capri.

If you board up steps at the rear you can see this; the leading edge of the *tailplane*, the small wing at the back, is calibrated with a series of paint marks where it meets the body of the aeroplane. These marks show the angle it is tilted up or down at. Why not turn to the man behind you, especially if it is your boss and say something like, Looks like a slab tail again, so hang on to your hat. Once the cabin crew told me that as one man stood here at the top of the steps while disembarking (what Americans call *deplaning*), the wind caught his toupee and chased it across the concrete apron. I hoped he'd had the presence of mind to pretend it was a rabbit.

You will recall though when we talked about the shock waves induced by travelling at the speed of sound, these might migrate around the flying surfaces and render the moveable controls at the trailing edge impotent? Well these slab tails do not need these trailing *control surfaces*, because they move, like those of a missile, in their entirety. Any consultant will tell you if you have a problem, you should circumvent it.

As we saw when we tried to take off, the force of air increases disproportionately with speed. When we take off, this means every extra knot adds lots more lift to our wings, while on the way down, every extra knot increases *drag*, the suction force pulling back.

Imagine you have a lightning fast van: if you launch like a rocket, the air cannot keep up and the space behind you, for a second, is completely evacuated. It contains nothing until the air rushes to fill it in. If the van takes off REALLY quickly it leaves a whole corridor of nothing, which applies a tremendous suction on everything around it before it fills in. If you move off slowly, the space behind you gets filled in real quick, as if by a fast worker with a shovel, so there is very little sucking going on. That suction applies to everything in sight, including the back of the van. This is why thin wings are faster, as there is less to grab onto. Car designers used to think during the art-deco period, or later when there was crossover from aviation design, that the back end of cars ought to be tapered like a droplet. This is because the suction applied to the tail end of a falling raindrop pulls it into the shape of a tadpole. This is entirely involuntary and only because the droplet is *squishy* enough to be pulled into this shape by the evil forces of drag. We would be most unhappy with the automakers if our own vehicles became more tadpole-shaped at speed. We would look most silly.

In fact all this does is to present a bigger surface both to the force of suction and secondly to *skin friction*. This type of drag is what you experience when you rub shoulders; unless she was so attractive you enjoyed it too much to notice. (The French call this *frottage* or something; they have a word for almost any preliminary of love you can think of, along with plenty for what happens afterward.) In the end they concluded cars went just as fast if you sliced them off at the tail like a bullet. Unfortunately this leaves no place for the shopping, so nobody took up on the idea. Except the Smart car, which does not go nearly so fast enough for it to matter anyway.

Though I make the descent sound torrid, generally it is a fairly leisurely affair, because pilots like to cut themselves plenty of slack. One thing I had noticed flying the 737 was something never appearing in the manuals but existing out there in reality anyway. What airline training departments like to do is to pick up on developments that cast light upon the flying condition and then incorporate them into the manuals, pretending they knew all along. They do this in the hope that brown-nosing will meet with just rewards, which usually it does. An English literary commentator once observed most people are in awe of power itself, regardless of who wields it.

I used to fly with a Formula Three racing driver and on one of those evenings when we got a free run into Hanover, I remember him querying whether we ought still be at 300 knots just fifteen miles from the airfield? We were throttled back, down low at a couple of thousand feet and at the point we needed to descend, the flaps and the landing gear were extended, nicely on schedule. It struck me this worked because at lower levels the air is thicker and you decelerate deceptively quickly. This was what it did not say in the manuals. At much higher levels the air is thinner and offers little drag. The Japanese man who skied down a slope of Everest discovered his parachute did not *begin* to slow his descent. He had hoped to use it as a *drag chute*, which is what they use to stop the Space Shuttle after landing, because it has lousy brakes. In an aeroplane if you carry too much speed into the descent, it is only too easy to carry it into the approach and the subsequent landing. A Southwest Airlines crew discovered this when they landed half-way along the runway at excessive speed in heavy rain. They stopped eventually, outside a gas station on the adjacent block.

As the descent seems to be looking after itself, let us look at a few more things while we have the leisure. Paperwork would be a good start. Here and there I mention my *logbook*. I have already touched upon the *navigation log*, while connected to each aircraft there is also a *technical log*. That is enough logs for a small fire. The logbook is required by the CAA or FAA (the 'Feds' as they are known in America), as an ongoing record of your flying hours. In it you are supposed to record details of each flight and these are supposed to tally with those recorded in the aircraft technical log, as well as with the *movements* recorded at every licenced aerodrome.

The CAA licenses aerodromes in an effort to control aviation, though what is happening among private flyers, as *microlight* aircraft become lighter and simpler, is they launch from anywhere and keep the scantest record. This is known as the grey market in flying. As long as they do not fall from the sky, everyone is happy. We used to operate charter flights to the road race at Le Mans, where every commercial operator in Christendom is trying to make a fast buck. Most people are trying to get there under visual flight rules, while flying through every cloud under the sun, in order to avoid paying airways charges. The CAA inspectors used to do surprise audits on aeroplanes and their crew, but what was most funny was they came by ferry: the travel warrants did not stretch to chartering an aircraft. We'd have done them a deal had they promised to keep quiet.

Toward the end I used to record each day at a time in my logbook, instead of each flight. Others I knew, whose life consisted of flying mailbags from Norwich to East Midlands each evening, did not bother at all. I remember an old air force captain permanently being leaned upon to keep a record of his flights in a Vickers VC10. From time to time he put in things like 'Brize Norton to Australia'. He was lucky to have the opportunity: before they introduced a college-based scheme toward a European commercial licence, one way of getting your *ticket* was to accumulate seven hundred flying hours of any sort. This was probably the greatest contribution the CAA could have made toward global warming and I thank them every time I turn down the thermostat. Light aircraft have a counter called a *Hobbs meter*, which runs like a taxi fare whenever the engine runs. Pilots from Europe usually went to America, where the flying is much cheaper, to accumulate seven hundred hours. Even flying gets boring after a while and some would take long lunches, but leave the engine ticking over in case their logbooks were ever cross-referenced with the meter.

What this means in practice is your captain today probably has more experience of burger and fries than almost anyone else on the aeroplane. Another I knew lay in bed at home near the runway, checking when local aircraft took off and landed, logging this flying as well. Not that any of this mattered much; I wish I had the chutzpa to have done it myself. When one 727 pilot in America was eventually involved in a minor incident, they discovered he never pursued a flying licence. He was like the guy in a white coat that checks into hospital and removes your kidney, on the strength of what he sees on the web. Personally I would rather have my kidney removed like this nowadays, as it is about the only way it will be done properly and inexpensively. I am never nervous flying as a passenger, until I hear there is a check captain up front. These are the training captains that sign off your performance. They are also on record for causing the worst accidents, which is only natural when they feel they are that much better than everyone else. While I worked at Heathrow a Malaysian 747 scraped a tail on take-off. It turns out this was only because the training captain pitched in with the legendary phrase, No! Do it like *this*...

The aircraft technical log records the uptake of fuel and oil and certifies the machine is in working order, while the documentation also records its original weight. This is done pretty much down to the last bag of sugar, so for instance the weight of the aircraft 'Prepared for service', which is before fuel, bags and passengers are loaded, includes pilots and cabin crew, along with their cases and any catering supplies. It even includes the oil in the engines, which in jet engines is not a tremendous amount. Many used to be lubricated by *total loss* systems, like lawn mowers that needed constant replenishing with oil.

When the passengers get on, they are assumed to be a standard weight, which includes their hand luggage. Checked-in baggage is counted separately. The notional weight of male and female passengers gets revised upward from time to time to reflect the realities of the McDonalds generation. I am going to get sued for that. If however anyone sees a contingent of Sumo wrestlers boarding and feel they exceed the notional allowance, you are permitted to challenge them and insist they be weighed separately. It is not going to be me doing the challenging.

The promising young singer Aliyah lost her life upon this technicality. Smaller aircraft at the bottom end of the charter market tend to come with dubious paperwork and newly qualified pilots, who cannot get a job on larger aircraft. Never believe a pilot when he says he prefers something smaller and slower. He is like the man in the Deep South who tells you he prefers being married to a goat. Unfortunately stars on video shoots come with equipment and bodyguards that are too heavy for smaller aeroplanes. They also tend not to listen to a two-bit captain until such time as he is skimming the palm trees.

A friend of mine (yes, I have one) was charged with operating the aircraft belonging to Bernard Matthews, the turkey king. I used to drive all night with turkey chicks destined for this place and sit outside eating a greasy breakfast, waiting for the place to open. He charged this pilot with organising a flight very early the next day for his fancy friends, whom he was taking to lunch in the south of France. At five the next day, without a word, they never turned up. They did turn up the next day, to find a cold aeroplane with a note stuck by condensation to the window saying, "Get another pilot".

People do charter aircraft at this level for all sorts of reasons. When I flew a business jet, typically old men would turn up and take very young women to the Riviera for the day. The old man would fall asleep first, shortly followed by the girl and a colleague of mine could not help noticing from the dashboard mirror, the lady appeared knickerless. Purely in the interests of confirming his eyesight passed muster, he invited the co-pilot to turn around and investigate. Robert refused however, on the basis the one thing sure to awaken her was discovering him fixated upon her crotch.

The only other paperwork I could mention are the posters the CAA still produce, exhorting people to fly more sensibly, in the way wartime posters used to cajole housewives to spin out rations of powdered egg:

STOP! You there! DON'T bust that flight level!

Or else:

Headsets...you know they make sense.

The CAA also produce a set of very worthy leaflets reminding us, if we did not know already, how sheep-like are the owners of light aircraft. These would typically say:

*We told you last year that the best way of assuring your aircraft will **not** take off is by loading it with two tons of lager, or letting that grass grow too long. To date only fifteen have died in such accidents ~ keep up the good work!*

They also produce exhaustive analyses of aircraft accidents, which pilots enjoy reading over a coffee in the crew room during quieter moments. Extracts from these are printed in the best-selling *Pilot* magazine and for many years accidents issuing in fatalities used to be highlighted in italics, so readers could omit those in which the aeroplane merely drove into the hedge. Every conceivable incident has to be documented. I have many favourites but one was the pilot 'running the engines up' at the airfield perimeter in Blackbushe. This is adjacent to the Basingstoke road, so it blew one passer-by clean off his bicycle.

These incidents need only involve the commander once the doors are closed up, when technically it becomes sovereign territory. During air rage incidents this means the commander has the authority to restrain the passengers or even better, to remain locked in the flight deck issuing orders. Advice on this involves a whole series of procedures before the genital cuffs come out. Most are couched in legalese, so if a cabin crew complains some guy made an adverse comment about her chest, I am expected *in extremis* to go out there and say, You appear to be a complete piss-head, in material breach of the Air Navigation Order and as a result, upon landing you will be arrested by an officer and detained in a fairly nasty place. The passenger for his part is expected to punch the commander upon the nose, while casting aspersions on his genetic make-up.

When it really gets interesting is when people either give birth during the flight (most likely to be one of the cabin crew) or else die on us. This can be most distressing for the cabin crew, who never expect a modicum of support from the flight crew and are rarely disappointed in this expectation. To try to alleviate this syndrome, airlines like every other type of company are employing 'people' people to help us all get along. These show us videos and get us to open our hearts, before reminding us that, Although the captain operated the wrong switch, that does not make him a dickhead as was suggested, but merely that he misinterpreted the visual cues... At the last place I worked they had recruited somebody with a doctorate in the study of advanced primates, which I felt was the perfect qualification for dealing with pilots. His first name was

Duncan and perhaps inevitably, I only ever referred to him as Dr Duncan Donuts.

The reason a birth on board is a nightmare, beside the mess, is the infant is then of no determinate nationality. Those that die on board are in an equal fix, not that they care about it. The cabin crew are encouraged to pretend this never happened, at least until arrival. Covering the cadaver with a tartan blanket and claiming he "looked tired when boarding" normally achieve this. Alternatively a bin bag can be used to cover either end. They often used to prop them up in the toilet until flights got much longer and passengers started saying, We knew the bacon paninis were suspect, but *fourteen hours?*

Whenever anything particularly special is loaded along with the baggage the captain has to be told about it and not uncommonly this would be a body being repatriated. This was especially common on the Dublin route, the Irish having an affinity for their native soil. A friend used to fly freight in small aircraft around Australia and used to say transporting cadavers was particularly unnerving at night, as they climbed higher and the pressure of air within the body produced one last gasp, or defiant burst of flatulence. There was one interesting story, though. Longer-haul aircraft like those of Virgin Atlantic have a *crew rest area* with bunks, usually below decks or at rear of the cabin. One of the cabin crew going back was surprised to find a gentle old lady who chatted for a while, until the crew suggested she return to her seat. To encourage this the crew member asked the lady where her husband was sat and went to inform him of her whereabouts. When she pointed out to the man his wife was with the crew, he said he hoped not because she was inside a coffin within the hold.

As distressing is the effect travelling has on animals. I took particular care these went in the right place and were separated from dangerous cargo. Consignments of dry ice would always be brought to the attention of the commander: this is a frozen form of carbon dioxide used for keeping catering fresh. It gradually boils off and fills the hold with gas and this had been known to account for the lives of several dozen of the turkey chicks that were transported from time to time. Lobster, prawn and eel were normally carried fresh in water, within polystyrene cartons whose tops were sealed with tape. Not always very well, for when one 737 arrived in Brussels and its forward hold was opened, the baggage handlers were met with a Biblical wall of water, along with a plague of eels.

Racehorses are frequently transported long distances to take part in races in different parts of the world, but are probably treated better than most of the passengers. Around seventy percent of all airfreight is carried in the holds of passenger aircraft, though the number of dedicated freighters is on the rise, principally to meet demand from overnight parcel operators. These will generally be retired passenger jets whose older engines are too noisy to meet regular service requirements. They tend to fly in the middle of the night, so like troglodytes their pilots sleep throughout the day. I was required to operate a standby duty at Coventry airport sometimes, as part of a postal contract. Coventry has no scheduled services but operates as a hub for freighters. As a result it is penniless and its terminal is made of compressed hardboard. The Pope dropped by on one occasion and a plaque attests to the fact. As I commented at the time, I only hoped he had not paused to kiss the concrete, replete as it was with hydraulic oil. It could easily have been the end of a beautiful career. Sitting here in the café at two in the morning, my fry-up illumined by ghastly lighting and the walls arrayed with flyers revived from the dead, it felt more like a passage to the underworld.

Cats and dogs would travel often, with or without their owners and I used during my external inspection to poke a friendly finger through the bars. At Palma there would be stray kittens frolicking beneath the terminal building and I would treat these during the turnaround to some of the crew meals. This soon stopped them. The baggage holds may or may not be warmed by air vented from the cabin and on occasions pets were consigned to the wrong hold and arrived as if from out of the freezer. There are stories of baggage handlers rallying around desperately with hairdryers, if only to be able to present a corpse to the owner looking more like a spaniel than a frozen haddock. The best I heard, which I like to think is true, was a story of a deceased cat being freighted back to London by its owner and the handlers, on finding it dead, scouring the catteries for a replacement.

DESCENT

Before we return to the descent for a quick recap, I did touch on the role of the controller and his or her care for their charges. I once took a light aircraft up to South Dakota and I arrived at my port of call early in the evening after a fly-past of Mount Rushmore. These presidential figures look grand in a Hitchcock movie, but aircraft are kept at a distance, from where they look about as impressive as embedded smileys like this: ☺☺☺☺. In a similar vein the Grand Canyon is about two miles deep, but aircraft are now forbidden from entering its maw. It hardly seems worth flying any more. After checking into this airfield I mentioned, in Dakota, it seemed a good moment to fly out over the Badlands. The air was so silky smooth, you could set the aeroplane up, hands off, and it flew itself. Beneath me was a lunar landscape, a place pioneers entered and never emerged. As I had only one engine, I could detect the concern in the voice of the controller, recalling his charge like a shepherd in search of a lost lamb. At times you see views beside which the fear of death pales, which is why we fly.

In fact the descent is possibly the best time for looking out of the window and often when it came to choosing which sector I might fly, as with the departure, I would take the view into consideration. There are places where the radio is very busy during the departure or arrival, so sometimes life could be quieter as the handling pilot, especially if the autopilot was engaged and it was an airfield you were used to. London, I told many visitors, is as remarkable a place to fly over as you might see anywhere. The town is overlain by an imaginary square and at each corner is a holding pattern. Depending on where you arrive from, you slot into one or other holding pattern. From northern Europe you fly along the Thames Estuary toward Lambourne, where the M25 meets the M11, while from southern Europe you appear at Biggin Hill. Transatlantic traffic appears at western holding points like Ockham, where the M25 meets the M3, or else Bovingdon near Hemel Hempstead.

For keen observers like myself, these holding patterns or *stacks* are a joy to spend time in, unless you returned from a night flight to Greece and your hopes of an early landing are dashed. From over Biggin Hill, you could see the Dartford crossing, the house Churchill lived in and at some distance, the racetrack at Brands Hatch. At Ockham you could see the Royal Horticultural Gardens and at

171

Bovingdon, the open prison situated on what had been the air force base. Did the inmates know they shared their domicile with a VHF Omnirange? Perhaps I could drop in one evening and give a talk upon it for them?

With a stack of arrivals at each of these corners all above 6,000 ft, departing aircraft from one of the two runways can be safely guided beneath, or left to follow their instrument departures. The task now for the controllers is to arrange for aircraft from each stack to be interlaced to the landing runway, like a string of sausages. This might take you meandering around the northern suburbs of London, before crossing to the south at Greenwich and turning westward for landing. Norman Foster recently completed a gherkin-shaped tower in the financial district and to emphasize its gherkin-ness, it was floodlit in green. This was one of the brightest things on the skyline when it was first lit and could be seen from as far away as Birmingham. The brightest permanently-lit feature of the town are the railway sidings outside Paddington, while the airport is surprisingly dark. Arriving late in the evening from the southeast and requesting a visual arrival, it was all too easily lost sight of. In which event you made sure you stayed south of the River Thames, so as not to give the game away.

Above London in daylight what most stood out were the cemeteries. Headstones are invariably white, with only a handful cutting a dash in black granite. Joe was always a snappy dresser, wasn't he? As a result these look grainy white in a sea of redbrick, or in London, a sooty yellow brick. I got to looking at these tombstones and comparing them to the myriad houses around and thinking, where have all the dead people gone? There is a constant supply of dead people down there, yet they are outnumbered twenty to one by housing. Worse would be flying down to Greece late on a Saturday evening, knowing you must be up all night. The length of the Adriatic Sea would be lit by thousands of seaside resorts and my first officer would remind me that at each of these, people were drinking and fornicating. While the two of us had to spin out a six-hour trip in the dark, amused only by a navigation beacon, yesterday's paper and a bacon panini.

Having read a little travel writing, when we got deep into the Balkans or Eastern Europe, if I saw an especially large blob of urban lighting I might ask the airways radar controller where it was. Then a woman with a heavily accented voice like a Bulgarian shot-putter would tersely reply, Is Dubrovnik. I would then turn to my co-pilot, his head visibly slumping toward the control column and say, Bigger than I thought. These exchanges would punctuate an otherwise reverential silence, illumined only by the flickering of screens and a glow from the overhead panel. Altogether it was like the mature writing of Samuel Beckett and I am convinced had it taken place in the Albery Theatre, it might run and run. For us it did run and run and I cannot believe I am contemplating doing it again. I shall insist on billboards at Manchester Airport that read, Returning from the West End, Colin Hilton stars in his smash-hit comedy "Bore Your Balls Off!"

I cannot persuade myself to continue our descent without touching upon UFOs. There was a Mexican crew who were convinced that their 747 did strike something they had seen, but could not explain. A great number of people I have flown with have witnessed such phenomena. I have myself, but only from the ground and in banal circumstances, waiting at Clapham Junction for a train one sunny afternoon. There was something high above, a pulsating light, so far away as to be indistinct. It would remain in the same spot and then move to another part of the sky at a speed and with a trajectory that I knew from flying experience was technically unfeasible. It was still there by Wimbledon, but there was nothing I could do about it, as there were no video cameras at the time. I could have pointed it out to any number of people, but all they could do was acknowledge what was known, that it was a source of pulsating light moving randomly from place to place.

That is the problem: we cannot get close enough. This is probably the way they like it. A veteran I flew with had been scrambled in a Meteor jet after a classically cigar-shaped object, which when he got close, took off like a harpy. A friend who flew the mail down from Scotland at night reported a light in his twelve o'clock, which radar confirmed as a stationary target. It disappeared and when the pilot inquired of its location, it reappeared in an instant some distance behind the aircraft, stationary again. No flying machine we know can do this. Either that, or if it is something we have secretly developed, then somebody is having a lot of fun with it.

Let us get the mechanism of the descent out of the way. At a point the computer has determined, the *top of descent*, you ensure you are cleared to a lower level by air traffic, select that level in the autopilot and punch the button. You might have to pre-select the level, because often you are cleared down long before you want to begin. Staying up at cruise levels saves on fuel besides allowing you to finish your dinner. Boeings go down of their own accord upon reaching this point, while the Airbus has to be told like a Yorkshire terrier. On the way down it is a question of badgering the controllers for successively lower levels, so you enter the beginning of the instrument arrival via what many call the *gate*, the right height. Otherwise you are struggling to dispose of height and speed all the way down. Ideally by this stage you will have discussed the arrival while examining the appropriate aerodrome *plates*, though there have been captains I have known to fall asleep during the *briefing*. Often I would not wake them until after landing, as they looked so sweet.

I cannot omit a word about *checklists* either. There are two types, a short version on a laminated card we use all the time and a more comprehensive version for dealing with failures of one kind or another. In the Boeings the big one is called the *Quick Reference Handbook*, because it is itself a condensed version of the technical manuals that tell you how things work. Between them all and a chat with your colleague, figuring exactly what has gone wrong can be like doing a crossword puzzle. The Airbus has a flight deck with TV screens and these list the required drills as appropriate, if there is an emergency. You have to be careful with them, as with all computers, because you can go through one set of drills requiring an engine to be shut down and then when you scroll to the next screen, you might find the other engine is in an even worse condition.

The laminated drills become known by heart and I can still recall some of the downwind checks required in the first aeroplane I flew some twenty-five years ago. Typically in the airliner there will be a pre-start check, an after-start check, a take-off check and descent checklist, followed by approach checks and finally shutdown checks. All are important, even the shutdown checks, as for instance if you do not turn the batteries off they might go flat, like in your car. The aircraft are supposed to be fitted with *chocks* behind each wheel, because overnight the hydraulic pressure supplying the parking brake can fritter away. I have known co-pilots board very large aeroplanes first thing in the morning and realise they were rolling slowly backward off the gate, all by themselves, as the chocks have been borrowed.

Finally I forgot to consider the very best reason for an unplanned descent, which is fire. Every three years crew have to revise Safety and Emergency Procedures, which involve trying to remember where emergency equipment is stored around the aircraft. It includes portable oxygen bottles, spare life jackets, loud-hailers, torches, crash axes, smoke hoods and so forth. You have only to learn how to float around wearing the life jacket once and my brother got to do this along with the company of a crew from Virgin Atlantic. He described this as the nearest he ever got to a wet tee shirt competition.

There is also the fire training, which used to involve regular goes upon an inflatable slide, which explodes from beneath every doorway in the event of an evacuation. Since one of the older captains built up some speed down this and hit the barriers like a downhill skier, breaking his ankle and ending his career, my last firm restricted the number of turns we got on this. You are also supposed to demonstrate an aptitude for climbing out of the flight deck suspended on a rope, but after a number of pilots got wedged in the window-frame or fell from a great height, this too was considered of dubious value. A constant of aviation is more people are injured practising than in emergencies themselves. The same is true of evacuations and pilots are reluctant to order these unless absolutely necessary, as all sorts of calamities ensue. What most passengers do is to stand in the doorway like children and turn to offer their turn to the guy behind. A helping foot from the cabin crew is usually all that is required. In the worst evacuation I saw on film, a 747 ended up sat on its tail on the runway. The slides deployed from the upper deck ended up vertical, instead of down an incline. This did not stop a number of passengers being assisted in freefalling to the concrete fifty feet below.

Since the age of five I have always felt people should not always do what they are told and this is a working example. It is also something the aviation authorities are going to have to grapple with more and more. There is a child-psychosis involved in most air-rage incidents, as the cabin is about the last place we get to sit and be lectured at by beautiful but domineering women. Or men. This takes us back to schooldays and in the same way adults returning to their parents for a weekend find themselves turning into teenagers, this is the best possible means to trigger schoolroom antics. Passengers realise expulsion is unlikely at 35,000 ft and this is one reason even chief executives embarrass themselves with infantile behaviour at times and why a court appearance comes as such a shock.

Much of this has to do with the excessive alcohol passengers imbibe, often in an attempt to quell nerves. I would occasionally go back to talk to those the crew had identified as especially legless and usually this convinced me the greatest danger was probably their sleeping for the duration. It was when passengers were drunk upon their own celebrity that trouble started. One ageing Scottish crooner I know to have defecated on the seats of an executive jet, simply to celebrate having the money to do so. Personally I might have given him a slapping, but who pays the ferryman? Other stars refuse to communicate directly with cabin crew, asking their PA to do this instead, though many are especially nice and some almost shambolic. I was seated next to Boris Becker once, but elected to read the paper instead of striking up a conversation, because the only thing I ever did with a racket was pretend I belonged to *Status Quo*. Stevie Wonder very wisely avoided his retinue using aircraft with propellers. When the captain was informed he had refused to board our aircraft for this reason, it left me wondering who had told him.

During the course of most safety and emergency renewals the video of the Bradford City Stadium fire is inevitably wheeled out and I have seen it now about four times. It has left me with the lasting impression I should never even consider watching Bradford City play football. I already knew how effective the radiation from fire could be, because I studied (if that is the term for it) at Sheffield University. It was renowned for metallurgy and my flatmate had been on a visit to one of the many steelworks since closed. By way of demonstration, one of its workers screwed up a sheet of newspaper and threw it vaguely through the air toward the furnaces. Before getting very far at all it would spontaneously combust. In older crucible workshops I visited in Sheffield, hundredweight pots of molten metal used to be pulled from beneath ground level twelve hours a day by men who sweated several stones each day and put it back drinking at night. The handles of hammers used to make scythes had been worn to the thickness of a toothbrush handle by the hours of human toil.

Periodically we were expected to find our way to the exit during a lifelike scenario. For smaller aircraft this involved somebody on the ground (in whom I detected a certain frisson of anticipation) leaving me inside a Piper Seneca and pumping it full of acrid smoke. It was not the nicest experience, though I had no greenfly for months afterward. In larger aeroplanes a mock-up of the cabin was used, with the sort of flickering red lights that I last saw in Santa's grotto. Interspersed among the seats were dummies we were supposed to rescue during our escape, giving us the opportunity to say, There's a soulless corpse here, else I just tripped on a manager. Finally there was the first aid course, which involved a resuscitation attempt upon a plastic cadaver, during which I became queasy and passed out, so they used me instead. I have omitted to mention the security course, though I alluded to it earlier in connection with plastic explosive. This ranged across the gamut of human depravity and after these briefings too, I would leave the building wondering whether life was worth living.

Fire has always been the bugbear, as aluminium burns quickly. During the Falklands war, one finding was that steel ships could take any number of strikes from Exocet missiles, while lighter alloy ships went up like a firecracker. This is basically because additives in alloys are the ones you see in sparklers, like phosphorus and magnesium. As teenagers we used to admire magnesium alloy wheels, without ever connecting them with the stuff that burst into flames on contact with water. Up until this point I had pursued life in the belief that water was used to put fires out. They discovered that the *Hindenburg* did not burn so rapidly when it crashed because of the hydrogen it contained (though it cannot have helped), but because its material was coated with an aluminium oxide, precisely what they use as rocket fuel. Hey guys, what can we use to make our airship shiny?

Another video featured a real life event, of which there are many in flying, in which a cigarette is dumped in a waste bin in a DC-9. This was overlooked when it appeared to go out, but later took hold and did its worst. The message in this one as in the next was not to doubt or dither. There was also the Lockheed Tri-Star whose cabin caught alight while taxiing to the runway in the Middle East. Until it stopped there were no fatalities, yet all on board subsequently died during the minutes it took to organise access for firefighters. Of most interest to myself was an industry video in which one captain whom I thought that I recognised was earnestly managing a response to one such scenario from his seat at the controls. Was he not the captain I had known who smuggled silk suits in from Hong Kong? I kind of hoped the screenplay would feature a sub-plot like in *The Pirates of Penzance*, confirming my suspicions. As ever I was disappointed.

During the fire that concerned the Swissair MD11 off the coast of Canada the pilots had to vacate the flight deck altogether when it began to drip molten products of combustion. There were two principal findings from the investigation. Firstly the emergency drills can be excessively long-winded at times like this, when rules should be thrown out of the window and the aeroplane put down anywhere. This contradiction in transport operations was identified earliest on the railways and to some extent in shipping. If you have a rule for everything, there is no room left for initiative and it has been observed that Hitler was most successful when he let generals think for themselves. On the railways, they found if they followed all of the rules the system ground to a halt. This was used as an alternative to strike action and was known as *working to rule*, literally doing things by the book.

The other finding was that the fire had been caused by the insulation around the wiring, which I think was called *kapton*. It was long since phased out of military use due to a propensity to catch fire, but unfortunately airliners are wired with a hundred miles of *looms* and are not worth rewiring like houses. The material has been replaced in recent manufacture, but the risk in existing fleets is considered acceptable. You have to remember that the pursuit of safety like all other processes of evolution experiences a growth curve which tails off, a law of diminishing returns. I have flown with captains now retired who recall accidents in living memory in which most passengers died because there were *three* different type of seat-belt buckle and rescuers took too long trying to figure out how each was released. I do not think I am alone in having felt patronised by people telling me how to adjust and release my seat-belt, though the simplest issues can be among the most crucial in times of duress. Like we have found on the railways in Britain though, if you nullify every risk the economics no longer stack up.

This view is increasingly being challenged at law however and is something society must really decide for itself. As it stands airlines make money only if involved in a cartel. Governments incline toward restricted access for them, as they are seen as a sovereign issue; our own is as likely to rescue BA as it was *Railtrack*, because if people turn up on Monday to find no train or aeroplane, it is government who gets the blame. We are unlikely ever to be short of manufactured goods or even cars, whether or not Ford goes bust, but while making aeroplanes constitutes a primary industry, like airlines themselves it is more a means of serving employment than making profits. It was Keynes who said during the Depression it would be cheaper to fill mines with banknotes and send miners after those in place of coal and this is about where we are now with the airline business.

It explains why governments refuse to tax the fuel aeroplanes burn, or why they are as keen to sign the Kyoto Treaty as they are to double the volume of air transport. The railways have been rationalised comprehensively during the last fifty years and offer a parallel experience, for they too were a benefit proven to have expanded beyond all reasonable commercial expectation, which is why their abandoned routes litter the countryside and each of their companies was bankrupted.

DESCENT

However, criticising our masters this way is about as low as we descend here.

APPROACH

The approach is the single most important aspect of flight. It is aptly named and could be compared with aspects of the approach to life itself, like an interview or the first meeting with the woman you might marry. Even in the operating manuals issued by Boeing, there is a fatherly entry reminding pilots the basis of a good approach is sound planning in the descent. Precisely to avoid the dangers I discussed of arriving too fast or too high: the word 'fast' itself connotes a certain disreputableness. These strictures are not without reason, for the majority of accidents are caused during this phase.

Most passenger guides to flying merely suggest the cruise is the safest portion of flight, so the risks are increased on the way up or down. This is a safe guess, like saying the most dangerous time to be in a car is when the engine is running. Pilots know intimately the approach is the most concentrated portion of flight and their own concentration rises to meet the eventuality. Were pilots wired to test physiological reactions, this is when the blood pressure would be rising and the perspiration beginning to increase. The crew may engage in desultory conversation prior to the approach and the volubility of this reflects the difficulty of the task in hand in inverse relation. Difficult approaches are punctuated by terse comment while familiar ones like that into Heathrow might be accompanied by silent sightseeing. Most biannual proficiency checks are accompanied by the analysis of a recent accident and in this chapter we examine that of a Boeing 757 flying to Columbia.

We saw how the inertial system and navigation computer directed the aeroplane along its course, as long as it knew its location before the flight commenced. This is important, especially without satellite navigation, because there are parts of the world where the aircraft has to find its own way. One of these is the North Pole, which airliners traverse regularly between say London and Los Angeles. For centuries ships had only a magnetic compass to guide them, though the magnetic pole, or centre of attraction, is not on top of the world, *true north*, but off to one side, *magnetic north*. What is worse, when you were nearly there the needle no longer pointed northwards, but at the ground. This was called *dip*.

You will recall those experiments where you put the bar magnet beneath the paper and the iron filings formed a *flux*, emerging at one end of the bar and entering at the other? Well the magnetism around the world acts this way too and dives at either end. It is this concentration of flux at the poles that interacts with solar radiation to produce plasma of charged particles called the *Aurora Borealis* or the Northern Lights. There is one at the southern pole too which we tend to forget about unless we live down there. The polarity of Earth (which end is North and which South) has reversed over aeons and Velikovsky suggested the world might have flipped bodily to cause this.

The upshot is pilots unerringly following the needle over either pole would end up like moths circling a lamp. I shall remind you why this happens. Whenever you fly or drive, you get an unconscious sense of where you are heading from where the brightest portion of the sky is. The sun moves so slowly as to provide a steady reference. I would notice the same with the stars during night flights, though as I mentioned before, on longer flights you did become aware of their own progress. The moth makes the disastrous calculation that your lamp is the sun, or possibly the moon. I say this because moths are supposed to sleep during the day, but ours is flying along minding its own business with the sun out there on its right wing tip. As it passes by the lamp the 'sun' retreats rapidly behind the wing and the moth imagines it is veering left and keeps veering right to correct this departure, eventually into the fiery flame. At least until we took up electric lighting, when we took to hitting it with a slipper instead. I flew with an older captain for a while and emerging from Edinburgh one night, climbing away with the mail, I felt a fluttering around my face and turned on my map light to find a moth on the air conditioning panel. I turned to the commander and said, Jim, would you like the *Moth on Air Conditioning Panel* checklist?

Actually there was not one of these, but there a drill for every other eventuality you could think of and besides, I thought it might help break the ice. When I came to fly the mail at night with beautiful co-pilots, as we settled into the route I used to find my mind drifting into fantasies about leaving the autopilot and making love among the mailbags, though the nearest I heard anybody get to this was slipping back there for abuse. During a check in the simulator the conversation turned to one especially attractive lady and the training captain, balding and overcharged with testosterone, let us know he most enjoyed those evenings flying back from Glasgow with her, when the setting sun would delineate the curve of each breast through her short-sleeved blouse. We should have turned ourselves in there and then for improper thoughts, but they used to say in the cabin that if every instance of sexual harassment were investigated, no aeroplane would leave the ground. During prolonged taxiing to the runway at Heathrow, members of the cabin crew would join us to chew the fat and one of these made veiled references to oral sex, of the kind that leave you wondering whether it might not actually be on the cards, then and there. The captain with me at the time was a young and particularly over-sexed individual and would have been only too happy for me to proceed. For my part its delight could only have been magnified by the circumstances, as I might have been the only airline pilot to be gratified on course to the runway. A sort of personal Everest.

When they migrate across land and sea birds navigate both by the sun and by this weak form of magnetism. Often they get confused on cloudy days and increasingly the modern world is being blamed for the destruction of their ability to follow the magnetic flux. In the same way, the noise of ships and undersea communication disrupts chatter between whales so they end up with the donkeys on Brighton beach instead of in the Arctic. Birds fly tremendous distances, the length of oceans, thousands of miles on the strength of a worm or two. This is why Lufthansa use the image of a stork as their logo, because of its tremendous powers of endurance. At times they get lost or encounter headwinds, becoming exhausted, but if they sink to the water they drown. If they chance upon a ship nearby they will smother it and seamen will tell you how every inch is covered by birds so weak you can hold them and they no longer care. The pilot of a vertical jump jet once put down on a Spanish trawler, though he was not too tired to enjoy a maggot. Should you salvage a ship at sea you legally own it and there was some argument with the Ministry of Defence, as the fishermen felt they were the new owners of a vehicle that could comfortably dispose of a basking tuna.

We are a long way now from our accident in Cali but what I was saying was the aeroplane, like the birds, continually knows its position. This is updated in flight, while you can enter any *waypoint* into the computer, like that representing the start of the arrival procedure, to send the aeroplane straight there to commence it. Unfortunately this crew sent the aircraft to a point behind them already passed and during the ensuing U-turn they collided with the valley. What I found spellbinding about the incident was the contents of the CVR tape, the cockpit voice recorder that provided the conversation several minutes prior to the accident itself. Let me first dispose of the expression *cockpit*. Early aeroplanes were formed of biplanes joined by a *fuselage* to the tailplane. The elongated fuselage was a tapered box into which the pilot could be lowered, through a cutout whose rim was trimmed in leather. As this resembled a pit into which fighting cocks were thrown, it came to be known as just that. In ten years of commercial flying, I have never found a fighting bird here, though mice and cockroaches are regularly seen in the galley. One infestation I came across was an aircraft with cargo including a consignment of maggots intended for a fish farm. During an unduly long layover at an airfield somewhere warm, these hatched into bluebottles, which escaped to occupy every orifice and ground the aeroplane for days.

The conversation between the pilots at Cali was one any pilot would associate with and covered the required syllabus. It looked at differences between long or short haul, besides analysing the effect each had upon lifestyle. There are the inevitable fears for retirement and the usual grumbles about both routes and rosters:

Capt	*I see Bill _____ took up long haul again.*
FO	*Yeah, those east coast routes are a drag...*
Capt	*What's the name of that beacon?*
FO	*Er, I'll check the plates (sound of rustling).*

Capt	*The guys on his third wife.*
FO	*How can you sit there for, what ten and a half hours?*
Capt	*They're leaving that descent a little late?*
FO	*I was here a month ago. I think it comes with the next controller.*
Capt	*Figured I'm kinda happy just flogging up and down to South America...*

Though I paraphrase, this is a flavour of the conversation preceding descent in any airliner, among pilots of whichever nationality. One of the things Dr Donuts suggested, though for all I knew he never flew an aeroplane with a rubber band, was the guys in the Potomac River incident did not know what they were about, because they engaged the stewardess in conversation on the way to the runway, when it was snowing outside. This pissed me mightily and I told him so. It was immaterial: accidents happen when people do *not* communicate, in this sphere as in any other.

They are not supposed to listen to this CVR tape until you die, by the way. Sometimes I did some in-flight crooning and then point out to the co-pilot that we could no longer consider crashing, because of the ensuing transcript:

Capt	*Now solitaire's the only game in town...*
FO	*What was that?*
Capt	*...and every road that takes him, takes him...*
	(Sound of muffled bang)
Capt	*er, down.*

There is an 'erase' button on the CVR panel and after a period bad-mouthing managers while routing to the gate, more paranoid types would stretch up casually to the ERASE button, while uttering some magical expletive like a grand wizard.

There are also cultural differences in communicating and western pilots have especial difficulty in flying as outriders to Chinese captains, for example. Oriental societies pay especial deference to age and so first officers are reluctant to question their interpretation. Age is problematical for flying and national policies are mired in employee rights issues. There is no specific test for senility during the bi-annual medical and unless you appear with a pencil up either nostril you are going to get away with it. At those times when the company took exception to things I had said they invited me to see the company medical officer and despite trying this ruse with the pencils I could never get myself dismissed. At Cityflyer, a regional airline in the UK, many of the captains were recruited from among those at BA who retire early. They continued on to the age of sixty-five and while some remained as sharp as tacks, I was told by co-pilots that others went visibly downhill. One of these co-pilots encountered a recent retiree at the shopping mall and asked what his plans were for the coming week. He began explaining a series of flights he imagined was scheduled for him, having to be reminded of his own retirement.

Returning to the East-West divide, when a Korean 747 came down shortly after taking off from London Stansted, oriental deference was highlighted as a contributory factor. Four years after this accident (when the captain's instruments proved unreliable but no-one wanted to tell him), thirteen local residents have been given leave to sue the airline for the distress caused by the megaton explosion it visited upon their duckpond. In the same week this legal finding was revealed in the papers, another awarded a resident near RAF Wittering a million pounds in compensation for the impact the base has had on house and home generally. People are no longer in thrall to the silver birds in the sky.

The fact many of the co-pilots in oriental airlines are Australian can be especially problematic, as this is a place where personal deference is unknown. My instructor in Toulouse was a man who wore a Stetson, commanded DC-3s by the age of twenty-three and played the trombone for a Vancouver orchestra. Pilots are idiosyncratic if nothing else and one I knew restored jukeboxes, keeping three in his garage. The first thing Greg asked us when we arrived here at the simulator was for a definition of 'human factors', the touchy-feely side of flying. Apparently it was calling the commander an ass-hole, but this time wearing a fixed smile.

Greg had instructed a crew from the Far East and refused to pass them, so Airbus got someone else to do it because the airline had just placed an order. They could hardly go back home without being able to fly them, as this is the stuff of international incidents. Usually when you order several aircraft the manufacturer will include training at their own facilities, which might be regarded as something of a cleft stick. Greg used this to hit his students. He said that during one exercise the inscrutable captain had taken off and instead of following the instrument departure, which called for a series of turns, he climbed into the blue yonder. Greg left this for a while and not wanting to challenge the handling pilot directly, got on the headset and asked the younger pilot to intervene and find out what was going on. After this happened he said the reaction required no translating whatsoever for the co-pilot was verbally karate-chopped in a way that made Oprah look a blue-belt.

I have only seen one safety video acknowledge this important interplay between pilots. When trainers refer to it at all they like to use guarded expressions like 'peer pressure'. Attitudes toward accidents caused by interactive failure are akin to those of Victorians toward sex. At that time gentlemen walking the length of the Haymarket could expect to be offered fellatio by half a dozen children, though this rarely appeared in guidebooks. There was no Rough Guide to Victorian England, with hot chestnuts and all. The safety video had been made I think by Air Alaska, who must be more open about relationships.

One of my most significant cultural shocks was emerging from a contract in Sardinia, where girls are chaperoned by hirsute fathers bearing arms, to Norway, where hirsute girls chaperone their fathers. Here I discovered that while Anglo-Saxons embrace drink and shun sex, Scandinavians engage in sex as a preliminary like canapés and purchase drink only furtively from government stores. I did a stint in Helsinki where the engineer from BA had been posted. He told me if you were especially friendly the locals might suggest you go home to service their wife, while they stuck around drinking vodka. This story was confirmed to my satisfaction when one girl I spoke to said she was regularly serviced by three gentlemen, from various walks of life, each of whom provided her with a medical certificate at the start of each month. These people treat sexual hygiene like we do flossing. And no, I did not become the 'fourth member'.

We have considered the importance of the approach and how it culminates every flight by reason of filling the interregnum between air and ground. Let us look at the physics of the process. Once pilots began *blind flying* in cloud, eventually there would be days when the weather obscured the ground. Inside cloud you might see nothing, though its density varies even within each layer and on occasions you cannot see the wing tip yards away. On the ground there have been occasions when I could not see the tails of parked aircraft from only a little further away. No aeroplane of any size arrives at airfields flying any less than a hundred miles an hour or a mile every thirty seconds. Trying to avoid obstacles on the ground at such speeds in vehicles that do not swerve but gradually *roll* into turns is an exercise that kills many.

The original way back to the airfield, for before *schedules* each flight began and ended at the same place, was to use your eyes and a map. The first flyers found their way back like nesting birds, by going a little further each time. I learned to fly at RAF Finningley up the eastern side of England and being flat, this was littered with power stations. Often you broke out above a sea of low-lying cloud and having no *radio navigation* equipment on board, we needed to call the radar controller for a *steer* to the airfield. They had accurate *approach radars* and using them could give you instructions all the way to touchdown on the runway. With larger aircraft like the VC-10, they could tell if it bounced upon landing and then would goad the crews by saying, Service terminates and your touchdown time was 11:53 and eighteen seconds, or 11:53 and twenty seconds.

A number of the instructors used to look around at the plumes breaking through the cloud above different power stations and *triangulate* their position. Three separate points are needed to figure out where you are and the police can track your mobile 'phones if in contact with three or more transmitters. Technologists discovered telephone networks are able to track aircraft too, because signals from each transmitter bounce off them and arrive at others, where they can be analysed. I call these transmitters, but telephone masts transmit and receive signals, passing them on like a relay race. They are neither simple receivers like your TV, nor transmitters like the remote, but a combination type called a *transponder*. (Those power stations by the way are long since defunct, as many ran on coal. The great cooling towers went for a pound sterling, so I considered buying one for posterity, or to organise the mother of all bungee jumps.)

Aircraft use transponders to assist radars in detecting them, by adding to the reflected radio signal with their own transmission. If air traffic asks you to *Squawk*, like a chicken, this sends a stronger signal again, distinguishing your blob on-screen from all the others. The same transponders are used by the military in *Identification Friend or Foe*. Incoming aircraft are interrogated by radar using a code, like asking for your pin number, and only the good guys are provided with the right response. In civilian flying by instrument rules these techniques are used so the controller can say you are *identified*, because until then they take no responsibility for where you end up. In fact there is a further caveat, which devolves responsibility for any collision with terrain upon the pilot, which is how it ought to be, because controllers are under enough stress already. The duty of a pilot in avoiding the ground is sacrosanct, except for the purposes of landing.

Back to the Air Alaska video, which was shown me during my command course, almost apologetically I felt. It is especially amusing because each scenario contrasts the pushy co-pilot, the understated co-pilot, or the co-pilot of your dreams. The pushiest is certainly the funniest for when the steward offers coffee he orders one for everybody. Then he gets onto the PA to introduce himself to the passengers while the captain is looking borderline apoplectic. In the next scenario a stewardess drops in and says one of her colleagues is having a difficult time at home and predictably the captain continues rummaging for his palm-pilot to complete the crossword, while the first officer jokes about periods. This is seen as the 'normal' scenario. In the ideal version the captain leans earnestly forward to recommend a personal counsellor, while the first officer rises to make the entire crew a coffee, while his hair looks considerably neater.

This training does not come without the opportunity for exercises in real life. Out there for instance passengers are ill advised to fly after recent silicone breast implants, because the reduction of pressure in the cabin makes crisp bags and implants expand like blowfish. This can rupture the suture along with the implant itself. Recently I heard from a crew member that on one flight a passenger had a breast explode, flattening one side of her chest while spilling the contents of the implant down the front of her blouse. This is not what you would want at the Oscars. Laughably the cabin crew had visited the flight deck for advice. I say laughably, because I could imagine them getting as much advice here as an orthodox Jew asking the way to a casbah.

Although our approach to London airport usually begins at six or seven thousand feet because of the wealth of departing traffic, typically in the UK it will commence at half the height, as most of the country is comparatively low lying. In places with mountains, like at Cali, the arrival procedure might begin at more than fifteen thousand feet. This is when it pays to remember to reset those altimeters from the *standard pressure setting*, which separated us from other aeroplanes, to the QNH or *local pressure setting*, which keeps us clear of the mountains by comparing our height to those on the map.

The highest altitude at which I was cleared for commencing an approach to the airfield was at sixteen thousand feet on the way to Santiago in Spain. One reason they did this was to pass over responsibility for the remainder of the flight. In Spain until recently they taught French in schools instead of English. Many people in the south speak no English at all and I travelled here once with a small black suitcase and was often mistaken for a Mormon and kept at a healthy distance. I bumped into a guy with a beard who was the son of the magistrate in Seville and spoke French. We were then able over a beer to conduct one of those conversations interrupted by spells when you have not a clue what some or other phrase means. I was distracted by a beautiful girl sat upon the knee of her beau and singing like a canary, as they do in sunny places. Noticing my plight he said, *Elles ont seulement leures jambes.* If I have it right this meant that these girls had only their legs, to which a response might be *De temps en temps c'est assez.*

This initial approach altitude, known as the *transition*, is where we reset our altimeters and commence the STAR or standard arrival that we briefed with reference to the plates. These instrument arrivals are often used in their entirety at airfields with little traffic, whereas in London they prefer to use the radar to interleave you with other aircraft and so maximise the flow. Like the standard departures, the STARs are really a fallback for places without radar, or places so quiet they do not use it much anyway. They create a nice orderly flow in the absence of supervision from the ground.

Many countries have military air bases that are underused and often they accommodate civilian traffic. They are usually well equipped with radar, as money was once no object. I remember when learning to fly I wore flying overalls with a kneepad the size of writing paper. One of the cadets used to cut a portion matching this size from the middle of larger maps each time he flew, like using toilet paper. If you read a book called *The Right Stuff*, you discover they had much the same attitude toward the fighter jets themselves. Youthful exuberance I guess.

To talk you through a *Bovingdon* arrival at London, which I have to fabricate to some extent as I do not have it before me, says you cross this beacon north of the airport at seven thousand feet. Then it directs you to route east and at seven miles beyond the beacon you should decelerate to 220 knots and descend to 3,500 ft, while turning right on an *intercept* heading to pick up the *localiser*. The reason I do not know it by rote is that Heathrow has a landing every minute and normally you are directed by the controllers onto the final approach track. To pick up on some terms, an *intercept* is a track toward a pre-determined route inbound to the runway, the way a slip road intersects the main carriageway of a motorway. The *localiser* we intercept here is a component of the ILS or *Instrument Landing System*: remember those radio ranges, the beams that told you to steer a left or right to stay on track? This is one of these, except very accurate. The Germans transmitted similar beams toward London, so bombers could follow them. Another aspect of the ILS is it has a vertical corollary called the *glideslope*, which guides you down a virtual incline toward the runway at the same time.

All this was only developed because it automated a process that used to be carried out by radar *approach controllers*, who talked you down in the same way. ILS equipment is expensive, especially if used to guide you down to landings in fog. On the other hand it involves no training costs and has no sick days, so expect more of it. Radar approaches are still used from place to place, or from time to time. As the controllers do not get to do practice often at places like Heathrow, to stay in shape they might ask you to be a guinea pig during some arrivals. Then all the way in, they are going:

> *Descend now to three thousand feet and make the heading 255, closing from the right, heading 275 on final approach track...drifting left make the heading 280...continue descent to two thousand feet...correcting nicely...check your gear and minima...on centreline, heading 280...service terminates and contact tower now on 118.70 and thank you very much.*

And you thank them very much too, for a job well done. This might have taken you to within two miles of the runway (more expensive radars take you much closer), by which time you hope to have broken cloud, during a stable descent down to what the controller referred to here as your *minima*. This is the lowest altitude by which you must have seen the runway to continue visually, without it being dangerous to do so. The exact height above the airfield at which this minimum altitude is set will vary with the quality of the equipment, or whether the flight crew and controller are qualified for the most accurate types of approach. (Basically the more accurate types of approach will allow descent to within a hundred feet or less of the surface.) The equipment on the aircraft and on the ground have to be up to the job and if it is really foggy, the aeroplane needs two of everything, even two working wipers. Nobody takes any chances with landing several hundred tons of aeroplane like this, when you are hardly able to see anything, so every aspect is examined minutely, even down to the topography of the surrounding area. The limit on planning permission for commercial building in the city of London is a thousand feet as a result of strictures imposed by the CAA.

The minima for each of these types of approach appear in the aerodrome plates along with all other pertinent data. At bigger airports there are so many types of approach or runway available that for flight planning they are considered to be separate airfields. We may look at the impact this has on *fuel policy*, what happens if you are fast running out of fuel, in the next chapter. I am making no promises. The reason incidentally they have to publish legal minima to say how far you go without seeing the runway is because there is little time to react and straighten up for landing. As you drop out the cloud you might mistake something else for either the runway or even the airport itself.

In a celebrated case a BA 747 captain coming down in fog mistook the urban lighting along the perimeter road for those of the runway at Heathrow. This is a lot easier to do than it sounds. During the recovery or *go-around*, the undercarriage came within thirty-five feet of hotels on this road and the moral of the story is do not build next to a runway. Often houses are built around airfields that have existed for nearly a century; in a while residents complain about the noise the way they complain of damp when living on flood plains. Conversely at Liverpool Airport taxiways had to route around a Tudor mansion dating back to the time of Henry VIII. The guide here told me how once, as an aeroplane passed by, over its noise one of the tourists had said, You'd have thought they'd have built the place further from the airport.

There was a predictable amount of huffing and puffing from British Airways themselves over this incident and from what I recall, the co-pilot had been under par with a stomach complaint, while relatives had joined them on the flight deck, which the airline will insist was a distraction. At the inquiry however if you said your first officer was sick, the airline would say the flight should have been cancelled, though were you actually to call and cancel it, the reaction of the company is entirely predictable. We saw how dangerous it is to take off in snow and many of the charter airlines fly 'Santa' trips to Finland. The crew of one 757 here discovered after more snow had fallen they had no data for take-off, but were 'persuaded' by the chief pilot to do so anyway. I have heard of cases in which pilots have been suborned in the same way even by the chief executive himself. This is the one time the big man will ever deign to talk to you, so consider it a privilege. In the case of the BA captain his defence was he should not be apprehended for practices going on routinely in airlines, which they are happy with so long as it suits them. He pleaded a genuine error in a pursuit in which error is unavoidable, while recovering the situation with only egos sustaining damage. The union recommended he resign despite taking his money and eventually one day he sat in the car and gassed himself. I do not hesitate to record the story and provide the hearing he was due.

Beside radar talkdowns and the ILS, other types of approach involve use of navigation beacons like the VOR and the NDB, which we mentioned in connection with marking out airways. As they provide less information and are inherently less accurate, they are more dangerous for approaches. Or perhaps less safe, in the way burgers are not disgusting but merely less delectable. If you use a restaurant, you might want to know whether it has a Michelin star. ILS systems have one and places with approach radars are mentioned too, along with selected VOR approaches, but airfields with an NDB are what the motorway cafe is to a great night out.

Let me clarify. You will remember how the NDB aerial produces a simple radio signal (for which reason it was called a *homing beacon*), interpreted from the flight deck by a pointer on a dial? Well this cannot only be used to guide you blindly toward the airfield, but also roughly in the same direction as the runway itself. It is no good breaking out of cloud to be confronted by a runway in the wrong direction. Now with the needle at top of the dial we are headed for the airfield, so if the landing direction is westward then we have to home in on the airfield from due east, with the needle still in the twelve o'clock position on the dial. We use the *clock code* when flying as it helps describe where things are, like other aeroplanes viewed from the flight deck. For example, air traffic might say you have traffic at ten o'clock. This means they see a blob getting close to yours and try to imagine how it would look from where you are sat. Then the crew both swivel to the left for a look, unless one is not entirely awake and looks to the right instead.

All this is like listening for the direction of the airfield and turning to approach it, the way you locate a dog in the woods. I have heard of cases where pilots have been stranded in cloud above the remotest airfield in Greenland, without a beacon to help them down, so the tower controller has gone out with his microphone and listened in the silence to where the aeroplane seemed to be coming from and talked it in like a shepherd. This is as intimate as it gets between a pilot and controller. That said I worked with a pilot married to a girl in the tower at Heathrow. There is an intersection with the runway you were occasionally offered for take-off enabling you to skip the queue, though to ask would be an imposition. I goaded this pilot if his wife was on frequency, by threatening to say, Jonathon wonders if he might use Block 79 for take-off, please?

In the very early days of aviation you had nothing but a compass, map and stopwatch, so you would have felt that NDBs or *non-directional beacons* (so called because you could home in from anywhere) were like the latest in video mobile technology. You might even want a dial with a coloured background that personified your lifestyle, unless you crashed and had no lifestyle of any kind. Pointing an airliner with a wobbly needle while descending into mountains in a thunderstorm is about as sensible as a hedgehog crossing the motorway. After anguished heart-searching the CAA finally omitted it from skills checks, firstly for the 747 and then for other types of aircraft. During these flights in the simulator they also wanted it done with an engine failed. I used to ask them if they wanted a Spanish omellete served at the same time.

The older trainers like to see it done, in the way they would still like children sent up chimneys. This casts them in a poor light, but in my own experience they have rather more integrity than many of the 'modernisers', while at the same time being more open to new developments. The thing about *non-precision* approaches is they will always lead to messy situations and within the last three years an aircraft arriving at Zurich was told not to use the main runway or its ILS, as at night it contravened environmental bye-laws. Despite the snowstorm in progress they were offered an older VOR approach to another runway, during the course of which they impacted a hillside and killed all on board. This is their swan song. As to the environmental aspect (and this means the audible impact), there is nothing so environmentally unfriendly as an airliner crashing in your back yard.

This particular approach, using a VOR beacon, is itself a step up from the NDB, because replacing the wavering needle is a more solid *beam bar*, which accurately represents whether you are drifting off a predetermined track toward the runway. In the Boeings the autopilot will lock onto this beam by itself, like with the ILS, leaving you to watch its progress as a casual observer. The Airbus requires constant intervention to maintain the track, which was a backward step. You could never find a trainer to admit this; in the way you will not persuade the man with a Mercedes the Porsche has a better chassis.

This touches upon the two singular failures of non-precision approaches, using either an NDB or VOR, in that they are adversely affected by the wind, which more easily blows aircraft and pilot off course, while at the same time they include no vertical component, the radio beam that guides you down an imaginary slope. Consider too that you ideally need guidance all the way to the runway, so the antenna needs to be thereabouts. Were it located elsewhere on the airfield like these navigation beacons, then aircraft can never be truly aligned with the runway. With the ILS, the radio antenna is in your face at the end of the runway and the glide signal, the vertical component, emanates from an aerial right alongside the runway where you touch down. Replacing beacons with the newer type of transmitter is sadly like any other safety initiative: nobody wants to foot the bill and the politicians are content with ritual hand-wringing.

Much the same could be said about security and it is during the approach that aircraft are most at risk to current threats, as they are flying a steady trajectory down a three degree slope, about as low and as slow as they ever get. The most recent attempt to bring down an airliner was the Israeli Boeing 757 fired upon while taking off from a resort in Africa. As we have seen from the CLIMB chapter, at this point the aircraft is accelerating toward high speed, while pursuing a trajectory that is as steep as possible. As we have seen, departures are also randomised by the intervention of controllers. In contrast, arriving aircraft are *vectored* or guided onto a long and straight approach, between ten or twelve miles out and beginning around 3,000 ft. If you wanted to organize a turkey shoot you could do no better. This is the fault of no one agency, but merely happens to be the way aeroplanes and airports have evolved. What to do?

You might think carriers themselves would provide insights like these. They eventually filter down to their employees, but do not hold your breath. The only things that move quickly in aviation are the aircraft. After 9/11 the radar controllers were obliged to *offset* the instrument approach into London, so instead of beginning out there on the localiser beam south of Canary Wharf, where the high-rise buildings are, they ran you parallel for a mile or two before intercepting the track to the runway. Pilots do it themselves anyway if they are lined up with one runway and wish to sidestep to another. I do not know who sat down with whom to come up with a game plan like this, but what normally happens on these occasions is the people on one side of the table imagine they are so important they cannot take 'no' for an answer. Then officials from both sides congratulate each other upon the solution, normally over a buffet. Nobody will have dreamed of consulting either a pilot or controller and if they do, the hunt is on for the three stooges.

If I could put that into perspective, the perpetrators of 9/11 chose Boeings, because these are simpler to fly and for this reason a likely target. They form the bulk of the global fleet and as an older and more established type, they are to the Airbus what a typewriter is to a word processor. This is from the view that for anyone with any form of training, what to do and just how to do it is more immediately obvious. I omit here the magnificent 777, also a part of a newer *generation* of aircraft, though even this has a steering wheel that anybody with a car would recognise. The Airbus has a side-stick, more like that of a PC, used for pointing the aeroplane instead. I like to think the thrust levers are not nearly so intuitive.

The aircraft that took out the Twin Towers would have been travelling, or they certainly sounded like it, at maybe four hundred miles an hour. This is a mile every ten seconds, so the offset into

London after the attacks would have delayed the eventuality by just twenty seconds. I guess all they did was simply draw the *extended centreline* of the runway and say, Oh, it's too near the city. If I can draw a picture in your minds of the solution, it was like hitting a moose in your car not dead centre, but six inches off. I considered pointing this out at the time, but things soon reverted to normal anyway. From what I hear on the airport bus (and the man on the Clapham omnibus is supposed to be an indication of public opinion in the UK) while the locked-door initiative was driven hardest by the United States, this is where the rules are most frequently violated.

This comes as no great surprise, as railways over there were decimated long before they were in Europe, so that society was adapted to the aeroplane a generation earlier. This means there is a preponderance of airline employees moving around the country needing the *jump seat.* In this environment, regulations are harder to enforce. The jump seat is what Leonardo di Caprio used in *Catch me if you Can*, the telling film in which a real-life fraudster posed for months on end as an employee of Panam, with nobody noticing. As with many of these things, the immediate response to 9/11 was to overrate the magnitude of the threat. Given any form of external threat, particularly attended by surprise, people are supposed to overestimate the risk of a recurrence by a factor of ten to one. In other words if you are hit by a car, you spend the next year overcompensating for the repeat match. As a teenager I was stood once on the pavement waiting to cross the road, when a disabled driver mounted the pavement and threw me at the wall with a blow a quarterback would be proud of. Since then I always keep a good nine yards from those mobility shoppers.

I am not going to delve deeply here, for you knew anyway that politicians have to be seen to be doing something, in order to be elected. What was refreshing about the response in the USA was agencies had the common sense to invite solutions from anybody, which is what their adversaries had been doing anyway. The nature of modern conflict is such that in aviation, as in every other sphere, we live in a wired world. A French cleric put it well. He said to begin with there were no networks at all and then they appeared progressively in the form of railways, highways, communication cables and eventually *radiotelephony*. He wrote this before the web and mobiles added layer upon layer. We are clothing the world in human consciousness and recent research into near-death experiences have proven minds continue sentient after brain activity has ceased, raising the possibility the mind exists independently, like music is distinct from the radio. The Buddhist scholar Alan Watts claimed human history itself had a life cycle, so the horrors of the Middle Ages were like the phase when kids pull legs off spiders.

Ultimately the way this is trending is security can only be assured by a Borg-like social mentality. The *Borg* is an entity in Star Trek comprising a community of individuals all cognisant of each other. This is what termites are like and it is the reason they are able to respond to external threats effectively, while building fabulous structures, but not always airports. There is a whole science surrounding the notion individuals create something larger than themselves once they interact in accordance to rules, like in a Mexican Wave. Who started that anyway?

The practical implications of this is that there has to be a more intelligent approach to discerning who is a threat to the common good, beside simple external appearances. When I worked in a branch of an American bank with an eclectic workforce, it struck me for example that people from Hong Kong were more English than the English, if that appears to make any sense. Not long after the fall of the Twin Towers, upon arrival at Milan I was informed a passenger had a particular need to retain his luggage, so that it would not pass through the customary channels like the remaining checked-in baggage. After all of the other passengers had boarded I descended the steps to do a little personal profiling. I was hoping for a retired bridge player from Iceland, so as to get away quickly, but what I got was a young and athletic man of Middle Eastern appearance sporting a beard, whose name was listed as Mohamed. And he especially wanted to see that large suitcase loaded.

Actually he would have fitted the description of almost anyone in London and I think he appreciated the irony as much as I did. What he was saying was the last time through here the cigarettes and so forth he had purchased had not emerged from random searches and this is half the problem: many of these airports are removing these goods for the safety of the travelling public and smoking them for the same good cause. The airport at London earned the nickname 'Thief Row' only after years in pursuit of the accolade. Once he boarded I opened the bag and there it was as he suggested, cigarettes, Walkman, mobile. I put it all in the rear hold anyway where I imagined it doing less damage. Never say never.

What I might suggest to trainers is instead of wheeling out videos of the last war, they ask why pilots know more about missiles from the news than from the company. Employees are prone to forget what the word 'company' means after all: a company of individuals associated with a common financial aim. Unfortunately it is those in companies longest who tend to assume ownership and disregard ideas from elsewhere, which is why inevitably they sink like the Titanic with all on board. There are exceptions. *General Electric*, the company Edison founded, is still intact a century on and making the most powerful of jet engines. (The name gives away its beginnings, but it was Tesla and not Edison who invented the means to power our world.)

Which brings us back to flying. One way the industry is trying to improve the uniformity of performance during the approach phase, so as to avoid accidents, is to use information on every aspect of each flight. As aircraft have become more computerised, not only are they able to upload software to alter how they fly, or the appearance of screens, they can also download digital data relating to specific events. These include the settings of most of the mechanical controls, along with sensory data from the instruments on the trajectory of the aeroplane at any moment. This is separate from the CVR, a voice recorder operated by a microphone on the flight deck. Along with other tapes this is included in the *black box*, which is actually orange to stand out, but it is called a black box because this is the scientific term for a self-contained part of a larger process. Your computer is effectively a black box: you know what goes into it and what come out of it, without needing to know what happens in the middle. The aeroplane black box is usually situated behind the rear baggage compartment, considered the place likely to sustain the least damage and fire.

Where best to sit as a passenger varies a lot. The 737 that crashed at Kegworth suffered high impact forces, which bent the forward and rear sections. As there was no ignition, the best place (if there can be such a thing) was in the middle by the wings, where the cabin was strongest. If the aeroplane catches fire, which they normally do, this is the worst place to be sat. The 747 that struck a mountain in Japan killed all but two or three at the very back, which is kind of logical. On other occasions people at the front are best off, because often the nose ruptures from the cabin and they get to step off ahead of all the mayhem. All I ever knew was I wanted no accident at all, because unlike autos whose dashboards were smoothed out years ago, airliners have plenty to embed in your skull. This is also true of the Airbus, with a flight deck laid out by Porsche. No airbags here.

Increasingly what is used to record each parameter is not a tape at all but a memory chip. I used to work for Wang Computer and the great professor Wang made his money not only from word processors, but also from *core memory*. People forget this, except those like Bill Gates, but in the first days of computing they used all sorts of things to record the *zeroes* or *ones* that make up digital data of any kind. Among the earliest and most successful was this core memory, comprising tiny doughnut-shaped magnets that were threaded with especially fine wire, exclusively by women, who proved more dexterous. Should you run a current through these cores in one direction they were magnetically polarised one way and if the current was reversed, it was polarised another way. Each then recorded a zero or one. The problem was if you ran another current to sense this polarity, you obliterated it anyway. This was a problem like Schrödinger's Cat. What this meant was uncertain itself, but I think he was saying we could never discover if the cat was asleep in the box because taking a look always awakened it. He should meet our cat.

Professor Wang's brilliant insight, which nobody else had spotted, was that this did not matter, because once you had the information and it was lost to the core, you could store it for half a second and then write it back. This is like you telling me a phone number: if you forget it, this does not matter because I read it straight back to you. The advantage of this form of memory was it was *non-volatile* and if you turned the power off, the memory was retained. As a result it was selected for the Space Shuttle, because if it ever crashed, then they might have an idea why. For all I know it is still there. Mr Wang is dead now, but while he was alive he had an email address and encouraged people to mail him. Out of deference to his technical objectivity and powers of original thought, I sent him one to say his voicemail product was crap and no one used it. This elicited a response from his PA, who said she did not anticipate a reply from Mr Wang. What she meant to say was she read my email and under no circumstances would she even consider showing it to the old man. I do not think I blame her; there were fewer defibrillators around in those days.

The best chief executives I have met have been open to insults of any kind. In my secret role as an inventor and having invented a full motion simulator (in the form of a large sphere which levitated on a cushion of air), I once visited a computer gaming exhibition. This was better than Blackpool Funhouse until someone rumbled I was a pilot and not a games developer at all. Before ejection, by which time I had managed to imbibe much complimentary champagne, compromising my performance on many rides, I met Blair Parkin. He ran a firm called *Trimension*, which was spun off from the simulator industry. They provide the projection systems you see in huge spherical cinemas at theme parks. Having sent him an outline of my putative design, I found him quite encouraging. He pointed out most industry-changing ideas come from outside. I like these sorts of people as they endorse a lifetime of uselessness on my part.

Before we leave off the approach, let's talk CFIT. This is the acronym for *Controlled Flight Into Terrain*, which for the public means flying into the side of a mountain, but with a certain style. Whether this is any consolation for the passengers I do not know. Nobody up there is holding scorecards. What it means is the flight crew were not where they thought they where. You would have thought they could never imagine they were about to collide with the ground, but unfortunately they often realise this, but too late. The foremost expert on deciphering the contents of CVR tapes is on record as saying the final imprecation he hears most often is 'Shit', said without fear or much conviction, but just the recognition they lost the game. For a pilot, this is all death in flight means and if you ride around mountains at high speed for a living, it literally comes with the territory. It is a game you must believe you can play. I have known captains toward the end of their careers confront the responsibility that faces them each day and decide they no longer like it, but hope to eke out until retirement. I have known others who after a lifetime of hairstyles adjusted to the demands of authority grow one down to their waist.

CFIT is gradually being eliminated by ground proximity systems, but given your speed in an airliner you only ever have a rough idea where you are in relative terms and terrain is never far away. The GPWS or *ground proximity warning system* is a radio antenna on the belly of the aircraft, which acts like a pinger in a submarine, firing off signals and listening for how long they take to bounce back from the ground. If it encounters terra firma suddenly, or occasionally when it detects another aeroplane passing briefly beneath you, the system shouts urgent homilies through the flight deck speaker:

> *Whoop Whoop! Pull Up! Whoop Whoop! Pull Up!*

Audio warning systems generally come with an American accent, which I quite like, because it makes you feel like a bit part in *Thunderbirds*. One South American crew were paying more attention to a football match they had tuned into when this alert went off, whereupon one of the pilots could be heard saying, Shut Up, Gringo! The final score was about ninety-nil to the mountain.

In automobiles, manufacturers have introduced the soothing tones of a woman, which is about as far as they got in treating women equally. Female voices have also been used for warnings in fighter jets. Different aircraft in the same fleet often have different *avionics* systems, which is an abbreviated way of saying aviation electronics. As a result you could never quite be sure how the aeroplane was going to sound until it started talking to you, which was quite nice in a way, like anticipating the first words of a child. There was the American guy, the British one who sounded like he ought to be on public broadcast radio programmes and another that sounded like Mervyn the Paranoid Android.

One more voice alert might tell you the aeroplane was sinking beneath the glideslope during an ILS approach (an uninspired *Glideslope! Glideslope!*), while others in the repertoire asked you not to sink after take-off (the equally unimaginative *Don't sink!*). Then there was a whole liturgy relating to why the aircraft was closer to the ground than it ought to be. If everything on the approach had gone as well as expected, however, the first we got to hear from any of these people was a warning at 2,500 ft above ground:

Two thousand, five hundred.

And then one hundred feet above our *minima* for landing:

One hundred above.

And then a point as low as twenty five feet above the runway when we had to decide whether we were landing or not, because it was happening in two seconds anyway:

Minimums! Minimums!

I really had to think to remember exactly how that alert went, not least because it varies from one aeroplane system to another. I think though the main reason was because it was always at this point in the aeroplane that your attention was so rapt as for you hardly to notice what was said, beside an unconscious recognition of its portent.

The aeroplane also provides height readout to help you put it on the ground:

Fifty... Forty... Thirty... Ten.

And if you screwed up the landing and floated:

Fifty... Forty... Thirty... Ten... Five.

It said that 'five' in a fairly pointed way. It would also shout *Retard! Retard!* at you, which was no reflection on your cognitive abilities, but a reminder to close the thrust levers. These utterances were made in an electronically accented voice like that of Stephen Hawking, which gets endearing after a while. Although Professor Hawking was offered an upgrade, he claimed people were so used to him sounding like the speaking clock that we all quite liked it. This is quite true and now whatever else the developers call it, we shall know it as the *Stephen Hawking* voice. He should have it trade-marked.

Computers at airports do something similar. There is a radio frequency they have you tune into called the ATIS, the *Aerodrome Terminal Information Service*, which is what you and I call a tape recorder. What it does is read out the weather and the runway in use over the radio, so pilots know in advance. It is a strange coincidence in aviation that the range at which you receive the ATIS coincides with the point in descent when you are busiest. This is also the time you will be informed a passenger refuses to emerge from the toilet. I have known them to lie down in the centre aisle, for reasons buried deep in their psyche.

Nowadays they also relay terminal data by satellite, which solves the problem. Modern ATIS systems also allow the tower to type this information into a computer, which reads it out. It is usually updated every half hour and at Heathrow is consistently late. Each successive batch of information is given a name so pilots do not mix it up, such as *Information Bravo* and then *Information Charlie*. At Christmas in London they give it festive names like 'Information Reindeer' and then onto 'Santa'. It gets that desperate. Sometimes people get to fancy each other just from listening on the radio. During a visit to the tower in London, Caroline _____ happened to call up and I could not help but notice them swoon at the sound of her voice. You come to recognise that of controllers too, like you do radio celebrities. Like with these celebrities, if you saw them they looked nothing like you imagined.

The transfer of data to synthesised audio has some peculiarities abroad, where the English is not quite idiomatic. Broadcasts in France speak of things like 'Few Cloudy', which they are too proud now to consider altering. The best was reportedly in Madrid, where crews arrived to find a robotic ATIS adding the following advice to the weather:

Caution, air traffic controllers on the job.............training.

I was going to tell you how they enhanced that GPWS system, the pinger. To such an extent they called it EGPWS. You guessed it! The *Enhanced Ground Proximity Warning System.* This really belongs to the navigation computer, because it contains a database of the territory you are flying over and projects it as a background shade on the navigation display, the screen showing your route. If that purple line with the aeroplane icon steers off the fairway into something red, this is a thunderstorm or a mountain. Either way this is no good. Whereas the weather picture sweeps from side to side like a wiper, by the way, terrain sweeps from the centre. Databases of terrain are not foolproof. Not many hills get altered over the years, but they do put up the odd concrete tower or steel mast from time to time and these can run to a thousand feet or more. Such information was developed for things like cruise missiles, which compare what they see on video to the knowledge they have stored in memory, confirming they are headed in the right direction. Airliners are similar except they are supposed to miss the target instead of hitting it.

That is about all we see of the approach. For passengers with a window it might be terror or inspiration, but I used many of these approaches to see what went on below in London: flowers at Kensington for Lady Diana, the lights of Piccadilly, a home match for Chelsea, new offices for the mayor, smoke from the collision at Ladbroke Grove, the fireworks on Clapham Common, but most remarkable by far, the soft transparency of a million points of light, in a city wakening to the gentle flux of dawn.

LANDING

It seems appropriate before we touch down and wind down shortly afterward, to review some of the aircraft systems that have developed, making the machine what it is now. There is something almost sexual about the concentration a pilot releases after landing, during the *roll-out*, when we coast to a halt, especially after the perfect *touchdown*. And the final touchdown of the day is going to be good whichever way you look at it, because it means we are going home. In the first airline I joined, before we packed up and also closed up for the night and took a cab to the hotel, there would be a 'landing drink'. We would raid the galley for a scotch and soda and reflect there for a moment on surviving another day. Not so much surviving flight as surviving life. Any of you could do this, even within the confines of your own home, by just finding yourself a suitable space. At the latest of the airlines for which I worked and which I hoped was my last, one captain took a glass of wine at the end of one flight and then got into trouble out of all proportion to any possible satisfaction the victuals provided.

I shall keep this analysis simple. When they decoded the human genome, they discovered it comprised as few as thirty thousand elements, when they were expecting many more. This is the number of instructions to determine quite what we are and they compared the number to the constituent parts of a typical airliner. The paper I read actually depicted an Airbus 320 in this connection, the last aeroplane I flew, back then in February of this year. It is true to say it has thirty thousand components, discrete elements with a form and function, but it is made of rather more if you take their constituents apart as well. It has around three million separate electrical contacts that are each plated in gold, so in many ways the modern airliner is like a precious jewel, a flying Faberge egg. All of that craft containing all of that craftsmanship and so many soon end up in the desert, where they sit out the recession like wallflowers, their beauty slowly fading as the fashion slowly evolves toward newer and more captivating models.

Take the word itself, *airplane* in American English and *aeroplane* otherwise. I have used the first of these only in the North American edition, for it is an ugly word which nonetheless evades the spell-checker. Anybody ever stopped to analyse the role of spellcheckers in cultural hegemony? Before we look at either word, what we are about here as passengers is the *airliner* ~ where did that expression come from anyway? Against my better judgment I left off for a moment to check this in the built-in dictionary here on the computer, only because it does not involve standing up. Although this marvellous software will tell you anything you want to know about the etymology of the sea cucumber, it merely lists the airliner as 'a large passenger aeroplane'. Brilliant. I cannot imagine anybody out there knowing that one.

Where I am struggling without the twenty-five volumes of the Oxford English Dictionary here in front of me is in deciding whether the term originates from the railways or the oceans. We are prone to forget the railways long pre-dated roads as the most reliable means of transport. In England railtracks were known as the *permanent way*, which begs the question of what happened to roads from time to time. Probably the answer was weather-related, as you do not need much in the way of cold and wet to make early roads impassable, especially after the churning of hoof and rim. There were parts of the country especially favoured in this way, like say the chalk downs that were both firm and well-drained. Otherwise you were into that game the Romans pioneered involving lots of carefully hewn stones piled one on another. The English never took to this and rightly perceived it was a lot of work for few benefits, like a weekend in Edinburgh. It was worth waiting for the railway for that sort of thing. People like me with no special role at work are simply known as *line pilots* and proud of it. Whether this related to a line across the ocean drawn upon a map, or whether it originates from the first permanent lines across country from A to B, those of the railways, none of us will ever know.

You would have thought operating this *aeroplane* in air was a given, though they also discovered it created lift in water and in these conditions they called it a *hydroplane*. Water is eight hundred times denser than air and these wings need only be eight hundred times smaller to support the same weight. Smaller in terms of overall area like a carpet, because it is the total extent of the wing that governs the quantity of lift available. The best demonstration of the hydroplane is a shark or dolphin. Each has a pair of fins to either side, while the dolphin has a tailplane, unlike the upright fin of the shark. Fish like those in your aquarium contain a bladder sac, which they squeeze to make themselves denser than the surrounding water, so that they sink. Anyone who has seen dolphins after a school of tuna will realise this may not nearly be quick enough and they use their fins instead as hydroplanes, twisting them to produce powerful lift forces to help them duck and dive. Bear in mind lift can be applied as either an upward or downward force.

All aeroplanes are designed nose heavy, so if the wings stall and lose their lift, the aircraft drops like a paper dart and gathers flying speed again. The only thing to stop it nosing down like this during the course of normal flight is the *tailplane*, which pushes down like a kid on the other end of the seesaw. If ever you board a jetliner by the rear stairs, take a look at it. Whereas the big wing, the *mainplane*, is curved on top and flatter beneath, the tailplane is flatter on top, especially at the front. They work in different directions.

The classical formula for lift is **half** x *Rho* x *V* **squared**, from what I recall. The Greek letter in the middle was I think the density of the surrounding atmosphere, though the thing to note is the *V* **squared** bit which says that lift increases out of proportion to speed. When Richard Noble developed the Thrust SST, the car that broke the sound barrier, they calculated if the nose lifted a little too much, it would suddenly develop an upward force, a hammer blow seventy times stronger than the force of gravity. Do you remember gravity? That was the force that, if you fell from a thirty-two foot ladder, would pull you to the ground in about a second. If you see anyone about to fall from a ladder, get that stopwatch ready.

That is all the equations we get to look at and even this one is probably wrong. People who do pure mathematics claim equations have an inner beauty, but from where I stand they are as ugly as a bare ass. When British Airways updated their corporate image and lost a lot of money painting their tails in ethnic art from places nobody could recognise, the tower controllers complained they could not tell which aeroplane was which. At night they rely on a pair of binoculars and the *logo light* that all aircraft have to illuminate the tailfin. Once while we were waiting to line up for take-off, the controller testily said, Follow the BA, I don't know what the motif is supposed to be. Their pilot replied he thought it was aboriginal art, whereas I told them it looked like Jackson Pollock's.

The *plane* is then simply a flat place, so the wing is literally a flat place that gives you a lift, like Amsterdam. Wings are nothing special and if you fitted hand grabs to a piece of hardboard (most DIYers use eight by four) and run down a slope, you could probably do something respectable. This is what Sir George Cayley had in mind, though he used his carriage driver to do the flying and after a while, the carriage driver left his employment. Next up was a mad German aristocrat whose name escapes me (Lilienthal, you idiot) who ran down hills with a giant pair of batwings. His last words were, Sacrifices have to be made. If you need last words in this business, make sure they belong to somebody else.

The Wright brothers noticed like everybody else that lift itself was not a problem. It was more a question of directing it. The weight of the aeroplane once supported only by air, which is very slippery stuff like oil, literally wants to slide off the side of it. The closest analogy I can give you is a floor tile with a rubber ball on top. It is going to need constant corrective action to stay put. You can improve things by dishing the tile slightly in the middle and you can do much the same with aeroplanes, but any aeroplane without a means of correction is eventually going to crash. Which all of them did until the Wright Flyer.

You can go to any country in the world and they will claim to have invented the aeroplane and Edison used to say the thing you could guarantee after developing any product were the people who claimed to have had the same idea. The work of those like Pearse in New Zealand and Pilcher in the UK are emblematic of those whose efforts were stymied either by a lack of resource or by accidental death. Inventions are each a testament to general endeavour, but in the end the prize belongs to those who demonstrate the practical reality, who persuade others to get off their backsides and try it themselves. This prize belongs to Orville and Wilbur. They were a unique augur of the twentieth century in developing a germinal idea from teamwork, like Madame Curie and her husband, or Watson and Crick. This itself was a new idea, a quantum leap in the application of human intelligence.

The way these ideas are manifest in the modern aeroplane is itself a cooperative venture, like the cathedrals of Europe. Aeroplanes are stunning in their complexity, the richness of their being, but as with these cathedrals this is only because they are a sum of parts each allocated to a guild of craftsmen and brought together only for final assembly. The layout of the aeroplane is almost ecclesiastical, almost parliamentary and this facet of flight was most brought home to me in bad flying conditions, when we are all on a pilgrim progress. Behind the cabin divider are the great unwashed, the latter day equivalent of the unread bucolic or journeyman traveller. Ahead of them occupying the sacristy are the great and the good, prelates and captains of industry, ministered unto by the cabin crew, who are themselves privileged cognoscenti with access to the higher courts. Among their number is the keyholder to the holy of holies, the inner temple, whose occupants communicate only indirectly with the laity by way of this mediation. Here at the foremost end of the building, dressed in their priestly robes and addressing formulaic incantations to distant oracles, or caressing the controls with seemly veneration, are the pilots who witness the manifest terrors of nature. They are here to propitiate the gods of thunder or those of the four winds; but above all to earn their paycheck.

Returning to more mundane matters, people had known all along that a set of tail feathers made things fly straight, after firing arrows at each other for centuries. All aeroplanes still have these feathers, but leave the bottom one off so that when the aeroplane *rotates* for take-off, nothing scrapes the ground. If you overdo this and pull too hard, the tail does scrape the ground. To meet the eventuality many have a skid beneath the tail, while Concorde has a tiny wheel. All new types of airliner have to demonstrate they can fly along the runway with their tail grinding the ground, yet still take off. In operational airliners this leaves an impressive trail of sparks, but also creates an impressive trail of paperwork. A scrape may puncture the fuselage like a burst tyre, so it cannot pressurise. The only warning in the flight deck this has happened on take-off or landing is the cabin crew, whose *aural alert* goes something like, Ere, did you hear that scraping sound?

We now have a pair of wings and a tailplane, the feathers, joined together by the *fuselage* or body. This used to be square because the people who first built them had been coachbuilders. They switched from wooden carriages to cars and aeroplanes when they saw the writing on the wall. The fuselage needed to be strong, as aeroplanes were dropped onto the runway from a great height by trainees, or by people who should know better. Even today I have known airline captains to put several backs out of joint. This usually means they have to take an empty aeroplane up with an instructor for a practice session. I have also known crews in the 'States so bored of the job that they put it down as hard as they dare. You will be relieved to hear this is rare, but pilots who misbehave because management upset them are not nearly so rare. I flew with a Mauritian pilot who told me crews would taxi around as slowly as possible to maximise overtime, or alternatively drive the aeroplane hard to waste its fuel. Others throttle right back in the air to capitalise on overtime. In the days when you took the northern route over the Atlantic because the *range* of aircraft was limited (the distance they flew without refuelling), some dropped into places like Iceland on a pretext, to stock up on salmon. Airlines pretend the behaviour is as about as likely as you making personal calls or using the colour copier for food recipes.

What really made square fuselages suffer apart from the landings was trying to pressurise them with air. My first commercial airliner was square-bodied and for this reason could not be pressurised in this way. It was known affectionately as the 'shed'. The very first metal airliner, the Junkers, was actually made out of corrugated aluminium, like the sides of a box. Corrugation is a feeble attempt at rounding structures off, like lots of ripples in place of one great curve, because the problem with square things under pressure is they bulge, which is okay for milk cartons but not for aeroplanes.

The piston engines on earlier airliners always needed to be some place cool, normally out front of the fuselage or wings. This is not an issue with jet engines, which are effectively immersed in their own source of cooling air. Imagine you are a jet engine, then the way I am going to keep you cool is to stand you up to your neck in water. Now pretend you are a piston engine, like in your car. There is no pond and instead I have to keep dowsing you with buckets. Obviously, jet engines were the way to go and the first pilots to use them in Germany, having been used to sitting behind a noise-factory, described the experience as being pushed along by an angel. One aviation writer said no pilot forgot their first flight in a jet. Mine was in a Citation, a basic aeroplane designed for the successful businessman with a licence. Instead of a deafening roar as you opened up on the runway, there was a muted rush of air, a subliminal whine and a thump, thump of wheels on the centre-line lights.

When I got to fly a large fleet of airliners, I could not help noticing during this *take-off roll* you could tell how new the airframe was. Newer ones with nice tight wheel-bearings and no loose joints rolled silently over the concrete, even at two hundred miles an hour. Older ones would bang and rattle, the vibrations accentuated by the fact the nosewheel was not far behind the flight deck. Hit the ground hard enough during landing and the *stanchion*, the nose-wheel stem, comes right through the cabin floor. (Passengers have surely been killed this way: they die every which way but loose. People also injure themselves in any way you can imagine. A medical student I knew once admitted a respectable spinster with a haddock up her private parts.)

When you do an external check of the aeroplane as the handling pilot, preferably before the aircraft gets airborne, it starts at the nose and runs clockwise, so I shall do that now. Take the forward doors for a start. I have known airliners pushed back in error with doors still open and the jetty attached. The results are unattractive, especially as the combination of aeroplane and jetty has a guillotining action. Moving along, the wings are filled with fuel, as this is about the only place left for it. Long-haul aeroplanes also use the tailplane, the wing at the back. Once they have done this they can pump it back and forth during the flight in order to keep the aeroplane balanced. In Concorde, the *flight engineer* or third crew-member spends a lot of time pumping fuel around like this.

The wing tip might have a *winglet* attached. This reduces drag slightly and saves on fuel consumption, which means aeroplanes travel further. Though what most makes aeroplanes travel further is how efficient engines have become. Your car engine is thirty per cent efficient at best. It spends most of its energy acting like a glorified heater, or producing lots of noise. Jet engines are the most *thermally efficient* machines around, well over forty per cent. Even this is not all it could be, which is why we have no oil left. At one point Boeing developed a stubby version of the jumbo jet, which seated fewer but went further, replacing passengers with fuel. In the meantime the latest engines made even the original version go further, leaving a number of operators with embarrassingly small 747s. This is the Boeing answer to the Betamax video recorder. Birds create the same effect as these winglets by the way, from fanning out their tip feathers. Nature always gets there first.

The undercarriage is interesting, as it derives from pit-props. The first jet airliner *type-rating* I studied for was at a building in Coalville in the county of Derbyshire. In front was a memorial to a dozen miners who died down a shaft on this spot. Among the most common questions you will be asked as a pilot is whether you intend to graduate to larger aeroplanes and also, how long the process takes. If you walk into a commercial school, in something over a year they can provide you with a *commercial licence* and *instrument rating*, which proves you can fly approaches without looking out the window. It takes around a further three months to fly a particular airliner. All this is as a co-pilot, more normally called a *first officer*.

Subsequently you fly in this role for a few years or more, convincing yourself you will make a better commander than half of those you accompany. Looks can deceive in this way. Larger aeroplanes with flights of longer duration include a *second officer*, a sort of flying tea-boy. They sit up front when there is little to do, like your dad used to sit you down with that plastic steering wheel on a rubber sucker. Only after a couple more thousand flying hours are you even qualified to command the aircraft as a *captain*, let alone experienced enough. Many airlines when you qualify as a commander take you off your current type and give you a smaller aeroplane to play with. It is not that bigger ones are any harder to fly, more the fact that crashing one is harder to hide from the press.

This rite of passage assumes there are the places available within the airline, that you are up to the job and you have the *seniority*. This considers any pilot to be as competent as the next, so promotion and demotion are determined by who joined when. It is an odd system that stems from locomotives having been operated by a fireman and a driver. Firemen themselves were recruited from among the cleaners. Those at the bottom of this pecking order could be relocated a dozen times in as many years. One thing certain was you were likely to work for the company for the next fifty years. In this context the nuances of who deserved what meant a great deal to qualified personnel. The same assumption in the airline industry hit the buffers when governments tried to prove their free-market credentials by weaning airlines off state aid. It does not matter if airlines are loss-making from the view of the unions, as they regard money as being there to make the world go-around and not to feather the nests of chief executives. They look as though they have a point. CEOs dislike pilots because they are stuck with them, like Mr Rochester with his lunatic wife in the east wing.

The other thing then is you do not graduate to larger airliners; it is like using a larger hire car. Pilots of long-haul airliners are on a higher salary scale and this again stems from the relationship with operating 'mainline' instead of 'branch line' locomotives. Long-haul crews claim they have more responsibility, or at least until short-haul pilots demonstrate they move more bums around on seats each day. (Terms like *mainline* are still used directly within the cloisters of many airlines and BA effectively operate a closed shop, in which membership of the British Airline Pilots Association is compulsory. It is not technically a closed shop as this is no longer legal: they just take the subscription money from you anyway.)

Back to Coalville and landing gear. Up the road there is a mining museum with many exhibits. Among these is a locomotive with no fire of its own, because of the flammable gas that so often pervaded coalmines. It was charged with steam at the beginning of the day, like a vacuum flask. Of more interest is the history of pit-props. You do not see how these could possibly lead to airliners, do you? I am not surprised, as the link is fairly tenuous. Among the earliest types of mine were those burrowed into valley sides, where ores were already exposed. Romans went for lead in this way. (I noticed from Pompeii that the columns of stones were stacked by boring a hole down each and filling it with lead to hold them like kebabs on a skewer.) With these mines they soon discovered the weight of earth above would bring the roof of the shaft down once they tunnelled out its contents.

A funny thing happened near Heathrow when they were extending the tube railway. They used a technique for tunnelling developed in Austria, which involved spraying the rock sides with concrete as you go along. This did not work in the loamy soils near the airport and instead caused an office to collapse down a hole one morning. As in, Miss Simkins, could you copy this pleeeeeeeeeeeeee. Much tunnelling is still going on around the airport in pursuit of the fifth terminal. One of my co-pilots had worked on the Channel Tunnel and because of the small world tunnelling is in Europe, this was to be his first line of defence in the event of redundancy Those loamy soils around Heathrow by the way: until recently you could see tractors planting lettuces around the airport perimeter. It was once host to the most fertile market gardens in England, the richness of the soils attributed to the fact it was among the best drained parts of London and had been used for centuries for the accumulation of both human and horse manures.

Originally then pit-props were used to hold the roof of mines in place. They were made of wood and so there had to be plenty of forest around. I believe some wood is better than others and I shall guess at ash. Putting the props in place (and removing them later) was not the easiest of tasks and the hammer often damaged the prop beyond repair, if it was not sodden already. Enter the hydraulic pit-prop, which could be manoeuvred into place and pumped up like the screw-jack which you fit your spare wheel with. These were manufactured and probably also invented by Dowty. They sold in huge numbers and then along came Mrs Thatcher and with a wave of her wand, Presto! the coalmines disappeared. Dowty looked around wondering what else apart from a weight of earth is awfully heavy and in need of support? Oh yes, the Boeing 747-400, aptly named, for it is four hundred tons of aeroplane regularly dropped from a great height. Dowty have since been taken over by the French equivalent to form Messier-Dowty. Originally aircraft suspension was made of loops of bungee cord around the axle supporting the wheels. For a while this worked.

Can we peer into those baggage holds for a moment? The fuselage has to be circular in order to contain the pressure and somehow we have to run the wings through its section. Wings have a cross-section of their own, a certain depth. Imagine they were leaves, then were they like those of a daffodil or aspidistra, they would be too floppy. I would say too thin, but they obviously do the job. The fleshier leaves of cacti are better, especially those with spiked tips which they cover with eggshells in Thailand. These are either curved or a little thicker and preferably both. This makes them rigid and this is how wings are constructed. Before this they flew biplanes, which are made rigid by stacking them and using bracing like *struts* or wires. Unfortunately this is messy and slows the aeroplane down. Airliners use internally-braced wings, which gives them cleaner lines.

The wings themselves used to be built around a *boxspar* like a girder that ran the width or *span* of both wings. The problem was it came straight through the cabin and one of the bugbears in flying a bomber used to be that walking between the cockpit and tail, you had to clamber over the thing. This would not go down well in business class, else the ticket would have to advise ladies to dress suitably, in trousers. Airliners also have long wings, the span of a 737 a hundred feet and a 747 twice that. There is no way you can transport such girders around the country. This is now the biggest stumbling block when it comes to building airliners. The Airbus is built by a European consortium of countries which are always arguing about who builds what. Eventually they are assembled in Toulouse in France, but they have to widen roadways or knock down railbridges and drive the parts around at dead of night, like Cornish smugglers. Either that, or they use a bloated aeroplane in which one fuselage can be fitted inside the other. Boeing carries out assembly inside a shed in Seattle that is supposed to be the largest covered structure in the world. What they also do nowadays is to use two separate wingspars, one for each wing. It is important if you build a pair of wings to ensure each is fitted to the correct side. Jet engines may have a blade like a sharkfin attached to one side or another, if testing showed they needed the air manipulated in some way or other around the wing. I have known 737s not to fly well and engineers to discover the fin was fitted to the wrong side of the engine. I imagined this to be feasible, as the engines look absolutely identical.

The two wings are bolted to either side of a *wingbox*, which sits beneath the cabin floor, between them. It also has structural depth to make it strong and if the wings are over-stressed, they will snap at the joint. Developing the 777, they put hydraulic jacks beneath the wing to bend it until failure and in this case it bent through thirty-five degrees before going BANG. Which is a nice coincidence, because in normal operation the wing tips of a 747 are designed to flex up and down throughout thirty-five feet. It is fun as a pilot to watch the wings flex and mine used to do this, but not nearly as much as those of bigger aeroplanes. These have longer cabins too, so that people at the back can see it twisting in flight, like a tube subjected to a giant Chinese burn.

I have seen stretched versions of aircraft undulate on the ground, sagging in parts as they hit the bumps. A reason for these stretches is that many new types of airliner are legacy models; in the way carmakers will introduce a new chassis or floor-pan and then exploit it shamelessly over ensuing years. The overwhelming reason for aeroplanes to develop in this way is their chassis is essentially the cross section of the cabin. This can be extended at any time by inserting *plugs*. Stretched versions are necessary to accommodate extra passengers on expanding routes or to adapt aeroplanes to a niche market. The Airbus 320 seats around two hundred and was stretched into the A321 to seat thirty more, but it was also shrunk twice to produce the A319 and A318, so as to address a market for regional and business jets respectively. Airliners of this type are used to shuttle executives for instance across the Atlantic, between the headquarters of Daimler and Chrysler.

The Boeing offering in this marketplace is the 737, which was introduced as a fairly small twinjet known as 'Fat Albert' back in 1968. It is still being stretched and internally redecorated thirty-five years later. A reason airlines welcome these developments is they do not have to retrain pilots. This is an enormous overhead and probably means they have to over-crew a fleet by ten percent, to account for time spent in the simulator or training on the line with passengers. While the appearance of such aircraft might change markedly in the cockpit, they remain the 'devil you know' when it comes to handling failures.

Passengers get unnecessarily scared when they see wings flex. Ever see newsreel of the Tacoma Straits Bridge? Metals are as elastic as rubber bands. Coat a ball bearing in soot, drop it on a tile and look at the footprint. The thing deforms like a tennis ball on impact but bounces straight back. I just read of a man in England who built the largest-ever ball of rubber bands, over sixty thousand of them. So many people asked him if it would bounce, he shipped it over and dropped it out of an aeroplane and onto the Arizona desert. It didn't. Instead it exploded like a bunker-buster and produced a nine-foot crater. The prairie dogs were most unhappy and called for UN intervention.

The wingbox is a useful space and is often used to contain fuel. In the 747 it is a whole room you can walk around inside and on one occasion, they found a wooden chair the engineer had used during a job and forgotten to remove. Tools get left all over the place on aeroplanes, not always as obviously as this. Forward or rear of this box is the *wheel-bay*, into which the main wheels are retracted, while there are also the baggage compartments. The wheel-bay can often be viewed through a spy-hole beneath the cabin carpet. You can use this to check the wheels are locked in place if the indicator on the flight deck says they are not. You do not want them collapsing on touchdown. Once after we took off we heard a bang, which I attributed to a pothole. If the same aeroplane operates on the same runway each day, it gets airborne around the same spot, which wears away the concrete. This put the heebie-jeebies up the passengers and indeed one had only recently survived a 747 running off the runway into Hong Kong bay. We thought we had best check we had not had a blowout and I was sent back to scrabble under the seats, seeking the viewer while assuring travellers it was entirely normal to see your co-pilot make love to the centre aisle. Tom Jones said to keep your hat on and I did.

The tyres on aeroplanes are very heavy, as I know from carrying spares. At times I would find we were hauling these without them appearing on the load-sheet and often people did not know where they had been left, much like your stapler. Those on Airbuses weigh around four hundred pounds, largely because the rubber is up to five inches thick. They are cross-ply as well, instead of the radial type on cars. This is good for sustaining the tremendous loads engendered by a heavy landing, but cornering is abysmal. On a wet runway if you make a quick exit via the *rapid exit turnoff*, sometimes you found if you turned the wheel or pushed the rudder pedals, you continued skidding in a straight line. The last time this happened to me was driving a truck full of turkey chicks across the Pennines at the dead of night. Whereas in a car on bends in the wet the steering stays intact and the back end goes, in a truck you turn the wheel and it has no visible effect upon your trajectory. Tell me in a single sentence what this word means.

The baggage holds used to be places you could climb into and if you ever find a disused aeroplane, some of those baggage bays have hatches into the flight deck or cabin. Pilots who are locked out often use this means of ingress. It also gives aeroplanes the feeling of being decked like a ship, which is great. The DC-10 had a crew rest area down among the baggage holds and to get there you used an elevator. How cool is that? Almost as cool as the spiral staircase in the 747; I always hoped to finish my career climbing that staircase. Bugger. The bags used to be thrown in any old how but now get preloaded into the unitary loading device, or ULD. When I studied for the Airbus I never remembered what half of these acronyms stood for, which younger guys found amusing. It was not so much the brain capacity; just that life was getting too short to give old dogs new names. I might say 'baggage bins' and irritate the trainers, or call the *Navigation Display* a television screen instead.

These loading devices are aluminium boxes that slide into the holds and are locked in place. As well as them there is usually a smaller baggage compartment for throwing late bags into all by themselves, which they call *rush bags*. These are the ones that will go to Bermuda by mistake. During my external check I might find a bag lodged in a corner that had been working its way around Europe all week. It is the old maritime practice creeping in again: the notion that carriers are doing you a favour by getting you there at all, let alone with your bags. The on-time policy of airlines dictates that you go whether or not cleaners, caterers or baggage arrive. I often thought, Great vacation ~ a week on the beach in Y-fronts waiting for a suitcase. During these debacles, when they knew baggage had been left behind, most flight deck kept their heads down and made no announcement, leaving passengers to spend the first afternoon of their vacation around the carousel. And why is it carousels everywhere have a tattered brown suitcase going around on them? Do they arrive each morning and say, Okay Charlie, pass the brown bag and let's get this thing rolling?

Now that I have mentioned incidental features like the rush bag compartment, I should also say that other minor features are added to aircraft once they are seen to be needed in practice. These might be fins here and there because the aircraft did not initially fly properly or recover like it ought to from the stall. If you look along the top surface of the wings, you might well see protrusions like shark teeth. These are called *vortex generators* and are there to stir up the air so it stays stuck to the wing. Otherwise if it took a vacation at this point, then those moving control surfaces you see behind them on the trailing edge find themselves in blank space, like we saw with supersonic shock waves. A way to view the stickiness of air is to look at a golf ball, which goes further with dimples. Otherwise the ball travels with an invisible tail behind it, which the air has yet to collapse into, having been pushed aside. This represents a suction force clawing it back. If you dimple the ball, it breaks up the closest air, the *boundary layer*, into spirals of turbulence with the motion and energy to go anywhere. The moment they feel drawn into this tail, they go there and reduce its effect.

Other features of aircraft added later have more to do with turbulent captains. A regional airliner I flew had sealed windows in the flight deck as its French designers had seen air-conditioned cinemas and gone the same way. It meant if you forgot to leave a copy of the load-sheet or needed a fuel receipt with engines running, there was no place for it to go. They then built a letterbox like a supersonic cat-flap in the side of the fuselage. In larger airlines you could heave the window back and rest your elbow there in order to look the business, as in 'Check out my wheels, Sister.' When you were not doing that you could lower paperwork to the ground and to meet this contingency some captains had a length of string. I used to fold the stuff into darts and wing it across the apron. Then I discovered as they retracted the concertina toward the air bridge, that you could screw the load-sheet into a ball and bounce it off the curve of the forward fuselage and into the goalmouth.

That about completes our tour of the externals, except for that noisy engine right inside the tail-cone, called the *auxiliary power unit* or APU. This is a small and self-contained jet engine designed to provide for power or conditioning on the ground. From time to time Boeing look at using it for extra thrust on take-off, without ever getting around to it. When cruise liners were in port before they set off, they had to get the kitchens and everything ready for that 'welcome on board' feeling and rather than plug a cable into the side (which you can do with an airliner) they ran the engines in *hotel mode*. Aeroplanes have many sockets underneath and would be ideal in a trailer park. You can connect warm air to one of these, from whence it goes into a recirculation bin where used conditioning air ends up. Airliners circulate a portion of air through filters besides drawing it from the engines, to meet airflow volumes required by the authorities during certification. If there is not a plug in the belly for connecting a conditioned supply at the gate (in case the weather is very hot or cold) then they can run a flexible pipe down the centre aisle called a *dragon*.

You can usually set the air drawn from engines to HIGH or LOW as well as OFF, in case the engine catches fire. It cannot stay off for long if you are cruising, because this source of air is needed to keep the cabin pressurised, so people can breathe. Consumer groups often accuse airlines of being stingy with the air supply but it does not really matter, for it is impossible to stop at least an element of circulation anyway. Beside which the filters are supposed to be especially effective. Passengers do complain they catch colds, but this is more likely because they are stressed by the whole experience and sat in the row ahead of the guy doing the snivelling.

The APU also supplies compressed air to start the engines. There are occasions pilots forget to start the APU at the gate, which is embarrassing when you turn that starter switch. Small jets have a starter like your car, as they are easily rotated, though for an engine weighing four tons an electrical motor would be too heavy itself. Instead we draw *bleed air* from the APU and pump it into a turbine, which spins the engine through a gearbox. If you wonder how a turbine works, try sucking down the tube of your vacuum cleaner, while your partner listens for the compressor inside spinning around by the force of air. Otherwise persuade your partner to do the dusty bit and then he can sue me instead. Early jets used by the RAF would have a ground supply of air for starting, and if there were problems then one technique was to start another aeroplane and direct its jet wash down the inlet. The APU can help in other ways, like providing air conditioning when you want more energy from the engines for a heavy take-off.

Before we leave the baggage story, let me tell you another of my favourites. I like this bit, when you all gather around my chair and Charlie toasts the marshmallows. Firstly let me preface it by saying that passengers have got wise to the baggage-left-in-London routine and increasingly use carry-on luggage instead, of vast proportions. (After the coffin is manoeuvred through those doors you can hand it to the cabin crew anyway.) Instruments like double basses often accompany musicians and airlines insist a seat is bought for them if they are to remain in the cabin. Infants under two can occupy the same seat as a guardian and I used to wonder whether a violin could be squeezed in like this along with the larger double bass. The cabin crew themselves use *wheelie-bags*, invented by an American pilot who used wheels on his overnight luggage. In a curious parallel, the man who replaced perambulators with buggies also designed the undercarriage system for the B52, which is laying waste to Iraq as I write ~ not only from the mouths of babes, but from those of bomb-bays too. Fitting the wheels of airliners into small spaces is a tremendous art, requiring all sorts of dislocations, especially when you have as many wheels as a B52. These are arranged not in the usual *tricycle* layout, but as a set of four like a quadruped. Each set can be turned a little during a crosswind landing, so the aeroplane can roll down the runway cocked off to one side like a trolley.

Supermarket trolleys are a good example of vectored forces. The *vector* is used a lot in aviation. Imagine racing down the middle of an aisle on the trolley, feet off the ground. If you see a small child centre-aisle and have no steering you must apply a sideways force to affect your course. A shaving foam might be used at this point as a *JATO bottle*. (This is a rocket the military fit to aeroplanes to assist their take-off and a group of American teenagers once claimed to have fitted one to an abandoned car.) You hold this canister amidships and twenty yards short of the child, hit the nozzle shouting, Break right Buzz, geeks in your twelve! At this point an impressive vapour trail spews from the canister and you squeeze down the side of the kid and are never allowed near the place again; I know this from experience.

Let us rewind the action: we took a run-up and accelerated the thing initially and then ceased applying force. According to Newtonian physics, we could continue all the way to Mars with this *velocity*, a combination of speed and direction. To avoid the child we applied *vectored thrust*. Releasing the foam applies an acceleration force that complies with Newton's law about every action having an equal and opposite reaction. The foam fires off left and drives the trolley to the right; if you traced a line along its path during the course of a second then momentum takes it ten yards forwards, while the force of the foam itself would take you one yard to the right in the same time.

Now go to the far end of the first line (the long straight one) and at right angles to it, off to the right, draw a line of one yard. Join the two lines and you have an elongated triangle, in the centre of which the child is seated. We have mathematically calculated the track of the trolley (along the longest side of this triangle) without ever having to see it confirmed in reality! The longest line is the *resultant vector* and these are called vector triangles. They are what NASA used to put people on the moon. Go there at weekends and you see them in the park with their trolleys and giant shaving-foam canisters. The main application of this for our purposes however lies in raising the nose to apply a lifting force from the wings, so as to alter the original momentum of the aeroplane.

The favourite luggage story I alluded to is of the Russian jetliner that sat alongside us once at Paris airport. It had an under-floor compartment like a walk-in wardrobe, off to one side of the doorway. It was arranged like this to adapt to the lack of infrastructure around the vast steppes of the Soviet Union: no jetties, no carousels, no ULDs. Passengers simply walk across the apron, suitcase in hand, greet the hostess and hand in their astrakhan overcoat. This is hung up nicely and the suitcase stowed neatly with the others, while the passenger passes suitably unburdened into a nice warm cabin, designed to defend them from the rigours of a Siberian winter. How utterly civilised. In a stroke, without ever intending it, they have met the urgent needs of the modern traveller. Like those countries without existing telephone networks that install the very latest digital systems developed elsewhere. Meanwhile back in Europe I am sat in the flight deck, delayed an hour because the baggage reconciliation computer has broken down and we have to perform a *baggage ID*, to account for every piece. This involves all the bags being arrayed on the apron and every passenger being led out in the fog to choose their own. While that happens a French policeman and his contingent like the Keystone Cops turn up and say they do not care what the airport has said, they want the passengers in luminous vests, or else two at a time, like we were unloading the ark of its animals. This gives me an opportunity to call him a cheese-eating surrender monkey, while he gets to escort me around the Bastille.

We are fast losing it. Let us go back inside the cabin and complete the landing. The approach usually begins around ten miles out, where the controllers tuck each aircraft underneath the glideslope, the imaginary three-degree incline. On the instrument this appears as a bar coming down from above, like the ceiling falling in, except as it hits the middle, the aircraft locks on and drives down the slope at seven hundred feet-per-minute. As it locks on and begins its descent, you hear the engines spool down a little, so the speed does not run away with you. If you are also on the lateral track towards the runway, the beam bar is also centred on the same display, so you have a cross-hair arrangement. When I passed through RAF selection procedures, they put you on a machine like this and moved a dot around a screen, while you moved the controls to put it back in the middle. It is a core skill for the pilot. On one DC-9 approaching Zurich, this instrument earthed out and made the cross-hairs centralise. The crew thought they were flying a perfect approach, except they were doing so into the side of a hill.

The airlines have really tuned into the sort of *psychometric* testing the military have used as an aid to recruitment for years. I often consider going along to these events just for fun. They usually involve grown adults playing with Lego. At one I went to at Britannia Airways, we had to role-play a board meeting to discuss how the food on an oil rig came to be contaminated with traces of oil. I first insisted we all have name cards in front of us with grand-sounding titles and when I got to speak, I did so in the style of J R Ewing, turning to my fellow applicants and saying things like, Grease my sandwiches with oil once more Bobby and your ass is history. I did not get the job, but they did put me in touch with a travelling theatre.

The actual *touchdown zone* is about a thousand feet into the runway, which seems a trifle odd. Runways are designated by their orientation, referenced to a magnetic compass. Those pointed due north for instance (360 degrees) are called runway '36'. Of course you can land or take-off on the same runway in the opposite direction, pointing south (180 degrees), so that from the other end the same runway is known as '18'. Just to make sure, there might be a big '18' painted on the surface itself at this end. I notice on the shortest runway at Heathrow they have painted '1,000' in huge letters to remind you this is as many metres of runway you now have left. When I learned to fly, we were encouraged to land on the *numbers*, while hobby-flyers organise spot-landing competitions, where they have to land upon a target. Weird.

They also send up balloons and try to take them out with their propellers. I must tell you more about party balloons. They rise until the gas inside is as dense as that outside, like the fish I described with bladder sacs. This is usually around five-thousand feet. At this level I have seen a variety of shapes whisk past the window, including a dolphin and a bumble bee. In these instances you ask the co-pilot if you are still sane and they say, No. Larger balloons flown by balloonists are not supposed to enter clouds or aerodrome zones, while to slow down they drag along tree-tops, giving a creditable impression of somebody crashing. Some have told me that being in cloud is particularly scary, as punctuating the silence is the occasional throbbing of invisible aero-engines getting ever closer.... and presumably farther, or else I would not have heard the story.

Airliners aim well along the runway so that if they sink violently on the way in, at least they crash upon the concrete. The main reason for this plunge, besides pilot error, is again the weather. You will be aghast at the constant threat that thunderclouds pose. They look ugly and black sometimes, believe me. They have ominous under-hangs known as *mammata*, which means 'breasts'. Even before getting into the aeroplane first officers would often shout across to me, Check out those mammata! Or words to the same effect. What thunderstorms cause in the vicinity of the ground is a peril called *windshear*. This is usually only vigorous enough to be a threat in places like the prairies, where the thunderheads build up to vast proportions. They rain so heavily inside that as the showers of rain fall through, they cool the air by evaporation, like when you hose the patio, or they splash water around a bullring. Much the same happens in your shower and if you would let me join you in there, purely for research purposes, I would be able to explain. You know how the curtain keeps getting drawn in and sticking to your thigh, making you worry how if Norman Bates turns up he is going to get a clear run? This is because the friction of the water droplets drags the air down with it and when it does so, the curtain acts like a wing or *airfoil*; as the air rushes faster down one side the pressure is reduced here and the fabric responds to the lift.

Inside the thunderhead the force of that drag combined with the cooling effects of evaporation make the air sink like a lead balloon. Huge columns called *microbursts* sink at a rate which no airliner can compensate for. If you are high enough this is not so bad and what most glider pilots do in sinking air is to drop the nose further and go faster, so as to fly out the other side before ground intervenes. The response in the airliner is a *go-around*, where you open the thrust-levers wide and haul the nose into a do-or-die climb. Of equal danger is the effect of this column when it hits the ground and splays out like a dropped carton of yoghurt. Instead of falling at seventy miles an hour, it travels the ground at the same speed. Air is frictionless like water and once it gets moving it takes some stopping. Waves in the sea only lose a half of their height over a thousand miles.

Aeroplanes fly with *airspeed*; they do not care how fast they are moving over the ground. This is why roofs have a habit of taking off in hurricanes, their *groundspeed* is zero, but their *airspeed* is a hundred and that is enough to generate sufficient lift (like with the shower curtain) to take them off. If an aeroplane happens to be overtaken by a localised gust of wind travelling a hundred miles an hour and it was coasting in at two hundred, then 200 - 100 (Dang! Another formula) leaves the aeroplane with only half its airspeed. This is insufficient to support it and exactly this scenario put down a DC-10 a mile short of the runway and obliterated the IBM PC project team. Since this accident key personnel from companies are not allowed to travel together. Which probably suits most of them. We once provided charter flights for a European tour by the Eagles; Don Henley, whose contempt for the others was infamous, travelled entirely separately. This is just the shot in the arm aviation needs: an airliner for every passenger.

If this has not frightened you enough, here is another. We have mentioned in connection with showers how a flow of air reduces pressure. An Italian called Bernoulli discovered this and I like to think while Archimedes was in the bath when displacement occurred to him, Bernoulli was having a shower. We have seen how pressure is a function of the weight of air and if there is less air immediately above the wing and more below, there is only one place for it to go. A side effect of this upward force of lift, which continuously reduces the air above the wing and squeezes it below, is *circulatory flow*. This has the same effect as a house party. If the lounge is crowded, people move upstairs. Everybody up there is truly spaced-out and those downstairs want a slice. The only way molecules can do this is around the wing tip and by the time they work their way around, the wing has disappeared on its travels. This generates a constant stream of aspiring air going around in circles, known as *wake vortex*. The wing sheds all sorts of spirals and the smallest (in which pressure drops viciously like in a tornado funnel) often condense air into fog and produce visible spirals. If you sit in the car parks littering the approach to runways you will hear the whip-cracks of these against a deeper undertone, long after the aircraft has passed. This is not Jean Michel Jarre, but the interplay of all these twisters.

Above all, the main span of each wing produces voluminous spirals persisting for minutes afterward like dust devils. One aerodynamicist said that if pilots could see them like the visible waves produced by speedboats, they might not fly at all. Due to their persistence, aircraft landing or taking off behind especially large airliners are provided with much greater separation by air traffic, like five miles instead of half of this. Even then I have known 737s rolled like kayaks by the effect. Big bumps shortly after take-off? That will be *wake turbulence*. It is what brought down the American Airlines A300 out of New York two years ago.

These then are all reasons why we land long and the *touchdown zone* is painted with checker marks to help identify it. Runways are generally inordinately long to address the needs of acceleration during the take-off roll. Usually they are more than long enough for landing, so much so that at Frankfurt they are experimenting with dividing the runway into two virtual halves for landings, some of which take place just beyond the midpoint. These do not take place actually while aircraft are sat at the beginning of the same runway, as that would be called an *overlanding*, which is strictly forbidden. I once suggested to a lady in the tower at Manchester that eventually this might be considered a good idea and she looked at me like I had suggested we get together to lick strawberry ice-cream off our naked bodies.

Alongside the touchdown zone on the grass is a set of lights which visually guide you down the required incline toward this zone, by turning red if you are low and white if high, or pink if you get it right. I was told that in Papua New Guinea they often appear white from any angle, because the lenses make the ideal culinary dish and are regularly removed by the locals. The runway itself is marked up in other ways but principally by coloured lights to make everything easier in the dark or the fog. Down the centre of the runway is a set of white lights and there are more of these down either side as well. Once at Heathrow they took out the central lights and I all but lined up with those along the edge instead. It is the little things that get you in flying.

(Should aeroplane undercarriages drop onto the grass you have to call out the engineers before you go anywhere. In long-haul aeroplanes you have no choice because the wheels sink under the weight of the vehicle. This entails deplaning passengers and baggage and defuelling the aeroplane to make it lighter. While this happens you can be filling out the paperwork. One charter airline in Manchester that was used to operating shorter aircraft took delivery of a bigger type and managed to drop two onto the grass in the space of a week. This is because the main-wheels are so much further back and the pilots were turning too early. Unlike in a car, you have to go past the bend before turning the tiller, as you are driving from way out in front. There used to be a ride at Blackpool funfair called the 'Mice' and this was like a roller-coaster except with individual cars. They had wheels set so far back it looked like you were headed off the tracks at every bend. It ought to be included in the training syllabus.)

Other lights around airports include centre-line lights that become yellow as you run out of runway, to assist with the rollout after landing in fog. Across the end of the runway is a set of red lights. See these sail by and you have blown it, along with all of the tyres. When you are safely on the taxiways these are edged in blue lights and if you come across a set of *wig-wags* or amber lights that flash from side to side, there is a runway ahead. This is a hint you ought to go no further without a very good reason.

Landing scenarios are of four main types. On a nice clear day, you see the runway from miles away. I would call this is the Californian type, but there is too much smog. Wild places like Scotland, where the air has been scrubbed by its passage over the ocean, have the best visibility. During this type of landing the runway grows continuously in the windscreen, its perspective smoothly enlarging, which at night looks very much like a video game. Showing passengers the view at night, some said it was as awesome as childbirth, though ideally attended by rather less blood and gore.

The second landing is typically European and involves dropping out of an overcast of cloud, when all is revealed. It is a good thing at this point if you recognise familiar landmarks. One American airliner was misidentified by air traffic and talked down to a landing at Brussels, except it was scheduled for Frankfurt. This would make you feel like you arrived at a black-tie event in fancy dress and swathed in toilet roll. There is enduring fascination in emerging from cloud at a late stage and hunting feverishly for the runway. Mistaking the airport is something student flyers excel at. One student returned to what he thought was Bournemouth airport and slipped into the landing pattern, informing the tower of his position, except he was talking to a controller fifteen miles away who was scouring the skies with his binos. What was especially funny was the CAA was at the first airfield doing an operations audit. Always the way, isn't it? An industry nostrum is that inspectors were never very good at flying, the logic being Bernard Shaw's dictum: Those who can, do. Those who cannot, inspect. I think this is an ill-considered slur on the finest body of men I have seen since the Dagenham Girl Pipers.

The third type of landing is in fog, when there is little to be seen by pilot or passenger. The first *blind landings* were achieved by an instrument landing system installed at Heathrow, combined with equipment fitted to a fleet of de Havilland Tridents. It was pioneered because the preponderance of coal fires at the time combined with London fogs meant the airport was barely open to traffic come the autumn. Before this type of landing could be contemplated, a comprehensive system of flight data recorders had to be fitted to each aircraft and monitored continually, to ensure the system worked entirely to the satisfaction of all concerned, not least the pilots. BA therefore have a wealth of flight data for all of their aircraft types and when Boeing 767s recently appeared to produce uncommanded flight manoeuvres, control movements the pilots never even asked for, American investigators turned to BA, whose 767s were continuously monitored.

During landings in fog the pilot is really looking for those pinpricks of light, the visual cues that the aircraft is headed in the right direction. *Approach lighting* extends half a mile before the runway and includes arrays of cross-bars, beside those along the extended centreline. These may be accompanied by a sequential series of stroboscopic lights that flash their way toward the end of the runway. They are not actually necessary, but like in any nightclub they do add to the atmosphere. A legendary French flyer once came in to land at night, his runway lit only by goose-necked oil lamps. When he lost sight of a few of these during the final stages, he could not work out why. Then he remembered they left the transport van somewhere around there and in a moment, rather than pull the nose up, he pushed it down hard and the aeroplane bounced on the ground and sailed straight over the top and that, ladies and gentleman, is entertainment...

SHUTDOWN

You spotted I missed out *crosswind* landings, but you did not think I was leaving it that way? When I have told you more about flying than you knew of the birds and bees? Gather round my feet in the dust and pay simple homage, or shower me with money. My needs are simple. The *crosswind* landing stems from the fact the runway points only one way, or at best two, while the wind is not nearly so forgiving as to do the same. We build the runway using our best guess as to where the worst of these winds are likely to come from. When it comes to typhoons, even the wind does not know where it is coming from and after landing in one of these, a mighty DC-10 was simply lifted by one wing tip and turned lazily upside down. I was not worried, commented one American passenger dryly, until they started to applaud...

I have been applauded just one or twice, the first time upon landing in Luton after a holiday charter had returned. The passengers on these flights were so stoned they would applaud your insulting their sister. Over the PA one of the crew would say, During the flight we shall be coming around with a selection of duty-free drinks and cigarettes, or you might like to choose a widescreen television or microwave oven. Few passengers would notice. As they boarded she might say to them, Tickle your arse with a feather? repeating it only if she had to with, Particularly nasty weather? As they left the aeroplane, she would pinch the backside of gentlemen here and there, making sure they turned around to confront whichever male passenger happened to be following.

Passengers themselves can be equally engaging and businessmen would often pass cards bearing messages like, Call me later at my apartment. As a heterosexual captain I could find this upsetting. Even the directors of major PLCs approached female members of the crew like this. Others were engaged more directly; one girl with a tightly bound hair-bun was informed by an off-duty police officer that this looked like an anus (without using the conventional Latin). The best I saw was on contract in Sardinia, from where we plied our trade back and forth to Geneva, among other places. We had a young and very blue-eyed Italian for a steward, whom we almost adopted for his gentle manner and innocent charms. He would drop by at the hotel on the way to Sunday lunch with the parents of his girlfriend, shirt and tie immaculate and Bible clutched in one hand. "Ivano," I would say, "You look a million liras". Then a lady travelling to Geneva spotted him, her husband away on business, so he disappeared to her mansion for the week. As you would if you were handed a business card on which was written, I can offer you a week of luxury and sexual gratification.

Things of this kind never happened to those in the flight deck, as the commanders were visibly too old and the first officers gave the game away with that hanging tongue. One of our seedier looking co-pilots had, after a girl from Virgin Atlantic left the jump seat she had earlier occupied in the flight deck, buried his nose in its cushion. This was bad enough, except she returned for her hat. Another had leaned across to see why the boarding was delayed and seeing an ample lady crossing the apron, turned to the captain and made some derogatory comment about her girth and origin. When she appeared at the flight deck door, the captain turned to him with the phrase, I wonder if you have you met my wife? And then they went flying together. On another occasion a first officer was disgruntled in some way by the driver behind him enroute to Luton airport. As he was overtaken he scowled, raised a digit and mouthed an unseemly suggestion to accompany the gesture. He recognized the driver later as the captain joining him to Palermo.

Being married I felt there was a rubber stamp across my forehead to this effect, though admittedly it might have been my complete absence of persona. I once sat as a passenger next to a beautiful lady who led a trading department, who in the course of the conversation scrabbled around to find the address of her hotel. I did wonder at this point whether her colleagues might be feeling she should not be getting warm and fuzzy with a uniformed officer in business class, but I did not overly care. When travelling in uniform this way, which is known as *positioning*, I might from time to time engage passengers in conversation, as it seemed the consumer-friendly thing to do. It had its compensations. On one such occasion I discovered I was talking to the general manager of one of the largest hotels in London that was owned by a firm I once worked for in

Cheapside. As we had many ex-colleagues in common I invited him to the flight deck for landing during a later flight and he left his card with the suggestion I drop in to eat some time. I capitalised on the offer six months later for an anniversary and was treated to dinner in the highest restaurant in town, along with lavish accommodation in a penthouse suite. Informing the captain with whom I worked the next afternoon of my luck, he turned to me quizzically and asked, Why did you waste it on your wife?

It never happened for me though, this sex at work, which was how it ought to have been. For anybody interested in playing the markets, the opportunity was there. Discussing it with some of these players, however, I discovered the gene pool was fairly restricted. One of the first officers collected name badges like locomotive plates in this way and he seems to have been something of a sexual locomotive himself, if his claim to have collected eighty inside two years turns out to be true. On his first day in Edinburgh a nominated representative presented him with all of the badges on day one, to save him the bother. Many of the girls who were more promiscuous, so far as I could see, were often more open and kind-hearted as well. If I read what he said correctly, the publicist Max Clifford said the most sexually expressive of his clients were often the warmest too. I shall let you know once my investigations are complete. At my last employer, I was told one girl would invite you for a glass of wine and as you fumbled nervously with the screw top, slip into the bathroom and emerge entirely naked. This sort of thing only happened to me in dreams and even then, I would be chased from the hotel by a rhino with three heads.

Sexual harassment has always been a feature of the airlines, which after all are merely offices with wings. The chief pilot of one of the better-known charter airlines in Britain touched up a friend of mine while flying with her, probably in pursuit of some or other trophy set for him by the lads. Pilots from the Navy often head up the flying side of many such airlines and coming from an organisation that excluded women entirely from ships, perhaps this was only to be expected. Likewise one of the cabin crew I knew had been expelled from a successful naval career on grounds of his homosexuality. I chanced upon an obscure satellite documentary once, devoted to the contribution of gay members of the US Navy during the last war. This was sufficiently engaging to keep me tuned in, unusual for a type of programme which (as Steve Coogan pointed out) would more normally be analysing mudslides.

Needless to say the charter airline involved in the harassment incident looked at who was most valuable to the company and then got rid of the woman instead. Even now I have flown with attractive women and knowing certain among the trainers to be a little oversexed, asked them whether they ever paused in the pursuit of their charges, if only to consider aspects of the flight in hand. Some of the pilots in senior positions would inform the women they could make or break their careers, so clearly somewhere along the line the casting couch has been replaced by a nearly-flat recliner.

You have to bear in mind when you move around the airline industry that the obligations of *omerta*, the bond of blood, or else the old boy network pursues you. One of the larger of the no-frills players in the UK has a flight operations director who was best man to a fleet manager at Heathrow. In turn his own best man was, Oops, the same manager. If ever I applied to join his airline, even if I built the best possible construction in Lego, he would be on the 'phone to his friend and flouting employment laws by asking for a value-judgment. I do not particularly mind companies checking I am not a carpet-chewer in this way, but it might be courteous to ask. Or am I just being naive? Answers on a postcard please.

The crosswind landing involves the aeroplane approaching while pointing off to the side in order to pursue a straight line, or *track*, when the winds blow sideways. It cannot land like this, though we have seen the B52 can at least point its wheels in the direction of the runway first. Other aeroplanes have to effect a turn during touchdown, a flat turn by using the rudder like in a boat, or a rolling turn in the conventional way. This lowers one wing and puts the wheels on one side down before the others, which is mildly entertaining. We were assured this would not scrape an engine, but in lower-slung jetliners with engines at the rear, digging in a wing-tip was always a possibility. In the DC-9 I was told you could easily chamfer the edges off the landing lights fitted here.

There have been many attempts at castor wheels on aircraft, like those of a supermarket trolley. There is even a helicopter with them. Even the main wheels of the 737 give just a little in this way. Any perceived advantage was always offset by the difficulty of driving an aeroplane down the runway while inspecting the flowerbeds down either side. If I have not mentioned it elsewhere, the futuristic satellite terminals at Paris Airport once had aprons punctuated by flowerbeds, since covered over with tarmac. Shame.

A further complication I might cover is landing in a crosswind *and* on a snow-covered runway. I did this at high speed in the simulator once with a man who had flown for the Antarctic Survey. He left the Antarctic Survey after having punched its chief pilot in the face. I like a man with opinions forcefully expressed. He advised me to go with the flow and land the aircraft almost sideways, so the *drift* experienced in the air was continued down the slippery runway. It seemed to work, as we were back in the simulator the next day. On the way in we would pass a French captain and his young female co-pilot as they were leaving and my own captain would say to her each day, You could make an old man very happy. I found this sexist, yet confusingly funny at the same time.

During the last chapter we looked at some of the external systems on the aeroplane and now we look at some of those inside. In the cabin from the rear working forward there is a galley with cupboards, tea-making facilities, a fan-oven for warming your paninis and space for the trolleys, which are snapped into place so as not to roll around. My brother commanded a flight once and on board was a ranking Israeli official and his bodyguard. They do not come more paranoid than this. When the latter heard this metallic snapping from the galley, naturally he thought this was a gun being cocked and leapt from his seat to put the hostess in an arm-lock. These are the kind of people who see suicide bombers where we see men dressed as Santa Claus.

Forward of the galley are the toilets, so arranged as to permeate airline meals with essence of lavatory chemical. In one of the larger 737s the toilets were behind the galley area at the rear of the aeroplane and had a common discharge outlet. The engineers during quieter moments of the night shift used to enjoy inviting apprentices to put a gloved hand down one of these to investigate a blockage. While they did this and without their knowledge, an engineer would lean into the bowl in the adjacent cubicle and grab the hand of the unfortunate apprentice, who imagined he was grappling with the thing from the abyss. While we are about toilet humour, I should tell you about the captain who would invite newer members of the cabin crew into the flight deck, having prepared a mix of apple juice and hot water in a cup, to ask whether they could not empty it, as he had been caught short at the controls.

The very worst of my excremental memories was the charter we operated to the Canaries, in an aeroplane which had neither the speed nor range for the job. The three-dozen oil workers aboard, fuelled with a litre bottle of vodka each, had already discovered the handset at the rear for the crew and had used it to lead their colleagues in impromptu karaoke sessions. With all of this exuberance manifest, it was no surprise for me to discover before our fuel stop in Portugal that the one toilet on board was overflowing with emissions from every orifice, which were sweeping the cabin like an algal tide. During these investigations I risked any number of Glaswegians throwing their arms around my neck to tell me I was their best mate, despite my spraying them with insecticide.

Larger aircraft have outlets that service-trucks or 'honey wagons' connect to, sucking out the contents or replenishing water supplies under pressure. That destined for the Canaries had a rubberised cap like the top of a Grolsch bottle, but upside down. Despairing of getting any help from the Portugese handling agents, the captain (who was the one who had laid out the chief pilot in the Antarctic) strode purposefully toward a hangar and helped himself to a barrel used for recycling bottle tops. He was equally impressed as I flicked the catch to release the contents of our toilet. As he stood at a pace of ten yards, these dropped the full height from the aircraft into the bucket, like a scene from an epic by Cecil B. de Mille in which the Egyptians are wasted by a tidal wave of effluent. We left it right there on the apron, ha ha.

Moving on, at the front end there is another galley and in between these two areas, rows of seats only interrupted by a door or two. When I first practised take-offs and landings for real, which had to be done by night, I travelled to Belfast where this exercise was to take place at three o'clock in the morning. Anybody who has travelled around Northern Ireland soon realises the people are exceptionally easy-going and have a sense of humour. They must have had, to put up with this. What most impressed me though was to look at nearly two-hundred empty seats stretching into the pallor of the fluorescent lights and to realise I was about to take them all airborne. One small step for a man, one giant leap of faith for the accountants.

One of our own captains lived on the outskirts of the town and at the height of what were euphemistically called the 'troubles', BA flight crew were advised not to mix with locals or divulge their occupation. I would have been only too keen to divulge my occupation in the circumstances, for fear of being mistaken for a squaddie. Our captain used to take great pleasure in joining these pilots in the Jacuzzi and in the broadest of Belfast accents, telling them he ran the pig farm they could see on the final approach and by the way, what did they do for a living? My own view of working here was people from any walk of life take you at face value. In the border country Protestants had offered me a lift because they said I looked more of a target than a card with black circles. I took a stroll down the river into the republican parts of South Belfast and while I got some odd looks, I was more interested in the homely terraces so familiar from Liverpool, where in 1851 a fifth of the people were Irish anyway. Fear only breeds hostility in people, as I always said before being mugged.

Continuing our look at internal systems, having seen all we want of the cabin, we move on to the flight deck. First we see the fire-axe, wielded closely by many captains after 9/11. We inherited aircraft from SAS in Scandanavia and these had leather holsters containing truncheons, since removed and sold by the engineers through adult sections of eBay. Also here, a *circuit-breaker* panel with fuses for anything you can think of. The big fear in aeroplanes is of electrical things catching fire, so each can be isolated. We had inertial reel seat belts on the 737 and released suddenly, they would whistle past your head like a lasso and sometimes catch one of these 'CBs' and pull it out. It could be any of them, an inadvertent process that resembled pinning the tail to the donkey, but in reverse. Once in

Rome an engine would not start, which was titillating, because jet engines always start, unless the sparking plug has been isolated by a flying seat belt.

Further along are boxes with emergency equipment required by the crew, like life jackets (yes, we get them too), torches, oxygen masks, fireproof gloves and a portable breathing hood for fighting fires with. Fortunately this was to be used by the co-pilot, though we all had to try them on. At least I did until once when I saw fleas spring from its inner recess. It felt good to put all of this equipment on and then walk around the training department singing the theme from *Ghostbusters*. We also had to put out a fire, though the airlines replaced the foam with water, which is not nearly so entertaining. This was done at a rig including a make-believe oven with a gas supply and igniter, so that the instructor could merely turn the gas off so as to convince trainees of their firefighting abilities. Either that or delay the ignition until after the gas had been running for twenty seconds, putting anyone off ever wielding an extinguisher in anger again.

In the *overhead panel* above the flight deck there are switches for the systems like electrics, hydraulics and air conditioning, arrayed neatly in sections with flow diagrams to show you what leads where. Among these were switches in red, designed to put you off using them at all. I did a type-rating examination for the Citation jet and among the questions was, What colour is the pressurisation dump-switch? As the manual was in black and white, I wanted to write "A shade of lilac" with an explanation on the reverse explaining my predicament, so as to be awarded the mark anyway. Directly in front of each pilot are the instruments we have seen already, like the horizon, navigation display, airspeed and altimeters, along with a clock that is too complicated to set. There is a big red light for accentuating warning sounds and a yellow one that lights up for less urgent failures. Each can be cancelled by pressing it and after one arduous night flight, when the fuel light illuminated in my car, I leaned forward to cancel that one too. In a flight I was given in a Harrier jet, having done some flying already I was alarmed to see an array of warning lights down one side during the take-off roll. Not wanting to disturb the pilot at this point I alerted him to these when airborne, but was informed that a selection of lights were ordinarily illuminated at the best of times.

These were older *analogue* systems on the Harrier and about as reliable as your old train set. The aircraft had a moving-map display that was precisely that: a map moving around over a projector. The simulator in these days was housed in a hangar and took the form of a giant model of the countryside. A projector screen around the cockpit was linked to a robotic arm driving a camera above the landscape. When maintenance men leaned over to replace a cow, from where I sat it looked almost Biblical. I had a go in the simulator before one in the real thing and it went quite well until my vectored approach, which took me through both the fence and a flock of sheep, where I left them untangling the camera.

I have recalled extracts from the war diaries of this squadron already. In one fascinating account less directly connected with flying, a pilot recalled laying in the bath with the tip of his penis above the waterline, smothered in jam. He then released a jar of bluebottles into the environment. (You have to remember this was before television.) What I found even funnier was an episode in a bar in Glasgow where seeing a number of crew with us, some naval ratings invited themselves over. After hearing this story they retired to a safer distance. On another occasion at the same hotel we found ourselves in the midst of a Star Trek convention, during a fancy-dress evening. I was making conversation at the bar with a Lara Croft lookalike and enjoying the conviviality until joined by an older captain who was unattuned to modern sensibilities. He looked her up and down before asking, Who are you? Pocahontas? The following morning as I went out for the paper and a quiet breakfast, it was peculiar to see streets peopled only by Klingons. Rather than cross the road I would say to them, We come only in search of newspapers and we hail you, salesmen of Planet Basingstoke.

In the centre of the forward console in the flight deck are the engine instruments and moving back toward the door, the pedestal containing navigation computers and the throttle quadrant. This is called the quadrant because it is an arc of ninety degrees through which the thrust-levers can be advanced and retarded. Also here are the speed brake and flap levers. Further back on the pedestal are radios and navigation receivers, where custom demands that pilots spill their orange juice. Pilots cannot be separated from coffee and until recently there was a cigarette lighter as well. Airbus provided a coffee-cup holder to one side, complete with a scientifically-designed cup with a large rim. Because this needed washing up afterward, the cabin crew stowed it at the back of a cupboard and gave you polystyrene like everybody else. Any first officer finding the Airbus cup took it home to drink beer. As a result the coffee spilt anyway in turbulence or around corners on the ground, this time all over the manuals and books of aerodrome plates. As a result these were often sticky and terrain contoured in brown might actually be a stain and had to be interpreted with caution. An aspect of turbulence which left me helpless with mirth, was watching the tray of food invariably in front of the first officer being spilled all over the flight deck. Airbus was like the CAA in providing salutary memoranda on different subjects, with titles like, How to Care for your Carbon Brakes. One that amused me said something to the effect that a Clean Flight Deck was a Happy Flight Deck. It would not have looked out of place as a wallposter in a temperance hall.

The more important parts include the sidestick, like that of a computer, but in this event to point an Airbus. As many pilots will tell you, pull and cows get smaller, push to make them bigger. This is broadly true in any aeroplane, for if you pull the nose up and have the power or momentum then you will climb. Moving the stick from side to side rolls the wings in the same direction and engages the aircraft in a turn. The rudder pedals do next to nothing and many airliner captains get cross if you touch them at all. They are used in correcting for engine failure, though even this the designers of the Airbus wanted done by computer. It was retained because there were so few decisions left for pilots to make. Boeings use a control wheel instead of a sidestick, which does exactly the same thing. Airbus pilots have a pullout meal tray in its place, but once the autopilot was engaged I found this control column made a suitable lectern for the broadsheets.

In any study of landings I cannot overlook those on water and the related art of landing upon aircraft carriers, which often amounts to the same thing. On the safety card in the seat pocket, as the Irish comedian Dave Allen pointed out, the aircraft in the water looks like a train that just pulled into a station, its passengers disembarking with an air of ennui. Once in the water most aeroplanes settle slightly nose-down or nose-up, putting one or other set of doors beneath the waterline, so the over-wing exits are favoured. There are all sorts of elaborate instructions to pilots for landing upon water, or *ditching*. The only recent instance was an Egyptian Airways 767 that was hijacked, exhausted of its fuel and landed expertly in the water offshore. This made for video footage that satellite channels show upside down and backwards.

My wife knew two of the survivors, girls who worked for MTV. For each it was the first leg of a world tour and the one who had not flown was assured aeroplanes no longer ended in shark-infested waters. What I found interesting was that some of the guidance issued by airlines contradicted aspects of the ditching that saved at least some of the passengers from further injury. One of the girls was more agitated than the other (no prizes for guessing which) and upon hearing the captain she had inflated her life-jacket. This both reduced her injuries and helped her leave the seat to float toward the rupture through which she escaped. Balanced against this, airlines use the logic it is harder to manoeuvre physically while encumbered by an inflated jacket and from my own point of view I can see a danger of floating to the ceiling and getting trapped there. These things are not easy to remove if you have tied them, nor easily deflated. I am saying nothing though: do you think I am some kind of emergency lifestyle guru?

Landing on carriers has to be done sometimes and in the simulator they used to try it in the 737 for fun. Pilots describe it as the ultimate buzz, like landing on a postage stamp with no option for missing. The earliest operations used catapults to launch floatplanes over the side and afterward recover them when they landed nearby. The earliest *flattops* were possibly British and the Royal Navy certainly invented the steam catapult. It is used in conjunction with an *arrester wire* and if you land airliners at military bases, you can expect to run over these. A feature of landing on carriers is the time the engines take to spool up for a *go-around,* or baulked landing. If you decide to abandon an approach at the last minute you have to have the thrust ready, so the first difference is you do not ease off the rate of descent but keep the aircraft coming down. Then before touchdown you apply full thrust in case you need to climb away, while letting momentum carry the aeroplane onto the deck. Good naval aircraft have strong landing gear and for this reason the Spitfire was considered hopeless and the Mitsubishi Zero a good all-rounder. Subsequently the arrester cable grabs the hook on the tail and if you listen carefully to films of this, you hear the engines roaring as the aeroplane judders to a halt. Footage of these aircraft missing the deck can be quite entertaining, unless you are inside. Among the most remarkable I have seen shows tons of hardware pushed over the side of carriers, to evade their capture in Vietnam. As I write during the second war in the Gulf, the use of carriers and carrier-borne aircraft look to be with us for a while to come.

At the end of our own *landing roll*, we dropped the thrust levers forward out of reverse and reset the speed brakes. Already I am unable to visualise quite how this was done, though it is less than two months since I operated my last aircraft type. This is how flying is. I sat with another pilot and neither of us could remember where the parking brake was located in a previous type, which between us we had spent ten years flying. The job is wholly repetitive and many of the actions required to perform it are automatic. Pilots do it for the time in between these routines; in the way you drive for the view, or for the satisfaction of taking bends. Although much involved in driving is subconsciously performed, it is performed with a satisfaction of its own. Eventually this can be true even of the landing, when your mind might be elsewhere. It is like I suppose playing the viola, when during those passages you rehearsed a thousand times, you let your fingers do the work while enjoying the sound of the orchestra, immersing yourself as an unconscious observer like the audience themselves. Talking of music, the reverse thrust might not be applied during the landing, as often it is proscribed for environmental reasons. We have dined with friends near to the airport, a mile or so north of the runway, where it is only the reverse thrust that can be heard. As the *petals* or *sleeve* of each reverser directs the jet-blast outwards and the noise in the same direction, this is not surprising.

For certification the manufacturers of engines draw a map of noise emissions and they do so with lines like those on a weather map. Any line joining places where pressure is the same forms contours called *isobars*, while *isotherms* join places of equal temperature. With engines they choose a hundred decibels and then join the points where sound falls to this level. Decibels were derived from the noisiness of a bell, the way *candelas* or units of light used candles. Anyway, this contour produces a line that snakes around the outline of the engine itself, bulging around the front, very close to its edges and then forming an enormous spout, like the jet efflux itself, behind the nozzle. The broader margin indicates places where you should not stand unless you want to be deafened, but also if you want neither to be sucked into the inlet nor ejected from the other end. Painted on the side of the engine there is normally a hazard diagram, showing people on the ground exactly where they need to avoid to escape either of these contingencies.

Taxiing to the gate the flaps, the parts that make the wings larger, are retracted to neaten things up but also because if we bring them in while on stand they could make mincemeat of body parts. The same goes for the thrust reverser sleeves with which some engines are fitted. You could probably guillotine a ream of A4 with these. At the same time on the way in, if this is the last *sector*, you might mentally stow the events of the day. On those rare occasions you may not have got on, perhaps because the other pilot felt the approach was not all that it might have been, this is an awkward moment. You can hardly stop and get out, but instead trundle along in darkness and silence following a set of green lights, like lovers disappointed in some tryst. You cannot even have a cigarette.

Aviation psychologists try to examine such scenarios but it can be like getting a frank confession out of a Mafia godfather. Remember that the clitoris was only formally recognised as an anatomical source of pleasure in renaissance Italy (what did women do until then?), while it took Freud to discover the unconscious longings previously hinted at only by great art. These considerations are in their infancy in aviation and discussing them meaningfully is like talking sex with a sub-postmaster. There is much literature on the subject and lots of diagrams and models to go with it. I shall mention only a facet or two, as the literature forms a separate study area in which I am not, like most blokes, especially interested. Most pilots dismiss it as psychobabble and smirk when it appears on their roster, like they had been called to see the headmistress. Many on the day in question went to lunch and did not come back. There was never any follow-up for this, though there might be were you to leave off between flights for a burger and not return. Inadvertently one of our pilots once thought he was returning from Madrid as a passenger and took an earlier flight; arriving in London only to discover he was operating the next schedule out of Madrid and subsequently incurring four hours of delay. I have done this myself, though not nearly with so much style.

One feature of human factors on the flight deck for instance is called *risky shift* and this says that if you put two pilots together who are constitutional risk-takers, then the effects are amplified beyond expectation. Anybody seeing five teenagers career down the street in a Mitsubishi Evo will need no aviation psychologist to explain this concept. By the way, you can see I am the guy writing to the local paper about Mitsubishi Evo drivers. In a *pension* once in Toledo I got chatting to a young man from Amsterdam, who helped me with translation. Turned out he was a pimp, though he let it slip with the air of someone there for a trade exhibition on shower curtains. He was perusing a magazine and told me two girls were not enough for a new Ford Sierra. At this point one of his charges turned up and I thought of asking him for staff discount. She looked me up and down like I was a shower-curtain salesman, which I thought was rich coming from a hooker. What did he do all day though? Rampant sex in the morning apparently after each girl had finished her shift, followed by the cinema or the auto pages while they slept. He had left Amsterdam as he felt crime was getting out of control. He told me to expect the full treatment for as little as ten pounds in the bars around the old town and while I did not take him up on it, in moments of reflection, like the young Saint Augustine I sometimes wish I had. I thought we were supposed to regret only the injustices we visited upon others in the twilight of life? Is there only me here wishing I had lost myself among a sea of Spanish breasts as a young man?

What can I say of the crews with whom I have worked as our flight draws to its end? Owners of airlines have been known to declare they do not worry about recruiting cabin crew, as there was always another checkout girl waiting. (This was probably the same guy who drew up the précis on corporate ethics.) Pilots in turn are viewed as prima donnas. This is great, because that is how we view ourselves. Chief executives might pen articles in the media complaining we were as inflexible as the old coal-mining unions, but then somebody would inflexibly pin up a copy in the crew room and they and the union reps would have to get together to resume their uneasy truce.

Sometimes girls would join the airline only for the uniform and one appeared in the News of the World, which got wind of the fact she had divested it among the pages of a girlie magazine, providing in a dozen pages more customer satisfaction than she might during any number of flights. As we checked into the Glasgow hotel the porters furtively waved the magazine beneath the counter with a certain glee and when the girl herself arrived it was if they had met Gina Lollobrigida. Unlike the others who reappeared in the bar for a drink, she retired to her room, clearly one who kept business and pleasure separate. I threatened to interview her for the pilot magazine, for a piece entitled *Where are they now?* Then I realised with a start that my libido was kicking in and instead I interviewed the man who designed the folding staircase for the BAC 1-11. How they loved it. In a less professional exercise altogether two guys, a girl and a video camera turned up at a Heathrow car park and filmed an adult video on the bonnet of a car selected at random, which I hoped was my own. As several cameras are already trained on the site it merely provoked the man in the portable cabin to pick up his telephone and inform the police that things were happening that seemed to contravene the tenets of his own religion, if not the regulations issued by the Pink Elephant Parking Company Ltd.

The saddest thing about the episode is there appeared to be neither reflective parasols, sound equipment nor screenplay. On one of the occasions I was not too mean to tune into the adult movies at the hotel, the storyline featured a girl whose bicycle chain fell off and had to be secured by a passing motorist, to whom she decided to offer sex. Now I can see why those people at the Royal Automobile Club are so into the job. You could always rely on the flight crew to try to figure out ways of activating the adult channel without paying for it. This developed into a battle of measure and counter-measure between crews and hotel chains, as earnest as any cold war. One captain had been a TV engineer and like an operative from Bletchley Park, he carried an array of cables in his flight bag to assist him in the task. Others would invite stewardesses around to watch, hoping this would give them ideas in the way a dog might be persuaded to fetch a stick. Even gorillas require more sophisticated foreplay than this.

The 'form' would be to clean as many drinks and mixers out of the aeroplane as possible and repair to one or other hotel room, but only after the bar was closed. This was justified upon the grounds that most drinks had already been provided to the airline in the form of promotions. Equipped with the same moral certainties some among the cabin crew made off with at least the gowns from their hotel room and in some cases light fittings as well. This is understandable when you are starting out and very probably setting up that first home. Now you know why every home features a Corby trouser press. Such stories however are entirely untypical of the majority, who work hard, see few rewards and are thanked too rarely. By and large those at the other end of the salary scale can be as bad or worse and the captain who turned up with an empty box, complained the room had no TV and then checked out with the first one probably trumped them all.

At certain night stops I heard of girls coming down to the bar with no form of underwear beneath their dress, or playing games of strip pool. Not strip poker, as there were no cards available. I also heard of parties where lights would be extinguished and invisibles orgies engaged upon. On one occasion I arranged to meet a gay member of the crew in the bar and in the space of time I had a shower, he had been across the road for perfunctory gratification. Nor would he mind me saying so. Where I was concerned it got about as exciting as a pint of mild and a bag of pork scratchings at the Teesside airport hotel, which is exactly what happened one birthday. Believe me this lifestyle has taken its toll.

At some fleshpots in Europe like Brussels or Cologne I was told there were gay villas where you checked your clothing in like you were going swimming. One thing I did use was sports facilities. You will be asking why I talk of sports and tea-making facilities while Pompeian orgies are going on. On the continent many saunas required you to be naked but most of the girls would baulk at revealing all to somebody whom they worked with but barely knew. At one sauna in

Norway hairy guys sat around like Vikings with legs akimbo, while I walked in wearing trunks with sailing ships printed upon them. Touching upon the fleshpots of Brussels, as the new centre of Europe it attracts not only senior military officers and politicians, but a retinue of Eastern European prostitutes, whose services are paid for with our taxes. At the bar I spoke to a delightful girl calling herself 'Teddy', which struck me as an unusual name for someone from Slovakia, but never mind. She joined me by chance in the Jacuzzi, complaining her photographs had been lost during development, those of her dressed in lingerie. As I could not see myself pictured only in a pair of Y-fronts I failed to see why she had taken these at all. (Actually I had done it once, but only when developing a prone-piloted aeroplane and requiring the proportions for the cockpit.) During the course of this conversation I missed the airport bus from the hotel.

For many cabin crew the job fits somewhere between being a small girl who wants to dress in a pretty frock and fly to places with palm trees and the dreary world of work, with the politics of the office and the drudge of marrying, bringing up a family and leaving your husband only to wonder where it all went wrong. For others it is more of a career and not so much a conscious choice as the chance to avoid working between the hours of nine and five. Many are recruited from among the ranks of entertainers on cruise liners, or dance troupes from theatres and as a result are both delectable and engaging. Others arrive from college, while yet others work for a year or two and wonder why, when they always wanted to be an air-hostess, they had yet to get it out of their system. There is naturally a significant gay community in the cabin, either because they bring qualities to the job that it requires or because the cabin is a seedbed of life less ordinary. Of course the flight deck is no less of a hotbed for gossip, but not for much else. One New Zealander of my acquaintance flew with an avuncular captain shortly before he was to retire and during the flight he leaned over with a twinkle in his eye and said he had discovered another of the pilots in the company was gay. When the co-pilot inquired who the other might be, he leaned further over and replied, Give us a kiss and I'll tell you...

Flight deck are drawn from many spheres too, many decidedly odd-shaped spheres. Before he died the legendary instructor Ron

Campbell, whose pipe rarely left his mouth, pointed out that over half of all airline pilots in the UK were 'self-improvers' who were not sponsored by the military or the airlines, but left other jobs and squandered their savings in this hopeless quest. For a while Carol Reed edited *Flight* magazine and was probably the first woman to do so. The magazine has charted the ups and downs of aviation since its earliest years and is read worldwide, almost exclusively for its recruitment pages. If you want to send a message to the global population of pilots, as one day I might myself, you do it in these pages and disguise it as a recruitment advertisement. I could promote this book in that way, while adding a requirement for a house-help. Whether the editor was connected with Reed Publications, who owned the title, I do not know. What I do know is that she suggested in a leader column that the industry could do without the pilots who sponsor their own training. I suspect she knew little or nothing about the industry and that this came from a gin-sodden retiree in father's village. I cancelled my subscription and Carol left after possibly the shortest tenure in the history of the magazine, having dismissed half the readership. The industry cannot do without self-sponsored pilots, for the reason there would be too few to fly its aeroplanes.

As within all elites there are people in the industry that hate this state of affairs, but then there are people who object to immigration as detracting from 'their' way of life. I am probably the type of pilot they feel a particular distaste for, but the world is moving away from theirs and nearer to my own. The pilots I have known and flown with have without exception been remarkable. Flying is a talent magnet that draws people to it in the way a century ago people wanted to learn how to drive. I worked with airship commanders and rock stars, Gulf War veterans and orbital scientists, or people who restored Bentleys and raced them against the late Alan Clark. Pilots are supremely motivated individuals and the women among them more so, in order to climb through the glass ceiling. The strangest bonds unite them, like the moment an aeroplane breaks the surface of a sea of fog in near silence, like a dolphin celebrating dawn.

A check captain put it well when he said to sit in the jump seat and watch a well-executed flight was like seeing an orchestra at work and this is how you often feel, like a part of a vast enterprise that can break the speed of sound and make it feel only a perturbation, a pause in the enjoyment of a coffee and croissant. This is why a Mach-meter is fitted in the cabin of Concorde, so passengers can see it ease the through that magical value of '1.00'. Sir Terence Conran was asked to restyle the aircraft and he said he wanted a flash of light to run the length of the cabin during this phase, like lightning sometimes does in reality. Flying south over France on one occasion we were alerted by the controller and told Concorde was about to accelerate across the Atlantic coast. Indeed its trail could just be seen arcing upward into the stratosphere, its afterburners feeding the tailpipes like alchemists, their lilac flames transforming gases into the golden dream of supersonic flight.

DE-PLANE

Our flight today is nearly over. Before we leave off flying and go our separate ways, there is more classwork to get through. I promised a look at flight training. A man named Link in the USA pioneered the use of simulators and the company he formed, as usually happens, went by the same name. I used to think Link trainers were so called because they provided a link of sorts to the real thing, though I think this is purely coincidental. Many people have surnames that presage employment, whether by chance or because it has imprinted their vocation subliminally since the earliest years. In many ways it is not odd at all, considering how many surnames spring from employment, like Cooper, Mason or Smith. I number a Brian Bankmanager among my own acquaintances.

The earliest simulators were a direct substitute for the hood that enclosed the trainee in dual-seat or *tandem* trainers. (Concealing the view from single-seat aeroplanes was always going to be a short-lived initiative.) The first of these training aids did not move at all and would be known as a *fixed-base* simulator. They provided a set of flying controls matching those in the real thing, which was easy when aeroplanes had uncomplicated systems, as most of the controls were used in common. The manufacturers of instruments for example would supply all of the main types, so that Sperry who pioneered the use of gyroscopes went on to manufacture most of these instruments, while in the UK Smiths are among the oldest instrument maker of any kind. For all I know they are connected with the firm that produces the clocks.

Once the flying controls had been arranged within the simulator, they could be connected to the instruments, so that it appeared to get airborne. This is no great shakes in an age of computer games, but in those days it seemed radical, one of the earliest commercially useful instances of virtual reality. Every other instance would be confined to the music halls and contrived with smoke and mirrors for public delectation. When the pilot advanced the throttles, for example, this wound up the airspeed indicator so as to create the illusion of accelerating down the runway; at the required flying

speed when the joystick was pulled gently back to raise the nose into the air, this activated the altimeter and vertical speed indicator. The same dials as the ones in the aircraft would be used, while those that were normally plumbed into the airflow would be driven by motors instead. Similar adjustments were made to instruments like the horizon and the magnetic compass, indicating the attitude and direction of flight.

Often for the benefit of the instructor (who would otherwise be clueless as to what went on inside) control inputs were relayed to a pantograph beyond. This took the form of a robotic pen or motored mouse, which trundled around a blank board or a sheet of paper, indicating progress in plan view. This is still true of the most advanced simulators today, which are connected via the computer to a printer, which can show the performance of the pilot in tracking some procedural route or other. Nowadays a view of the elevation or vertical progress of the flight is easily derived, though this was not the case in early years.

As much as anything the aim of the simulator was to accustom pilots to pursuing the task in the absence of visual cues, which can be quite alarming at first. We all sense which way up we are by a combination of visual and pressure receptors; what was called 'seat of the pants' flying was predicated on this basis. This is not the most reliable indication by any means and is frequently overruled by the visual picture in the event of contradiction. The best demonstration of this is those rooms in funfairs that rotate around a seat, which is suspended on an axle. One effect of this is to convince people that they are being swung upside down, when in fact this is happening to the room itself. Another effect is to induce the sort of nausea that requires the walls, floors and ceiling to be regularly cleaned of vomit. It is no way to earn a living, so these Victorian devices are largely dying out. Thanks to computer games, people are now able to vomit in the comfort of their own homes.

In an attempt to harness a measure of fidelity from the corroboration of sensory data, Link decided to throw in a little dynamism in the form of bellows. I have a vague notion the impulse was connected with the manufacture of church organs, as these were on the leading edge of bellow technology. The only other application of bellows that springs to mind would be the firing equipment used in foundries. Added to this holy provenance was the fact that many early flyers in the USA were earnest chaps connected in some way with the church. The Wright brothers' own father was a bishop of a non-denominational organization; invariably it was the adherents of low churches in both Europe and America that often made technical advances. This fecundity would often be tied to improving the misery of their condition, as well as to an unerring belief in the rightness of their ideals. The Wright brothers ate nothing but dried ham and eggs during their months at Kittyhawk. On the big day itself, December 17 in 1903, had they chosen not to go flying at 10:30 but to ride into town for waffles, events might have unfolded differently. They might have gone into fast-food diners instead, leaving Ronald McDonald a free run at powered flight.

The bellows in the Link trainer were able to tip it so as to simulate a climb and descent, while leaning it one way or another also provided a sensation of rolling into turns. I think they also rotated upon their axis to assist the sensation of turning. I only know all of this because the footage is occasionally interleaved with other newsreels in music videos to augment the entertainment, without any hint of the notion that we shall look equally naive to subsequent generations. The overall impression of the trainer as viewed from the outside could give only a hint of the misery and confusion attending its occupants. I have watched modern-day simulators for extended periods from this vantage point and there seem to be prolonged periods of dormancy, punctuated by frenzies of random motion.

Later with the introduction of TV screens in the wider world, some of the simulators were fitted with a rudimentary visual system marking out the runway with dots of light, which at night is about how it looks anyway. The bellows were gradually replaced by hydraulic rams, which are fiercely responsive. The geometrical arrangement these jacks assumed was like a tetrahedron that could either tip the simulator (or the 'box' as many crews know it), twist it, or else pump it up and down. The technical term for the last motion is *heave*, which is entirely appropriate. The control-response is both quick enough and sensitive enough to simulate even encounters with cats-eyes on the taxiway.

The software required to synthesise (for the concept is also known as synthetic training) the trajectory of aircraft in flight was assembled during the early days of space travel, which in turn had its origins in guided-missile systems. Anyone who has seen Tom Hanks in *Apollo 13* will recall that even the lunar module used an artificial horizon and a joystick like that of the Airbus to establish its direction. One thing missing from original trainers, the feeling of accelerating down the runway, could be recreated in the absence of visual cues by tipping the pilot backward, which also pins you to the seat. This technique is still used and reinforced by the motion of the graphics, it produces a sensation which is indistinct from the real thing. The equipment can never recreate a force exceeding that of gravity, whereas in a fighter jet almost ten times this can be sustained. When trying to design my own simulator however I did figure that if you were tipped most of the way backward even the feeling of gravity applies a force that can only be achieved on the level by a very powerful car. Work it out using the standard value of thirty-two feet per second, per second. Then come back and tell me just what sort of car that would be.

Put all of this together in an expensive box whose interior reproduces the flight deck of different airliners and you have an effective training tool. Now that newer aircraft have computer screens to replace many of the dials, little is required to differentiate narrow-body aircraft like the Airbus 320 from long-haul or wider-bodied airliners like the A340. This has four engines instead of two and apart from a software substitution to reflect this, all the simulator requires is for the two thrust-levers to be replaced with four. Simulators are now so realistic that what is called 'zero flight time' training schedules are allowable, in which all of the training on a new type of airliner is conducted in the simulator and the first time the aircraft is flown in anger is with the passengers. This is not as alarming as it sounds, for a pilot with operational experience goes along for the ride. I heard of one captain at BA who prefaced his welcome with, Ladies and Gentlemen I thought I would let you all know this is the first time I have flown this type of aircraft.................today.

Pilots transferring to a new type of airliner might spend as much as fifty hours or more in these boxes, being put through the mangle. My only grievance with them is they have no toilet, which seems to me a bit of an oversight, while secondly they use a fixed temperature which feels too cold when things are going well and decidedly warm once engines begin failing. The way the industry is being driven by software may eventually usher in a truer form of meritocracy, in the way publishing and music production is moving relentlessly down to where the action is by a combination of cheap hardware and potent software. This is how many of you come to be reading this book in its original form. Someone out there has already filed a patent for a hole-in-the-wall machine to print and bind a paperback with the subject matter of your choice, all of this *on demand.* What it means for aeroplanes is with a decent joystick and pedals plugged into your PC, along with the right software, you are virtually flying the Airbus in every sense of the word. The most recent add-on for the A320 to go with the Microsoft Flight Simulator software was so authentic, I found the guide friendlier than anything the company or manufacturer came up with. Many airline pilots use the equipment to keep their hand in for the real thing. I do not: I like my reality real. These virtual airliners can be linked over the internet and airlines like MyTravel (who are teetering on a bankruptcy they also wish was simulated) issue a schedule of work, so that hobbyists can get up and sit in the attic to fly to Greece at all hours of the night. I have no doubt that with a few rough edges knocked off they would be better at it than I could ever be.

This raises the question as to whether the complement of crew could ever be reduced further. Salaries are a very significant part of the cost of running any airliner, usually running to around forty per cent. Driverless trains have long been a feature of many light railways and in fact the Victoria Line underground was designed for driverless operation, though never enacted because of union and public resistance. Uninhabited model aircraft have already crossed the Atlantic Ocean and a tentative use of full-scale aircraft of this type might be to move parcels or other freight, for which there is an ever-expanding market. Most pilots do not want to fly this stuff anyway. Admittedly this is a long way off as only now are trials being conducted to coordinate the use of uninhabited aeroplanes in commercial airspace. Do not imagine either that scaling up such experiments is unduly difficult. The colour image of the nose of a 707 burying itself in a headlong rush toward the camera, that is etched upon many memories, dates back decades ago to when they remotely flew and deliberately crashed a retired liner to test out the incombustibility of a new type of kerosene. It did not work, but that only made the footage look more like we had hoped, a symphony of explosions to rival the innocent joy of *Thunderbirds*.

Not long ago the use of any sort of remotely piloted or autonomous air-vehicle looked circumscribed, though two Gulf wars and a revolution in computing have changed that perception drastically. Success in the second of these conflicts, which as I write seems assured, was due in the main to a picture of the battlefield itself provided by a range of remote sensing and communications technology. Whether this will trend toward airliners with a single pilot is more uncertain. It certainly ought to, but I cannot see the numbers being reduced beyond that. Passengers as a breed would be distinctly unhappy to discover there was either no pilot at all to share their fate, or else she was on the ground. Would they want the flight guided by a computer with no feelings either way? The best possible reason for eliminating a complement of crew is that even between them they can mishandle failures; offset against this is the fact that the human mind is an analytical tool par excellence and having two of them seems even better. The best example of this ironically was the crash of a DC-10 at Sioux City, which I happen to have visited. This aircraft had all of its hydraulics drained by an engine blade that separated during the cruise and ruptured the lines. This left it without control surfaces of any kind, though the three pilots figured out a way of manipulating the engines to direct the vehicle, say by applying more thrust on the port engine to turn right and vice versa. No computer would have thought of this, though subsequently a project at NASA was tasked with making software control the engines as well as flight controls in this way.

Pilots then fulfill the terms of what Hamlet said to a tee, being at the same time both base and sublime. An old joke among pilots considers the best combination for flying modern airliners to be one man and his dog, or perhaps one woman and her dog. The function of the dog is to bite the pilot when they touch anything. As things stand though the job is in many ways increasing in complexity;

there are more ramifications to almost every aspect of it, in the way the hospitality business is no longer a room and a fresh towel, but a cornucopia of practices from reservations systems to health and safety. The flight deck now calls for an array of skills and judgment which the panel of any law court would be proud of. Besides this, the overwhelming reason for two flight crew and a complement in the cabin is the emergency. Anyone having seen *One Man and His Dog* will realise four hundred passengers take some corralling. The severest failures on airliners, when most have only two engines, invariably include one of them going wrong. The exception is fire, which usually has its source here anyway. During times like this, just pointing the aircraft in the right direction can occupy one or other of the crew wholeheartedly. In the way though that the autopilot relieved much of this burden when introduced, software can be expected to ease it more. It is used normally in association with *fly-by-wire* systems that eliminate the cables connecting the control column in front of the pilot with the control surfaces themselves. Replacing this heavy and unwieldy arrangement are an input device, computer and wires, which lead to actuators driving the control surfaces that are hydraulic right now, but look to be electrical in future. While this type of aeroplane is in the ascendant, at the moment it remains a minority in terms of the global fleet.

Back at the first full day of flying by the Wright Brothers, this comprised four separate flights, like many of my own working days used to, the longest just under a minute in duration. Then they were anxious to pack up and return to Dayton to join their father for Christmas. There is never a perfect time to test a flying machine, in the same way there is never a perfect time to write a book. They had to contend with a steady wind of around thirty miles per hour; it is amazing the craft made any headway at all. It took only sixty-six years to consummate this take-off with a landing on the moon. The first event was witnessed by one of the brothers (I can never remember which), four coastguards and a small boy and the other by the largest global audience in human history. Each was as fraught as the other. The winds were really too strong for the first flight and there was no guarantee the aircraft would not nose over backwards and drop the pilot from some height. In the case of the lunar landing, the astronaut remaining in the orbiter gave his colleagues only a fifty-fifty chance. In the end they landed in the wrong place anyway, virtually out of fuel, while a computer failure above the surface sent the pulse of Neil Armstrong from seventy to one hundred and fifty beats. It was the decision of one man, then twenty-six, whether this failure could be ignored and a landing completed. The supreme aptitude of humankind to invent tools and escape its condition was put to the test in a split second, a condition that characterises the development of aviation generally. Nowadays a third of the personnel in the space programme are pushing sixty and the baton has passed again to individual enterprise, of the sort that took us into the air firstly in a balloon and later in an aeroplane. It is the lure of prizes and the prospects of tickets to space that is as ever powering the drive toward the commercial exploitation of space.

The history that lies between the covers of the first take-off and the farthest landing is entirely coherent. Each machine used a means of directing thrust, of creating a flow of gases and using the reaction proceeding from this to move from point 'A' to point 'B'. This was the other achievement of the Wright brothers, they determined what engine was required for sustained flight and built it along with the vehicle. This is real vision, making manifest in the short term what will be required eventually. They had calculated a need for eight horsepower. The Saturn V moon rocket was later to require five-thousand tons of thrust (the largest airliners produce eighty), but the same painstaking calculations of what was required for the journey had to be made. In aviation, carrying too much fuel requires fuel in itself, along with a heavier airframe.

The Wright brothers had no immediate customer for their craft and that is the other thing about invention. It was done to satisfy their own curiosity, though having done it they felt their efforts needed rewarding. They did not set out to make a fortune. During testing at Kittyhawk, they suspended work on Sundays. Having achieved flight, they actually put the machine away for four years to ensure the patent was as thorough as the design. When eventually they recommenced work on flight in earnest, they became bogged down in a dispute with Curtis, who stole a march by replacing the use of *wing warping* to make the aeroplane turn, with ailerons instead. These are not intrinsically better, but altogether more practical in view of the materials in use. Nowadays engineers are trying to eliminate control surfaces to replace them with smart materials that warp to electronic signals. The Wrights incidentally applied their patent to the whole notion of powered flight and such self-aggrandisement invariably ends in tears, for all inventions are essentially divisional. If I say I invented the car and the patent examiners decide that your own experiments were trending in the same direction, then I might subdivide my claim simply to protect the four-wheeled version, as I rate its chances most highly. You are then free to pursue the three-wheeler. Curtis would claim his machine with ailerons was an entity in itself. He would say the Wright brothers only succeeded where Europeans failed because their method of turning was superior. He had been working all along on one that was superior again; as such it should be recognised as distinctive.

The great aviation adventure therefore stalled at an early stage. Not too long afterward, one of the brothers died at an exhibition flight. Prior to this, the first tentative customer had been the military. They were not especially keen but as nobody else wanted it, they were badgered mercilessly. Military conflict was always the greatest incentive to flight and the First World War, albeit occurring in the wrong place, was the shot in the arm the aeroplane needed. Since the American Civil War, armies had used observation balloons extensively and the British Army maintained a separate corps of men throughout the period including WWII, when barrage balloons were used to protect London. Up until the point the *Hindenburg* crashed, the airship still looked like a harbinger of war, if only for propaganda purposes. Its vulnerability as an offensive weapon had been disproved during the previous conflict, by the upstart aeroplane. The first casualty came down a few miles south of my home in Hertfordshire.

What began as observers taking pot shots at other aeroplanes, developed to the point where at the end of hostilities, machine guns had been synchronised with the propeller, to fire directly through it. Germany made this a fine art and in the next war, the Me109 had a gun that fired from the hub of the propeller itself. Meanwhile the bomber developed a life of its own, apart from being simply a machine from which you happened to drop bombs. The design criteria in this case focused upon its range and weightlifting abilities. These are supreme requirements for passenger aeroplanes as well and it was therefore no mistake after each world war, that passengers were carried in surplus bombers. Even the Boeing 747 was designed as a freighter; the Douglas DC-10 was the first such transport to be designed with no military strings attached, but the company who manufactured it was always a prime air force contractor. The Airbus 380, a product of this century, may be the only large airliner produced exclusively for civilian use. Airbus wants to get into the military market, but nobody wants its products. Besides this, the 'merchant fleet' or whole transport systems requisitioned by government for war purposes is set to grow, especially now European governments cannot afford to operate their own military versions.

The fighter aeroplane however had no possible use after the first great conflict and Tommy Sopwith was left with hundreds, nearly all of which he sold for scrap. This is why barnstorming got to happen at all, as aeroplanes have always gone through phases when they have little or no residual value. They take a lot of planning and finance to put together and if their appearance does not coincide with one of material prosperity, they are as worthless as a hencoop and often end up used that way. And while they sit out the recession, the competition is designing leaner and fitter birds. Unfortunately the trend is set to worsen as the value of investment in aerospace rises. When I went to collect a type-rating certificate for my latest aeroplane, the Airbus 321, while we waited in the library the first officer I graduated with teased me with the value he had discovered for the aircraft: around fifty million dollars. He did this only to scare me in case I goofed up. You know the feeling when you wheel that new car off the forecourt and drive it home like you learned only yesterday? Well sometimes it is that way with airliners, though in this case they have to be considered with a certain indifference, because you cannot worry unduly about clipping a verge, much as you cannot worry constantly over the fate of its passengers. You have been taught how to do the job and are relied upon to do it. You owe it them for placing that trust in you: this is called the *command* of a ship and pilots called aeroplanes 'ships' for many years, though the fashion has died.

It was only slowly after 1918 that biplanes were abandoned for *monoplanes*, because of the years of financial depression and the absence of imperatives to speed aeroplanes along, while the internal environment of the cabin did not develop much more quickly. Hand in hand with this of course the piston engine itself had to develop and manufacturers relied on the success of the motor car for many advances. It is no mistake that Rolls-Royce or BMW have always been connected with aero-engines. Rolls currently has a third of the market. Into WWII a great number of biplanes were still operating, but the Germans had made great strides in the intervening years. Manufacturing capabilities were denied them and they focused upon the basics, encouraging the youth of the nation to take up gliding. Do not forget that the Wright Brothers attributed their success to this study. Secretly the Germans used the cover of the machine-tool industries to gear up for a future with sleeker and more persuasive forms of flight altogether. Israel and South Africa have impressive indigenous industries because access to aviation markets was denied them. Necessity is the mother of all such inventions.

Once war had begun the British found a response within them and often in terms of aviation it revolved around individuals. The British invented individualism above all else. There was Hooker with a supercharger for the Merlin engine that Rolls produced, which itself already envisioned future requirements. There was the anonymous civil servant who insisted on the production of higher-octane fuel to feed the engine and there was Mitchell, providing the Spitfire to carry it all. None of this would have availed without the efforts of everyone toward survival and these were badges of endurance in which all could share. One flying ace said he was not geared up until appreciating the temerity of an enemy that dared come flying over *here* on our patch, to cause mayhem. A precursor to the combat was the Spanish Civil War, used by the contemporary 'Axis of Evil' as a testing ground for mass bombardment. The axis was a little indistinct and should perhaps have been called 'Axis Plus' or else 'Axis Lite' after the implosion of Italy. Anyhow, dropping bombs on people as Picasso depicted them doing in *Guernica* is not a nice thing to do and the aeroplane always seemed to be used as the juggernaut for such ventures, up to and beyond the *Enola Gay* and its ill-fated mission to Hiroshima. I remember the account of one eyewitness, a young girl at the time, who said she looked up at the blast and seeing all the colours of the rainbow, was spellbound by its beauty.

The other thing the militarisation of aviation eventually did for civilian life was provide it with a supply of pilots. This is drying up faster than oil, a process that can only accelerate when the military begin using uninhabited vehicles with a vengeance. Talented but spotty teenagers using a computer, video and joystick will fly these aircraft from the ground. Anyone want to go on vacation piloted by someone who never left terra firma? Here is an extract from the glory days of American aviation, when you left off flying Phantoms in the Vietnam war and slotted yourself into a Boeing 727. It is from a book called *Pilot's Guide to an Airline Career*. Under its medical requirements section, the first heading asks "Are pilots really supermen?" It is a favourite of mine and actually yes, I think pilots really are supermen. Otherwise it lists the required attributes thus:

"The actual requirements of most airlines can best be summed up as follows:

> WANTED: Young man between 23 and 27 years of age. College graduate with engineering degree. Air Force or Navy flight experience in multi-jet equipment. ATR license with Boeing 707 or Douglas DC-8 type-ratings. Must have Ivy League look, 5'8" to 6'3" in height, weight 180 to 210 lbs. A full head of closely cropped blond hair, blue eyes set far apart. Athletic build with deep tan. Must be well liked by everyone, with a proven history of leadership in all contacts."

From Pilot's Guide to an Airline Career, W L Traylor ©1968

Looking at this, I could see it being seized upon feverishly by both the Hitler Youth and my previous employers alike. If there is anyone out there who wants my own resume with a view to a job next charter season, cut this one out:

> JOB WANTED: Old man the wrong side of forty. College graduate with the lowest possible mark consistent with

passing. Left RAF to drive motorbike to South of France; aeroplane had mostly one engine. ATP license with Boeing 737 or Airbus 320 type-ratings. Look of second-hand motor dealer, not even 5'8" in height and overweight. A full head of no hair, blue eyes set too close. Homer Simpson beer gut with 'filet of haddock' tan. Universally hated by everybody, with a dubious history of leadership in all contacts.

Any takers?

If nothing else the book reminds me of how unchanging the aviation market is from generation to generation. Plus on the cover is the silhouette of another favourite, the Boeing 727. In the way *Thunderbirds* produced a series with a different layout and various numbers of engines, so did Boeing. This is probably why they did it. The 707 firstly with four engines, driven by Scott, the 727 with three, flown by Tracy, the 737 with two, flown by Colin and the 747 again with four, occupied by Virgil. A good friend of mine used to fly around wearing the sash from his *Thunderbirds* outfit. He also had a rubber piggy nose and jam-jar glasses, which he insisted I wore before calling the cabin crew in to request a coffee. We shall never see his like again. I hope not anyway.

Talking of what pilots wear, I returned from Belfast once with a captain whose baggage was checked onto another flight so that he had to request permission to operate in a yellow polo-shirt and then expected me to do all of the walking around in the rain. I thought of amending the in-flight address to say that a crazed motor-dealer had taken command and was threatening to take us to Guernsey without a firm order for a dozen Nissan Micras...

But I did not. The 'sixties were something of a golden era of aviation (as indeed they were for just about everything else), as military jets had evolved their engines to superstar status and problems with pressurised cabins and supersonic wings were ironed out and anything seemed possible, even sleeping with the next-door neighbour. During night-stops in Brussels, whenever I was not in the Jacuzzi with call girls from the European fringe, the next best place was the aviation museum, which was free. No contest really. From the ceiling here hung my one true love, a Caravelle once operated by Sabéna, which until it went bust last year was the national airline of Belgium. It distinguished itself even among European airlines by never having made a profit in its entire existence except for one year, when the accounts department made a mistake and were severely chastised as a result. They were known colloquially as Such A Bad Experience Never Again, though in truth of fact they were no worse than any other airline.

I suppose I have to make an exception here for Qantas, who have yet to kill anybody. Remember the part in *Rain Man* where Dustin Hoffman will not get on the aeroplane because it is not Qantas? A friend of mine went for an interview with this airline and they told him the company divorce rate exceeded ninety-five per cent and asked did he still want the job? Being Australian he asked when they wanted him to start. I like antipodeans. One New Zealander told me how they arranged a surprise birthday for a girl in PNG and hid in the basement cellar until she returned from work, so they could all surprise her. They certainly did so, for they emerged to find her naked and smeared with peanut butter, which the dog was going for in the way only dogs know how. I could think of worse birthdays: most of them in Teesside.

The nineteen-sixties were also something of an environmental party-time, when fuel and drink seemed endless and the parents, or in this case the children, would be picking up the bill. Aviation has always been a bellwether of the economic cycle, an albatross that forewarns of stormy skies ahead. It takes forever to pick up once the bull-market kicks in, but the perceptible emptying of seats is the surest sign of corporations losing their nerve. This produces training and recruitment cycles as far out of sync as the manufacture of aeroplanes themselves. Until recently Easyjet were giving pilots golden 'hellos' of thirty-thousand pounds, whereas now you are removed by security unless you have flown for four-thousand hours and provide your own Lego. Joining the airlines is akin to surfing: catch it at the right time and you can be promoted to captain within six months, in a single stroke demoralising everyone who just sat out the last five years. Because of the seniority system the airlines have to use all sorts of excuses to allow this to happen and these are of the calibre you and I often used to avoid cross-country. From New

Zealand? Insufficient European flying experience. On the Boeing? The fleet is static and we have no simulator time to transfer you elsewhere. Colin Hilton? You have no communication skills and besides, you are too busy with the newsletter.

After 1960 dawned, aviation literally exploded. This is when the hijackers got practising for the seventies. There was a time I used to get ready for school to the sound of Jack de Manio and the news was routinely prefaced with a hijacking to Cuba. Why? Could they not lay on more schedules? Again there is an elaborate sequence of events to be followed by crews to meet this contingency, but many of them smack of Biggles meeting MI5. There are references to things like 'landlines' which to the rest of us are telephones. If ever you land and the tower asks you to "Contact me landline", it means you goofed up or your dog has been run over; it is as reliable as the policeman knocking on your door. The big imperative with hijacks used to be that you hung on in there with the passengers once on the ground. I guess that was not an option in the air anyway. This stiff upper-lip policy was revised after a hijacking where the crew hoofed it at the earliest opportunity, which actually delighted the passengers as it meant they were definitely going nowhere. Frankly I objected to the policy all along. Passengers in the post-modern world are supposed to be breaking down the barriers of formality and taking a more enlightened view of their role in a more cooperative venture altogether. Why should I not be allowed to lead from the front and slip down my post-modern rope to the safety of the tarmac?

It was around the early years of the Carter administration the atom bomb dropped, except this one was not called *Fat Boy* but 'airline deregulation'. Until this time they were happy for the main routes beyond the USA to be divided between airlines based in each region. It meant Panam in the southeast got to fly the South American routes while TWA might operate say the Atlantic routes and United those over the Pacific. There were a half dozen of these 'majors' though I do not exactly know who got what. Both external and internal markets were horse-traded between each and together they had monopolised the slots, the landing rights at major airports or *hubs*, so that no one else got a look-in. The system relied upon a *hub-and-spoke* network where you flew from any region to the centre and on to your destination, the way that when I was in Richmond I would have to travel into town first in order to get to Biggin Hill. This has fallen from favour with larger airlines nowadays because of its inherent complexity and the compound effect of delayed flights, none of which mattered however in the days before competition. Ironically the no-frills operators have revived the technique except that each regional airport now represents a sort of hub, while you do the 'spokes' by travelling a huge distance at either end of the flight in your car. This of course has only been made possible by improvements in the roads, a sort of coordinated response to transport that the government never intended but stumbled upon anyway.

BA benefited for an age from monopolising Heathrow, which is the biggest international hub in Europe, until a limited initiative by the Thatcher government turned it into more of a cartel. While airlines like bmi currently want to expand the arrangement where only two US and two UK airlines operate across the North Atlantic from here, this is only because they want to be a part of a larger cartel in turn. The airline business is like a giant Venn diagram ~ remember those? Overlapping cartels, cartels inside cartels... cartels like the ever-spinning wheels within the windmills of your mind. Restricting access to international routes is a web of *bilateral* agreement whereby the national airline of one country gets to operate to one capital if that of the other country operates the reciprocal.

In practice what that meant for years was that airlines like BA overcharged you by many multiples of the actual cost of delivery, not so much for the fun of it (though that must have been a happy by-product) but because they were a vehicle successive governments used to raise excise and to provide employment to people in this industry instead of another. It no longer looks so tenable a scheme once prices have been reduced by open access. On the international stage, countries like Singapore or the United Arab Emirates have taken the first steps and opened up their destinations more widely to other airlines. This seems to have improved the quality of service if anything, at least if the awards are a reliable indication. Among the consequences of earlier restrictions was another concept called *cabotage*. On the roads this meant that if you took a truck with a load to Paris, it came back empty so that a French truck could do the same in reverse. Until recently the rules applied to aircraft charters, so when an Italian football team wanted us to fly them from Milan to Naples for a match, we could not, because this was an internal flight and had to be operated by Italians wearing strange hats.

What Jimmy Carter did was to rock the boat and open access to internal routes, the home turf of the majors. The most conspicuous success following on from this was Southwest Airlines, which was nonetheless initially restricted by the process to operating within its own state of Texas. Although much of their success was founded upon Stetsons and a sense of humour, British airlines have taken more convincing to shed the formalities. Take their crappy magazines. At least BA accords its crews some column inches, but then they go and write things like, The view from up here can be quite fabulous and often I say to Tristan, there is no better career that a young man could entertain...The best I have read (and only because I have sub-chartered for them), is the magazine produced for Virgin Atlantic. Airlines never produce their own magazines, as they lack imagination. At least this one has something relevant to say, in which passengers might be interested. A significant number of their passengers fly out to New York just to go clubbing and then to fall asleep on the flight home on Sunday. Do they ever want to read about how a small vineyard in Kent has successfully imported a means of fermentation from the Haute-Garonne?

Part and parcel of the deregulation of the airline infrastructure is the reconstruction of the air traffic control network. Huge swathes of airspace are reserved for the military, wasting a great deal of fuel on one hand and on the other slowing the inevitable development of uninhabited vehicles, which anyone with half a brain can see will be more decisive in the next war anyway. It wastes fuel because airways have to take pronounced doglegs around this airspace, so that for instance every airliner flying north from London has to steer around the eastern side of the country beyond the Pennines. Added to this cost is the legacy of the ruling that each country owns the airspace above it, which means that every tinpot corner of Europe with the exception of Lichtenstein (was there not a Peter Sellers film about this place?) provides for the control of airline traffic generally. It stands to sense that if some of the contestants in the Eurovision

Song Contest leave you aghast, then a uniformity of equipment and expertise can hardly be called upon from Shannon to St. Petersburg. There is an attempt to address this cost and complexity on all levels. The European Community is driving a bulldozer of an initiative across the continent called the *Single European Sky*, which is also progressing at about the speed of a bulldozer. On a national level in the UK, the government has tried to sell off a portion of the National Air Traffic System to a group of airlines, as part of a public and private finance initiative. The group of airlines was especially interested in this as a means of controlling their own destiny, until such time as it no longer looked like a money-spinner, whereupon it disappeared from the bar at closing time faster than your mates on a stag night.

The training required to anticipate the boom-and-bust in aviation often requires the sort of duck-tape repairs I would often see used in the baggage holds. Originally airlines took on cadets from school and sent them to Oxford Air Training School, the airline equivalent of a public school. I am surprised they never put a lacrosse team together. The place is going slowly bankrupt, mainly because we have upset all of the Asian and Middle Eastern countries upon which it relied, while the European national airlines can no longer afford it. After 9/11 Aer Lingus withdrew their students peremptorily. BA used to have their own cadet training college at Hamble in Hampshire and people who went here like to drop it into the conversation, in the same way students from Oxford do (perhaps in the hope of basking in the reflected glory of certain other colleges around these parts).

Aside from this route into the airlines, what was known in America as the 'instructor ticket', where you garnered your own flying experience, has been replaced in Europe by a modular course that nobody can afford. It is therefore financed by the airlines, which get their own back by paying you like a burger-flipper for several years or else threaten to take you to court should you attempt to leave. You like to think the guys up front are happy and so do I, though there are times they are quite put out. Angry pilots are not nearly so safe as happy pilots, though the airlines like you to imagine they are as inert and functional as the autopilot itself. The last fatal accident BA succumbed to stemmed from a barney in the crew room that was carried onto the apron and into the aeroplane itself, before ending in a field just outside of Staines.

I suppose anyway that young people do not want a career as an airline pilot any more and I do not blame them. The philosopher Kierkegaard said he would rather his son become a monk than a journalist. I think I have that the right way around. Nowadays when I sit my nephews and nieces upon my knee, I tell them not to fly an aeroplane, but to become David Beckham instead. Fortunately they are more interested in computer games, which is exactly how it ought to be; kids nowadays spend too much time outdoors. The ennui of modern living is a trend airlines have been slow to adapt to in recruitment and a manifestation of this 'disconnect' is an absence of respect on the side of both employer and employee toward the other point of view. For senior managers airlines are a vehicle they use to capitalise upon the merry-go-round of deregulation whilst there are cherries to be picked, so as to retire and sell out the share-options at the earliest opportunity. The shares in Go which were purchased internally for tens of pennies later realised fourteen pounds apiece when the company was disinherited by BA.

For pilots meanwhile the airlines are there to be fleeced for experience or type-ratings and then to be disavowed like a mistress for the more alluring promises of another. Quite a number at my last employer conspired to complete very expensive training on modern equipment like the A330, fully in the knowledge they were leaving in the immediate aftermath. Then again airlines are often ambivalent enough to let it happen. The motives of these fresh-faced people can only be guessed at, but many see the type-rating printed up in their licence alongside others as a form of trophy, a goal in itself, no matter who pays for it or what opportunities have been denied others. I have known private pilots to complete all of the training and formalities required for the issue of a licence, entirely at their own expense, yet to eschew the actual qualification; the satisfaction being sufficient, like virtue, unto itself. But then these I suppose are a different breed.

For a generation the service mark of United Airlines, Boeing's own carrier, was 'Come fly the friendly skies'. Then one day some advertising exec asked what was so friendly about holding for fifty minutes in a Los Angeles stack, next to a guy with flatulence? Perhaps instead of posing as a world favourite, BA should be advertised as the least detestable? I have sat in uniform on flights and endured the rage of apoplectic businessmen bewailing the shortfall in service or communication and I have to say that I would agree with some of them, while at the same time letting them gently in on the fact they were beginning to look silly. As often as not it is the flight crew at fault, or specifically the captain who sets the tone. The airlines have made a cracking job of showing these people how to manoeuvre a machine over the past fifty years, but not much else. They have modelled them upon the precocious mathematician that forgets to change his underwear.

The situation is even more lamentable now that the crew is physically as well as emotionally separated from the cabin, by a door with a combination lock and video-entry system. Why anybody would aspire to locking themselves into a small place with someone they might not like for ten hours and calling it a profession I do not know, but it is probably as good a metaphor for modern society as any. On a wider scale, at the moment the industry is either enduring the birth pangs of a new way of working or the death throes of the last, I am not sure which, while for many of the majors survival itself hinges upon union votes among pilots, crew or engineers upon the extent of wage cuts. The outcome is often complicated by the extent of the rewards that chief executives have made themselves, like the men who found the cash box before the Titanic finally sank. Key to the current disputes are *scope clauses*, terms of contract that say if the majors try to reduce cost using regional jets on *thinner* routes (those with fewer passengers and not needing so wide a cabin), then they are not going to get away with paying the reduced salaries that go with them. As it stands, pilots at airlines like United can juggle days off with holidays and take an entire month for themselves, so you have lost a twelfth of their productivity before you even sit down with pen and paper.

It is no surprise that the pilots are defending this fiefdom with the bluster of Saddam Hussein, nor that they would be prepared to bring the whole thing down around their ears. Their hatred for the management is universal. I walked across the terminal satellite at Paris to talk to a guy operating a showroom-new Airbus for US

Airways. He was less eager to talk about its virtues than to castigate his employers for the mess they were making of *Chapter Eleven*. *Chapter Eleven* by the way refers to the protection of a company from creditors; for a while they get away without paying their bills. I have tried this with the telephone company.

Chapter Eleven is followed by *Chapter Twelve*, when the bogeyman arrives to close you down. The impact of this stage upon communities in America or Australia for instance is on a par with that of the Black Death in Europe, which eliminated a third of the population at a stroke. I did recently take a meal out and on the next table were flight attendants who had worked for American Airlines for nineteen years, along with their husbands. On a global scale however European governments are continually moaning about how US subsidies (of the kind they themselves are too mean to pay) are undermining their own inefficient airlines like BA. Meanwhile after their dubious support for a war in Iraq the Americans do not care much any more about what goes on in continental Europe, while traffic to the Far East has been suspended recently by an outbreak of a deadly flu virus, ironically spread around the world most expeditiously in the cabins of airliners.

Meanwhile the haggling goes on with the insurers as to whether the destruction of the Twin Towers by different Twin Aeroplanes constitutes a Twin Claim or merely a single misfortune. So there could be no better time, really, to reflect upon what civilian aviation (let alone military) has brought us, or brought us to, during a century of its development. There could not be a better time to write about it and the fact that this book coincided with a period in which I left one job that I enjoyed and started another is a great felicity. As a guide in life I suppose that, whatever you are doing, if now feels the time to do it, then you cannot be going all that wrong.

It was one of the English travellers and writers, either Laurens van der Post or Wilfred Thesiger, who said that the car and aeroplane were the worst of human inventions, because they had opened up every interior to mass tourism and so facilitated human migration, which together were destroying cultural diversity, all that has made us human in its various facets. I would add that each is doing much the same for animal and plant diversity. In recent experience in the

Middle East, Donald Rumsfeld has been relying on warfare based upon the 'access all areas' allowed by flying machines on the one hand and telecoms networks upon the other. Lumped in there of course with telecoms is computing, which in many ways is the same, like a mushroom and its tendrils. Air transport along with rocketry, its bastard offspring, is what has made American global hegemony possible. States only go to war if they think they can win and the notion of Plato, that they are naturally at war, has held since his day. If you build the deadliest of three-tiered triremes, you are less likely to use it to ship watermelons from North Africa, than to use it to allow the *continued* shipment of watermelons from North Africa.

Whether either of the Wright brothers foresaw all of this it is hard to know. Certainly Ford had doubts about the wisdom of introducing the automobile after seeing the Scorpio. As the Wrights wrote in their own book, all they did was to reveal an underlying possibility that lay there to be discovered already, like Michelangelo claimed he was removing only the excess marble from around figures already there. Life moves on and what the Wrights achieved will be eclipsed anyway by forms of movement through three or more dimensions that do not involve this primitive need for engines that breathe air, or airframes that must displace their weight in order to support themselves. Show us a flying saucer instead and we may just be captivated, if not captured.

When I passed through Heathrow recently, I realised none of my colleagues even knew I was gone. One purpose of this book is to remind them that I have and to avoid the cost of buying any of them a drink. I could see from those I met that they wondered why it was that I left and the fact is, I awoke on one grey morning and opened the curtains to see fourteen Canada Geese flying low past the church tower, heading south in vee-formation, when one of them honked and I took it as a sign. They looked so free.........

POST-FLIGHT

I wondered for a while whether to call this *Dead Man Flying*, but outside America (and come to think of it outside prisons where executions occur) it is meaningless. It seemed appropriate because as I went to hand in my uniform, in the earnest hope of not wearing one again, the meeting took place in a galleried building with an atrium surrounded like a prison with elevated walkways. There was no netting to deter suicides, but I did feel like banging my cutlery against the railings. The reason we met here was that Heathrow itself was bordered with armoured cars after a(nother) security alert and its offices were poised for evacuation. I returned there recently to use a pair of complimentary tickets and as I neared the M25 and its breakneck traffic, I began to feel the stress that all aerial travellers feel begin to accumulate.

I discovered that a road atlas was still packed in my baggage, along with a pair of scissors and a set of tweezers, both of which were now proscribed by new security measures. I purchased a bubble-wrap envelope to include all of these items before making my way to the toilets in the Queens Building, opposite the offices that BA occupy, so as to place the envelope behind a radiator. I intended to collect it upon my return, but this did not transpire. When they replace the radiator, they will look back at a turbulent era in aviation and decide they were the tools of an aspiring shoe-bomber. (I briefly considered capitalising on their loss by making them the subject of a Tolkein-style treasure hunt, which could at least have been more entertaining than the book itself.)

On the way over to Milan, a place I seem attached to by a rubber band, I perused the pages of *Flight* magazine. There were a dozen articles to catch my eye, which together form a reasonable snapshot of aviation right here, right now, as Fatboy Slim might say. They could be put into a time capsule and sealed along with the contents of my bubble-wrap, as they are as representative a selection as any historian of aviation could aspire to. Instead I shall share them with you briefly and afterward we can go our separate ways, like holidaymakers who swap addresses knowing, or at least hoping, that none will ever be followed up.

They are from the edition for the last week in March, of 2003. I intend to deal with them in the order they appeared in the magazine. The comments accompanying each headline are all my own, as you have come to expect by now:

Engine-failure 777 busts ETOPS limit An incident over the Pacific in which a long-haul aircraft continued flying for three hours and thirteen minutes to the nearest alternate airport, using the one remaining engine. This was just inside the maximum approved flight time over the ocean on a single engine. A commentator a few years ago made three personal predictions, including the loss of a Concorde, a collision over London and the ditching of a twin-engine aeroplane. In my view predictions like these are about as useful as suggesting a chimpanzee will eventually perform the entire output of Wolfgang Amadeus Mozart.

Singapore Airlines 747 suffers major damage in Auckland tail scrape This is the second jumbo they have damaged in recent years and as Oscar Wilde said, to lose one aeroplane is a misfortune, to lose two looks like carelessness.

Boeing: fake ILS signals 'are not one-off events' The manufacturer discovers that the system sometimes indicates aeroplanes are on the glideslope, when actually they are not. They concede this may have caused accidents in the past. Slightly alarming this one and rather like questioning the Catholicism of the Pope.

Losing face but saving lives Correspondence from a New Zealander suggesting the loss of an Air China 767, in which the pilot has been blamed, looks likely to be repeated as long as a fear of losing face remains ingrained in Asian airlines.

The usual suspects appearing alongside these titbits are Russian airlines lurching into crisis, or foisted with airliners they do not want, Chinese orders switched from Boeing to Airbuses as the wind changes direction, another maverick in Holland reviving Fokker, business jets and helicopters suffering tumbling sales, another smartass comment from Michael O'Leary, ATR claiming passengers prefer propellers, regional jets stretched again along with scope clauses, another US major filing bankruptcy, more environmental clauses from the EC, the crash of an Osprey V22, North Atlantic poised for deregulation, another quarter of profits for Southwest Airlines, another airline with a no-frills approach no-one thought of before and Colin Hilton claiming to be building a form of flying car.

And that is about it. As Marcel Proust once wrote, A work of art is never finished, it is only abandoned. I am singing from your hymn sheet, Marcel. The continuous evolution of flight along with the continual recollection of amusing anecdotes from my own brush with its development crowd my mind daily, whereas this was supposed to be a swansong; or at least a Canada Goose-song. I have notes on scraps of paper urging the inclusion of one or other omission, like the following addition on long-haul flying:

> Knew a navigator who was advised there was a bomb on board, at the 'Critical Point' over the Atlantic, when it was as far to continue as to turn back. Ruined his steak dinner.

I intend to eschew them all. Go and find out for yourself how the impact of computers changed *yield management* so that instead of employees flying around the world for nothing, passengers are doing it instead. Or how the term 'engine failure' is translated as 'Bad harvest-moon' in certain Japanese flying manuals. Two scraps say it all, though. Drive along the A34 and if you are careful going north you see the spot where Geoffrey de Havilland flew the first machine he built; people like him virtually saw the entire development of aerospace inside a lifetime. Concorde itself retires this year, a century on from the first flight. After completing this document in its original form, I noticed that it ran to one hundred and eighty-eight pages, while my call-sign as a trainee was *Bravo 188*, so I seemed myself to have come full circle too.

Above all, for me as for all others who have flown and dared look out the window, flight itself is a change of perspective. When I took up pleasure flyers in Ipswich during open days, many commented that everything looked more attractive from up there. Our world is viewed increasingly not so much from ground level as from street level, or from the perspective of the motor car. This distorts our view like any other perspective; while we feel that motorways increasingly dominate the landscape, from the air they appear as faint capillaries.

Aldous Huxley once wrote that the single new sensation the technology of the twentieth century had brought us was that of speed. Much later again, nobody seeing the Earth from the perspective of space could regard it as nearly so expansive as it once seemed. Flying does this for the rest of us, enlarging possibilities at the same time as shrinking the cultural capital of humankind. In this it is no different from any other human venture, beginning with our experiments in the Garden of Eden; whatever we gain in one sphere seems always to diminish us in another.

In the best tradition of the Academy Awards, there appear overleaf nearly all of the pilots with whom I have flown from time to time over the past twenty-five years. A number may be missing, as for a while I was not sufficiently motivated enough to bother recording them. They can be known collectively as the Unknown Soldier.

Typing them in, I was reminded of the scene in which the schoolmaster Mr. Chips, played so diligently by Robert Donat, is passing away and recalls the many hundreds of smiling faces with which he became familiar over the years. I regard this exercise with a certain end-of-term nostalgia and indeed considered adding Creek, Dawson to the list. Many indeed were my students and in the best public school tradition, which is rarely departed from within aviation either, they are listed by surname. From the going down of the sun, to the taking of the car park bus, we shall remember them. Where surnames appear without a first name alongside, these are usually those trainees.

Where I thought I recognised the surnames I might have added first names to them, but remember that the guy talking here is the one who mistook Dirk Bogarde for Humphrey Bogart, Charles Bronson for Charles Manson (or was it Henry Mancini?) and Tim Rice for Tim Curry. Accordingly, should you see entries in the list like Beckham, David they probably actually refer to an Albert Beckham with whom I flew twenty years ago. You may laugh, but I nearly appended the name 'Bowyer' with 'Lee', who played not for my last airline, but for Leeds United. My wife was once horrified to discover I had addressed one of our Christmas cards to the neighbours with 'Jim Bowen' instead of 'Jim Bywater'. The first was a game-show host while the second was our neighbour (and incidentally the man who headed up the introduction of the Ford Anglia. Go easy, Jim).

Omitted are the many whom I took on pleasure flights, who 'had a go' at the controls. It was two of these people alone who struck me immediately as 'natural' flyers. One was a sixth-form girl from Ipswich, who at 5'1" feared she was either too small, or that her blonde hair was not closely-cropped enough for the airlines. The other was a young female secretary, with absolutely no interest in taking up flying. We salute her wisdom.

The records should correspond with your own and if you recognise yourself and want a first name listed, contact mail@colinhilton.com or send an anonymous insult instead. Most of you will have flown at Ipswich, since closed, or else Blackbushe. Finally, so as to arrange the names in separate column-widths, this occasionally required me to abbreviate them. This is due to no sang-froid on my own part, but is merely your own fault for having such long names. Can I congratulate Mr. Lai here and now for his efforts in this regard?

Ladies and Gentlemen, I'm Colin Hilton, You've been a wonderful audience, Goodnight.

Abberton, John
Abbott, Nigel
Adams
Adamson
Adlington
Aitchison, Stuart
Aldred
Alexander, Stuart
Allen
Ambler, John
Ames
Anderson, Dave
Angell, Stuart
Asquith, Eddie
Austin
Austin, Jamie
Bainbridge, Howard
Baldwin, Mark
Barber
Barber, Pete
Barford, Leslie
Barnes, Geoff
Barnes, Mike
Barnes, Robbie
Barnett, Dave
Bartlett
Barton, Neil
Bate
Baxter, Ian
Beadle
Beadsmore, Will
Bedford, David
Beere, Tony
Belcher, Simon
Belcher, Tony
Bell
Benichou, Gregoire
Bennett
Bentley, Nick
Berridge, Jeremy
Berry, Tim
Berwitz, Peter
Bevan, Malcolm
Bevis, Phil

Bickers
Bird, Dicky
Blades, Tony
Blech, Robin
Bliss
Blunt, Alex
Bonner
Boothby, Neil
Boulter
Bowman, Shona
Bowyer, Tony
Bradley, Brian
Bradly
Bradshaw
Brady, Chris
Brewer
Bristow, Gary
Britchford, Dave
Britton, Andy
Brook, Stuart
Brough, Joe
Brown
Brown, Frank
Brown, Robert
Brydon, Alistair
Bucholz, Graham
Budd, Robert
Burn, Laurie
Burridge, Andy
Butler, Neil
Buxton, Chris
Byrne
Calvert
Cameron, Jamie
Cardell
Carling, Max
Carmichael
Carter
Carter, Greg
Cash, Brett
Cathcart, Steve
Cavalli
Chandler, Chris
Chandler, James

Chapman, Ed
Chapman, Rob
Chidwick
Chinnick, Andy
Chrisp, Peter
Clark
Clarke, Titch
Clatworthy, Matt
Cockerill, Lou
Cole
Collingbourne, J
Collins
Colwell, Matt
Cook, Alistair
Cook, Sam
Coppens-Browne
Cosker
Coulson, Simon
Crawley, Neil
Crook, Nick
Cullen, Iain
Cumming, Malcolm
Curd, Jessica
Curd, Jonathon
Curran, Judith
Curran, Paul
Dabbs
Davidson,
Dawson, Mike
Day, Peter
De Bank, Neil
De Gutis
Deer, Alan
Delahunty, Bill
Dickens, Mal
Dixon
Dodd, John
Dow
Drakeley, S
Driver, Pete
Duffy, Mark
Dummer, S/L
Duthie, F/L
Dwyer, Howard

Eaton, Mark
Edlin, Stuart
Edmund-Jones
Ellerbeck, Tony
Empson, Ian
Erry, Darius
Evans, Martin
Evans, Pete
Evans, Richard
Ewer, Ewer
Fallon, Paul
Farrant, Brian
Fernandez, Paul
Fisher, Roger
Fitzgerald, Ian
Fletcher
Fletcher, Dave
Flintoft, John
Foan, Andy
Fonseca, Andy
Forbes, Ian
Ford, Marcus
Foreman, Tim
Foster, Paul
Foxley, Andrew
Frampton
Francis, Dab
Fussell, Robbie
Gange
Garman, Jenny
Garman, Mark
Gibson, Mark
Giles
Giles, Rob
Gilson
Gliddon, Ian
Goldman, Cass
Gomez, Al
Gooding, Bob
Goold
Gradidge, Andy
Gratton, John
Graves, Rob
Greenwood, Fiona

Grice
Grievson, Clive
Griffin, Keith
Griffiths
Groves, Les
Guilbert, Dave
Haigh, Jeremy
Hamlington, Brett
Hands, Jonathon
Hansen
Hardie, Dave
Harper, Euan
Harris
Harris, Mike
Harrison, Neil
Hart, Alan
Hart, Mike
Hart, Nick
Hartley
Haslam, Fred
Hawkins, Martin
Hawskwood, Neal
Hayman, Geoff
Hayward, Ian
Heath, Steve
Hedges
Heffer
Herbertson, John
Herholdt
Herlihy
Heymann, Tim
Hill, Alan
Hill, Andrew
Hill, Deborah
Hind, Jon
Hinkley
Hoare, Nick
Holman, Dave
Hooker, Keith
Hooper-Smith, Steve
Hope, Duncan
Hore, Brad
Hornsby
Horton, Rob

Howell, Phil
Howie, Rob
Hull, Don
Hull, Susan
Hunter
Hunter, Mike
Hutchings, Lorna
Hutton, Bruce
Huxtable, Chris
Ibbetson, Ian
Irvine
Islam
Ivett, James
Jackson, Andy
Jamieson, Bob
Jeffery, Phil
Jenkins, Mel
Jenner, Anthony
John, Hugh
Johnston, Al
Jones, Jonathon
Jones, Keith
Jones, Martin
Jordan
Judd, Simon
Kelly, Frank
Kelly, Paul
Kincaid, Alan
King, Steve
Kinsella, John
Kmiciek, Jan
Knight, Cyril
Kosky, Mark
Kropascy, Nick
Lai
Langston
Lavous
Leach, Andy
Lee, Colwyn
Lever, Chris
Leyshon, Anne
Lintott, Dave
Little, Bill
Lloyd, S/L

281

ROLL OF HONOUR

Long
Lonzardi, P
Lord, David
Lowman, Bill
Lunt, Chris
Mackie, Phil
Mackinnon, Ian
Magson
Mahoney
Maidment
Marchington, Phil
Marsden,
Marsdin, Mike
Marshall, Ian
Marshall, Tony
Matthews, Dave
Mattimoe, Ian
Maxwell
McCann, Mike
McDavid, James
McFadzean,
McGrath, K
McHugh, Sean
McLeod, Olus
McPhie
Mehr, Arjan
Merlin-Jones, I
Michaelides, E
Middleton, Ian
Mills, Debbie
Milne, Dee
Mitchell, Craig
Moffat, Steve
Mollison, A
Monahon, Sarah
Montgomery, P
Moore, Andy
Moran, Simon
Morgan
Morgan, Neil
Morley
Morrell
Morris, John
Morris, Johnny

Morrison, Trevor
Morton, Harvey
Mulligan
Munro, C
Murphy, B
Murtagh, Mike
Murtagh, Ronan
Mylam, Ian
Myland, Tony
Nagle, Chris
Nanton, Richard
Nash
Naz, Faz
Nejatbakhsh, H
Neyland, Rob
Nicholson, B
North, Matthew
Nutcher, Chris
O'Reilly, Mike
O'Toole
Osman, Paul
Oultram, Andy
Owens, Dave
Pearson, Jim
Parkinson
Paskett, Graham
Patel, Girish
Patel, Simon
Paterson, John
Patterson, Ian
Payling, Rob
Payne-James, J
Pearsall, Mike
Pegram, Jim
Peplow
Perry, Mark
Pickering, Dani
Pigden
Pillai, Satya
Pitcher, Jim
Plaistowe, Rob
Plant, Adrian
Platt
Pooley, Rob

Powell, Steve
Preston, Mike
Pucher, Andrew
Purry, Jeremy
Ramsay
Ramsdale, Tim
Rank, Mike
Ratcliffe, Dave
Ratcliffe, Paul
Richardson
Ridyard, Clare
Roberston, Dave
Robinson, Mel
Rodgers
Rogers, Nigel
Rowley, Phil
Rowntree, Bob
Rush
Russell, Lee
Ryder
Ryman, Emma
Saint, Ernie
Saker, Fred
Self, David
Seymour, T
Shafto, Jeremy
Sharman
Sherman, Andy
Shiel, Ian
Shipton, Glenn
Silver
Simmons
Simpson, Clive
Sixsmith, Andy
Skelton
Slaughter
Sloane
Smith
Smithers, Steve
Sneddon, C
Snell
Sokolowski, G
Sowik, Andre
Sowik, Steve

Spain
Spring
Spurrier, Sean
Stanley, Ken
Starkie, Mike
Steenson, Eric
Stephens, Paul
Stevenson
Stewart
Stirling, Gavin
Stopp
Sumner, Ian
Sutherland, Guy
Sutton, Kevin
Sutton, Nick
Sykes, Mike
Talwar, Nij
Tann, Chris
Tarmar, John
Tarrant, Dave
Tate
Thatcher, R
Thomas
Thomas, John
Thompson
Tigwell
Tilling, Andy

Tiquell
Tregaskis, N
Trow, Phil
Tuffin
Turner, Chris
Turner, Ed
Tytler, Phil
Underwood, M
Vema
Venus, Andrew
Vetch
Vors, Kamy
Voute, F/L
Waite, Roger
Wakes, Chris
Walker
Walters, Sean
Ward, Nigel
Ward, Steve
Warnock, Clive
Warren
Watkins
Watts, Derek
Weeks, Mike
Welch
Weld, Chris
Wells

Wheeler, Ian
White
Wicks, Russ
Wiggins, David
Wigginton, K
Wilcox, Alistair
Wildish, Chris
Wilkinson
Williams, L
Willoughby
Willson, Gene
Wilson
Wilson, Alan
Wilson, Chris
Wilson, F/L
Wilson, Preston
Winten
Witherick
Wolokoff, Greg
Wood, Daniel
Wood, Mike
Woodhouse
Woolam, R
Wright, Mike
Young
Young, Trevor
Zottl, Tony

LIFE ON THE EDGE

Captain's log, June 5th, 2003, 0400 hrs. Am unable to sleep and wander to the nerve-centre of my *Enterprise*, the back room in Alderley Edge. Already it is light and a breeze is playing at the limes at the end of the avenue. I noticed during recent approaches to runway 24 at Manchester that the Edge seems to rise out of nowhere on the border of the South West Lancashire plain, much like the town of Ely stands proud as the 'ship of the Fens'.

The statistics section of MS Word says this book has undergone 850 revisions and comprises a hundred thousand words. These were assembled during the course of four weeks, but spent many more in the hangar being knocked into shape. To get them to a point where they can roll off the litho printers at *Printout* took three months. The editing was undertaken in A4 format on-screen and converted to a PDF file. From here it was imported by Terry at *City Graphics* into Quark Express on another Apple and scaled to 75%, so as to fit an A5 format. The typeface is *New York*, which I found pleasant on-screen, while lending the text a certain New English combination of reflection and rectitude, like something by Henry Thoreau. This produced three hundred pages of text, though I set out to produce only two-thirds this number.

The increase was a fortuitous by-product of reformatting the document and proves, if nothing else does, that we know nothing of how things work until building them ourselves. During the process I came to appreciate that what is taken for granted in a paperback is the outcome of considerable effort not only in putting words on the page, but in editing, proofing, layout, design, printing, marketing and retail, much of which goes by the generic name of 'publishing'. The test pilot of the 707 said a single flight was worth a thousand speculations, while the prototype Zero, though the most advanced fighter, was hauled from the hangar by a water buffalo. If you liked the book as a reader, buy another for someone else. If you liked it as a publisher, do something about the next thousand for me.